TIPPI

TIPPI

Tippi Hedren
with Lindsay Harrison

WILLIAM MORROW
An Imprint of HarperCollins*Publishers*

 For information address HarperCollins Publishers, 195 Broadway, New York, NY 10007.

HarperCollins books may be purchased for educational, business, or sales promotional use. For information please e-mail the Special Markets Department at SPsales@harpercollins.com.

FIRST EDITION

Designed by Bonni Leon-Berman

Library of Congress Cataloging-in-Publication Data has been applied for.

ISBN 978-0-06-246903-8 (hardcover)
ISBN 978-0-06-265613-1 (ANZ edition)

16 17 18 19 20 DIX/RRD 10 9 8 7 6 5 4 3 2 1

To my very special parents,

Dorothea Henriette Eckhardt and

Bernard Carl Hedren;

to my sister, best friend, and confidant,

Patty Davis;

to Melanie Griffith,

my "daughter of great fortune";

and to every single one

of my beloved animals,

past, present, and future.

CONTENTS

INTRODUCTION

My name is Tippi Hedren.

It's 2016, and I'm eighty-six years old, happy, busy, single, content, and healthy (for the most part, but more about that later).

A few weeks ago I came across an old steamer trunk I hadn't opened in decades and decided to take a look inside. There were some spider webs, and an empty half-gallon plastic milk container in one of the drawers. (Your guess is as good as mine.) Then I began opening the rest of the drawers, and it was like Christmas.

They were filled with treasures, a testament to the fact that I never throw anything away.

There were two yellowed, disintegrating family Bibles.

There were grainy old black-and-white photos of:

- my daddy, Bernard Carl Hedren, with his Masonic Lodge brothers. Tall, slender, and handsome, purebred Scandinavian, a quiet, stoic "good man."
- my mother, Dorothea Henrietta Eckhardt Hedren, German/Norwegian, with an angelic face that always looked its most natural when she was smiling.
- my older sister Patty and me, with our matching blond hair and Peter Pan–collared blouses.
- my paternal grandparents. They lived with us for a while when I was a little girl, but I hardly knew them. I remember that they weren't well, wore black a lot, and rarely spoke. When they did speak, it was never in English, always in Swedish, and they seemed to stay in their room all the time.
- me among the other members of our Lutheran church choir.
- several group shots of our large family. These photos are similar to some you may have as well, in which you have no idea who half those people are.
- me in my first wedding, happy and hopeful at the age of twenty-two.
- me and my beautiful daughter, Melanie, when she was a little girl.

Other memorabilia included:

- Two carefully bound locks of blond hair in an envelope with the words "Tippi—Age 8."
- A single strand of hair in a small black plastic pouch labeled MELANIE'S FIRST GRAY HAIR, AGE 14.
- My diploma from Huntington Park High School in California.

- My Girl Scout membership card. My Girl Scout uniform hangs in my office, and I immediately slipped the membership card into the pocket with my Girl Scout knife.
- Several hand-printed notes on lined school paper, addressed to Mom and signed "Love, Tips."

The treasures went on and on, and I kept every one of them except the milk container and that web-accessorized steamer trunk. I've got some scrapbook shopping to do.

At around the same time, the Hollywood Museum happily borrowed (obviously with my permission) my Golden Globe, engraved "Most Promising Newcomer, 1964," and the dress form with my exact measurements that the legendary Edith Head created to design my wardrobe for my first two films. I was a little surprised they wanted the dress form—it has some rips and tooth marks from the day one of the lion cubs found it in my bedroom and promptly stalked and tried to kill it. The Hollywood Museum didn't seem to mind a bit.

All of which added up to a whole lot of memories and a whole lot of food for thought.

I've been interviewed and quoted and written about more times than I can count since the early 1960s when I starred in *The Birds* and *Marnie* for Alfred Hitchcock, a man I look back on with admiration, gratitude, and utter disgust. Despite his efforts to thwart my career, I went on to act in more than eighty film and television shows. I've been a wife, three times. I'm a mother and a grandmother. I've been a model and an animal rights activist and a humanitarian. I have a lot to say.

So maybe, I decided, inspired by all of the above, it's about time I stop letting everyone else tell my story and finally tell it myself.

As I write this, I'm sitting in the living room of my home just north of Los Angeles in Acton, California. It's best described by an amazing fortune cookie message I chose one night after dinner at a Chinese restaurant shortly after I moved here: "Hidden in a valley beside an open stream, this will be the type of place where you will find your dream." I framed that little message and hung it on the wall of my bedroom, where it's one of the first things I see when I wake up every morning.

I'm looking out of a room of wall-to-wall windows at the spacious, secure enclosures of the big-cat preserve I named Shambala, a beautiful Sanskrit word that means a meeting place of peace and harmony for all beings, animal and human.

One of our tigers, Mona, is lying in the shade on her side of the chain-link fence just a few feet away. She's statuesque and beautiful. She's also a cat, so when I call her name, she might come to me, or she might stay right where she is and simply give me a look that says, "Hello? I'm relaxing right now. Maybe later. Maybe not." I get exactly the same attitude from my domestic shorthair indoor cat Johnny Depp. Someone once said, "Dogs have masters. Cats have staff." I'm staff, and proud of it.

Shambala takes my breath away every single day. And every single day I'm in awe of all the roads and detours it took for me to get here, almost as if, without knowing it, I planned it this way.

One

The population of Lafayette, Minnesota, my hometown, was approximately two hundred on the day I was born, January 19, 1930, at the beginning of the darkest depression the United States has ever experienced. Lafayette was too small to have its own hospital, so I had to travel ten miles away to the hospital in New Ulm to come into this world.

My parents named me Nathalie Kay, but from the very beginning my daddy called me Tippi, a nickname for the Swedish word *tupsa*, which means little girl or little sweetheart. It made me feel very special when he called me Tippi, and I chose it over Nathalie as my first name as soon as I was old enough to talk.

Mother was a schoolteacher back then, and Daddy owned the Lafayette general store. "General" was the operative word—he sold everything from candy to tractors out of that modest wooden building. I adored my parents and have never wished for one moment of my life that I'd belonged to anyone else.

My sister Patricia Louise, four years older than I, was a good sport about giving up her only-child status when I arrived. Our age difference kept us from being very close while we were growing up, but we've more than made up for this since we became adults. In fact, I'm honored to be the godmother of my niece Heidi, one of Patty's five children, three boys and two girls—David, Heidi, Steve, Beni (named after our daddy Bernard), and Tipper (named after me).

The demeaning Depression that was prevalent throughout the United States hit us as hard as it hit everyone else. Daddy lost his store, and when I was four or five we moved to Morningside, a streetcar suburb of Minneapolis, where Mother got a job in a department store and Daddy's health began to decline. He had a tremendous number of medical issues that eventually led to seven operations in ten years, but he still managed to live until he was eighty-seven. Mother lived to the ripe old age of ninety-five. We Scandinavians tend to stick around until we've accomplished everything we set out to do. I apparently told her one day when I was a child, "You know, Mom, when you smile, you feel happy." She loved that observation, and she lived it. Her life wasn't easy, but she never complained, and thanks to her example, I grew up with no patience for long-suffering martyrdom, in myself or anyone else.

I was a painfully shy little girl, a pair of green eyes peeking out from behind my mother's skirt when there was a stranger around. So it makes perfect sense that on the first day of school, when she dropped me off in a room full of children I'd never seen before in my life, I was out of there in the blink of an eye, sobbing and running to catch up with her before she was a block away.

How they coerced me into going back, I have no idea, but I came to accept school as one of those things you have to do until you're told you don't have to do it anymore. I wish I could say I grew to love it, but that never really happened.

I did the best I could to participate, though. I even played the violin in the school orchestra at Edina Junior High. It's a mystery to me where that violin came from—my parents certainly had no money to buy one, and I'm very sure we didn't just happen to have a violin lying around the house. I'm also very sure there are few situations more excruciating than a beginner practicing the violin. I can still picture Daddy sitting in his chair, completely hidden behind his newspaper, and that newspaper starting to tremble the instant I began raking my bow across those strings.

As far as I was concerned, what we were being taught in school paled in comparison to the education Patty and I got at home. Our mom was a wonderful homemaker, and she taught us everything from cooking and sewing to the proper way to clean a house and keep it clean. I enjoyed those skills then, and I enjoy them now. I'm a natural-born nester. I designed and decorated every square inch of my home at Shambala, and I am as excited about finding a unique piece of furniture or a table runner at a thrift store as some women get about finding designer shoes and clothes, which were once such a major part of my life and career.

We learned a lot about love at home, too, and integrity, responsibility, and morals, and keeping our word. Our parents weren't overly affectionate, but we never ever doubted that they loved us to the core of their souls.

We didn't have a car or even indoor plumbing. I was too small to navigate the dimensions of our outhouse seat, so Mom kept a little white porcelain potty for me—one that had belonged to my grandmother, trimmed with gold flowers—behind the kitchen door. Our parents worked very hard for what we did have, and we learned to earn our way through life with no sense of entitlement. We were aware that they couldn't afford to give us everything the other kids had, but we never felt deprived or inferior or frightened because of it, since they never discussed money in front of us or made their burdens ours.

Patty and I were expected to be well-spoken, to always be clean and presentable, to be well-mannered and respectful, to follow the relatively strict house rules, and to be good girls who attended the Lake Harriet Lutheran Church and Sunday school every single week. We happily complied—Patty, the brave one, because she wanted to, and me because I was so timid that I wasn't about to cause trouble.

In fact, I was so obedient that Patty still occasionally teases me about it. Mom told us when we were very, very young that if we got home from school before she came home from work, we were to write her a note telling her exactly where we were and what we were doing.

Mom apparently arrived home from work one day to find a note taped to the front door:

Dear Mom,

I just finished unlocking the door, and I'm inside the house.

Love,

Tips

I don't remember it, but all things considered, it wouldn't surprise me. Anything to follow orders and make Mom and Daddy happy, and the thought of rebelling never occurred to me. I was perfectly content to just do whatever it took not to disappoint my parents and then immerse myself in the privacy of my room to read and listen to music on my secondhand record player.

When I was four or five years old my favorite song was "When the Moon Comes Over the Mountain," sung by Kate Smith, a singer with a beautiful rich contralto voice. I listened to it over and over again, quietly singing along until I'd learned every word and every note.

One night my parents had a few friends over for dinner, and I made a spontaneous decision to entertain them. They were sitting at the table when I made a sudden dramatic entrance into the dining room and burst out with "When the Moon Comes Over the Mountain," complete with hand gestures and arms spread wide open, appropriate for my solo concert debut.

I'm sure I was intending that some combination of that song and my performance would send my small audience into rapt, spellbound awe. Instead, it sent them into instant gales of laughter. This was apparently the most hysterical thing they'd ever seen. And I of course ran to my room in tears, devastated and utterly mortified.

The scar it left was small but deep—it's about eighty-two years later, and to this day I could no more sing alone in front of other people than I could levitate and fly out the window. Logically, I get it. I'm not sure I could keep a straight face either if a four-year-old child suddenly made an entrance at a dinner party and began belting out a romantic ballad at the top of her little lungs. Emotionally, I'm still working on it. I've even taken private voice lessons and been assured that I have a perfectly wonderful singing voice, but just the thought of opening my mouth to sing by myself in front of other people, no matter how casually, sends me right back to that moment in that dining room a lifetime ago and stops me in my tracks.

It did inspire me to make a promise to myself, though, to never ever make a child feel foolish. And it's not as if it shattered my career plans.

I think I just assumed that when I grew up I'd be a wife and mother, since that's what girls did. But while my schoolmates also talked about wanting to be nurses or teachers or hairdressers, the only thing I was sure I wanted to be more than anything else was a figure skater. It was such a pretty, graceful, magical thing to watch, and I had to know what it felt like to actually do it.

Somehow my daddy managed to find a pair of figure skates for me, but affording lessons was out of the question. Fortunately, two of my friends, Harriet and Mary, were kind enough to invite me along to their lessons, and I'd sit on the sidelines, intently watching and listening and soaking it all in. Then every day when I got home from school, and every single weekend when my chores and homework were done, I'd take my skates to a frozen lake near our house and practice for hours on end, enthralled by the peaceful freedom of it and the sensation of flying and being so completely alive as I glided across the ice.

I had talent. I had passion. I had determination, and I had discipline. Unfortunately, I had also developed plantar fasciitis in my left foot that had to be treated, and an emergency appendectomy a year later, both of which cost me months and months of practice thanks to my doctor's "absolutely no skating until you've recovered" order. As far as a potential career was concerned, it was too much time away at too young an age for me to ever make up for, and I sadly gave up that dream, while Harriet and Mary both went on to perform in the Ice Follies. I was happy for them. I admit it, I was also a little envious.

But those skates traveled everywhere with me for many, many years, and no matter where in the world I found myself skating,

I would always close my eyes for a minute or two and be gliding on that quiet, frozen Minnesota lake, a child again, when life was so simple.

One day I was blessed with an epiphany, or whatever a life-altering realization is called when you're ten years old.

I was walking up a hill on my way home from school, carrying my books, not consciously thinking about anything at all.

Years earlier I'd developed the bad habit of biting my nails. I'm sure it was a physical manifestation of my shyness, my anxiety, my fear of pretty much everything. I didn't know how to analyze it, I just knew I hated it.

And all of a sudden, on that hill, I made a silent declaration to myself: "I'm not going to do that anymore."

I knew I meant it, and I was right. I never bit my nails again. I've had long, beautifully manicured nails ever since, an asset that became important in my life a great many years later.

In itself, the simple act of giving up nail-biting wasn't exactly an epiphany, but the essence of it went far beyond that. Somehow this triggered a much bigger realization in me, at ten years old, that things about myself I didn't like, that I felt were getting in my way and not serving me well, weren't *facts* about me, they were *choices*. With self-discipline I could *choose* not to put up with them and make whatever changes I wanted. If "I'm not going to do that anymore" could stop me from biting my nails, maybe it could stop me from being shy and fearful, too. Confident, fearless people seemed to be having a better time than I was, so why not give it a try?

I tried it, and sure enough, I liked it. It felt great to "just say no" to my habit of living my life on the sidelines. By the time I started my freshman year at neighboring Edina West High School (Morningside had a grade school but no high school), I had lots of friends. Three in particular—Mercedes Skaaren, Roseanne Bellows, and Caroline Povell—remain close to me to this day. We were BFFs before that term was even coined, and what's lovelier than friendships that literally last a lifetime?

I even had the sweet, thrilling surprise of my first love.

Richard McFarland was an "older man," a sophomore when I was a freshman. It was an adorable, age-appropriate romance, and I felt like a princess. We went to parties and school dances together, and school dances in the 1940s meant dancing to the most wonderful music ever. I've heard it said that we measure every kiss from every lover in our lifetime by our first kiss from our first love. That may be true. I have a crystal clear memory of the exact moment and the dreamy magic of that first kiss. I talked to Richard not long ago, and it gave me those same butterflies to hear that he remembers it, too, all these decades later.

Richard and I also had the added intrigue of being in a star-crossed relationship—his parents didn't approve of me. They were wealthy pillars of the community, and they had their hearts set on their son falling in love with a debutante. I had a lot going for me, but I wasn't even an *aspiring* debutante. We didn't let their disapproval stop us, and we had a chaste, wonderful two years together before circumstances beyond our control pulled us apart.

I imagine there are moments in all of our lives that we look back on and say, "That's when it all started."

That moment for me was a seemingly ordinary trip home from a seemingly ordinary day at school, early in my sophomore year.

I stepped off the streetcar at my usual corner in Morningside, in front of the drugstore that had the best milk shakes and hot fudge sundaes in town, and a woman I'd never seen before walked up to me.

"My name is Ella Jane Knott," she said as she handed me her business card. "Would you please ask your mother to bring you down to Donaldson's department store at her earliest convenience? I would like to have you model in our Saturday fashion shows."

Me? A model? Seriously? I was stunned, ecstatic, flattered, giddy—you name it—and I don't think my feet touched the ground as I ran home to share the news with my parents. Mom couldn't have been happier to take me to Donaldson's to meet Mrs. Knott and the rest of the people involved with their fashion shows. If I remember correctly, I started modeling at the department store the very next Saturday.

Of course I knew absolutely nothing about modeling, so I simply learned the same way I learned to figure skate—I watched and listened. I loved everything about it, and I was determined to be good at it. Before long, photographers were asking me to do print work, which was every bit as exciting.

Most unbelievable of all, though, was that I was having so much fun, getting to wear pretty clothes and be fussed over, *and getting paid to do it*. For the first time in my life I got to experience an amazing phenomenon called "spending money." And because it was a brand-new sensation for me and I was young and foolish, I couldn't spend it fast enough, especially on cashmere sweaters. There was no such thing as too many cashmere sweaters as far as I was concerned, while my frugal parents were still having to watch every penny of their hard-earned limited income to make sure we always had food and electricity and a roof over our heads. I was awful. I hope it matters that looking back, I feel terrible about it, and that one day I had the joy of buying them a car and many other things they would never have bought for themselves.

Shortly after my sister Patty graduated from high school she married a young man named Bob Hanzlik, a professional football player for the Philadelphia Eagles. I was the maid of honor in their wedding, and it was as if I had a premonition about how that was going to work out—I sobbed all the way up the aisle, which must have been very confidence inspiring for the bride and groom. Then the day after the wedding, we had the biggest snowstorm of the year in Minnesota, which, looking back, turned out to be an ill omen for that marriage. But that's another story for another day.

Still, I may have been the world's happiest fifteen-year-old girl in 1945. I was a model, my boyfriend and I were in love, I had wonderful friends and ice to skate on and parents who never once discouraged me from spreading my wings. And then one day it was all pulled out from under me.

Daddy's health was becoming more and more fragile, and the brutal Minnesota winters were becoming too hard on him, so we were going to move to the warmer, more temperate weather of Southern California.

Just like that.

I was devastated. Southern California? Were they kidding? They might as well have said we were moving to Pluto.

The girl in me who adored her daddy wanted whatever was best for him.

The teenager in me who was thriving right where she was, thank you very much, just wanted to wake up from this nightmare and go right on with my life in Morningside. Even while we were packing; even when they assured me that yes, of course my beloved cat Peter was coming with us; even when Daddy left for Los Angeles ahead of us to find a job and a place for us to live, I kept waiting for that moment when they'd announce that they'd changed their minds and we weren't leaving after all. But that moment never happened.

I was worried sick about my cat's taking such a long trip, but a very dear friend and neighbor of ours down the street, Mr. Weber, built a strong travel carrier that even had a little space outside so that Peter would be safe and not have to be confined the whole way across the country. It was so kind of Mr. Weber, and I've never forgotten it.

The move didn't seem real to me until Mother and I arrived at the station to board the train to L.A. Two hundred people, including my beloved Richard McFarland and every friend, every teacher, every schoolmate, every neighbor, every fellow model and Lutheran and Girl Scout, everyone I knew in this world showed up to see us off, and my heart broke with every good-bye.

I cried all the way from Minneapolis to Omaha.

I was sure my life was over.

Two

I've always enjoyed my own company and been perfectly content being alone. In fact, the only times I've ever been lonely were those times when I was with the wrong person. It's a blessing I especially appreciated at the age of fifteen, brand-new to Los Angeles, where nothing was familiar except my parents and my cat, and Peter was an outdoor cat, no needier for companionship than I was.

By the time our train arrived in L.A., Daddy had found an accounting job and a sweet little house for us in a residential suburb called Walnut Park. I was homesick, but there was no point in indulging in it—it wouldn't change anything or make everything okay again. I just busied myself helping Mother set up housekeeping and bracing myself for my first day at a strange new school.

I was starting my junior year at Huntington Park High, and I wanted to make a good first impression. The night before, after a lot of trial and error, I laid out my wardrobe—my favorite cashmere sweater, the perfect matching plaid pleated skirt, sparkling white bobby socks, and my most fashionable penny loafers. I was a nervous wreck as I walked up to the double-door school entrance, but I took a few long, deep breaths, put a smile on my face, and marched into that building as if I owned the place.

It became immediately apparent that I might as well have put on a pair of bib overalls and ridden in on a mule. Everywhere I looked, there were girls in tight dresses with lots of cleavage, stiletto heels, makeup, and professionally coiffed hair piled high on their heads. I couldn't have felt more out of place, and my impulse was to turn and run right back out those doors as I did on my first day at Morningside Elementary School. But "I'm not going to do that anymore." I wasn't there to fit in and make friends, I was there to get this whole school thing over with, so I squared my shoulders and dived on in.

Luckily, I had a higher priority to tend to. A few of the people I'd worked with back home had referred me to some modeling agents in Los Angeles, and one of those agents, a woman named Rita La Roy, signed me and began sending me out for print ads. I was finally back in the familiar territory of photographers' studios again, and L.A. started seeming not so bad after all.

It started seeming even better when a boy named Jimmy Lewis came along.

I'd promised Richard McFarland that I would never forget him, and I've kept that promise to this day. But there's a certain "out of sight, out of mind" approach to life that comes with being a teenager, and Jimmy Lewis was too irresistible to pass up. Like Richard, he was an attractive "older man," a year ahead of me in school. Like Richard, he was smart and fun and funny. Like Richard, he had wealthy parents—his father was a very successful attorney and his mother was a society matron. And unlike Richard, he and his parents lived only two blocks away.

It was one of those sweet young romances that started out as a friendship. Jimmy taught me to drive. He loved taking me to Newport Beach on weekends to show off his Star racing boat and teach me how to sail it. We spent a lot of time at each other's houses, and his parents didn't mind one bit that there was a very large economic difference between our two families. His mother, who seemed to sit and knit all the time, was happy to teach me to knit as well, and I turned out to be really good at it. I actually knitted myself a forest-green knee-length dress, fitted through the waist and flared at the hem, with long dolman sleeves. I was so proud of it, and it annoys me that I lost track of it somewhere along the way.

(Apparently this passion for knitting runs in the family. At about the same time I was learning it from Jimmy's mom, my sister Patty was becoming an avid knitter, too. She ended up supplying me, her children, and her friends with awesomely beautiful sweaters for many, many years.)

I graduated from Huntington Park High School in 1947, thrilled to have it over with. I wasn't especially interested in going on to college, but Jimmy had his heart set on going to Pasadena City College to major in business, and he wanted me to come with him. I was still enjoying every minute of modeling and had every intention of pursuing it. It was hardly a full-time job, though, and college might be kind of fun if Jimmy and I were doing it together. So sure, whatever, I was off to Pasadena City College, too, to major in . . . maybe art or something.

And what do you know, it was fun. The campus was stunning, the classes I went to were kind of interesting (from what little I remember of them), and Jimmy and I were getting closer and closer and falling more and more in love.

I was even approached one day, out of nowhere, to apply as a possible candidate for the Rose Parade Royal Court. What fun! The Royal Court rode on an elegant float in that magnificent, legendary parade—who wouldn't want to try out for that? I filled out the application in the blink of an eye.

Now, here comes the embarrassing part. Apparently the Royal Court committee carefully checks up on its applicants, and they discovered that I wasn't qualified to be a candidate because I wasn't really a resident of Pasadena. But wait, there's more. They investigated a little further and found out that because Jimmy wasn't really a resident of Pasadena either, and we'd used his aunt's Pasadena address on our school applications, we also weren't qualified to be attending college there in the first place.

In other words, we were busted. No Royal Court for me, and no more Pasadena City College for either one of us.

Needless to say, I took the end of my formal education incredibly well. Jimmy made other college arrangements, and I kept right on going with my modeling career, even getting a tiny, uncredited role in a movie called *The Petty Girl*, a romantic comedy starring Robert Cummings as artist George Petty, who in real life was known for his paintings of calendar pinup girls. Toward the end of the film, twelve of us fashion models, each representing a month of the year, were featured in a musical number with the movie's female star Joan Caulfield. I was January, aka Miss Ice Box.

It was fun. I thought no more about it than that. Not once did it enter my mind that more films might follow, or that I even wanted them to.

Modeling was what I loved doing, and like most American models, I felt I needed to be in New York. I wanted to be in New York. I felt myself being pulled there, and I wasn't about to put up any resistance. I was sure that if I stayed in California, I would continue doing modeling work here and there and end up marrying Jimmy. Worse things could have happened—he was wonderful, and I loved him. But every time I pictured a future with him, I pictured myself as a society matron, doing a lot of knitting, going to charity galas, and in the back of my mind always wondering "what if?" It was too early in my life to start piling up a collection of unanswered what-ifs, no matter how much in love I was.

So one morning, in the true spirit of "nothing ventured, nothing gained," I picked up the phone and called the best of the best in the modeling world, New York's legendary Ford Modeling Agency. They explained where and to whom to send my portfolio, which was pretty extensive by then, and I shipped it off that same afternoon without telling a soul about it, in case nothing happened.

Two weeks later, the call came. Eileen Ford herself wanted to meet with me, as soon as I could make it to the East Coast.

"Ecstatic" doesn't begin to describe how I felt when I hung up from that call. I immediately flashed back to the thirteen-year-old girl who'd stepped off a streetcar in Morningside, Minnesota, and had her whole life changed by a total stranger with a business card. Just like then, I wondered how I could be so lucky, and just like then, I couldn't wait to tell my parents.

They were wonderful, so supportive and there to cheer me on, never standing in the way of anything that would make me happy, even if it took me three thousand miles away. They simply wished me well, reminded me how much they believed in me, and promised to take good care of Peter.

Jimmy wasn't nearly as pleased as they were, but he knew me too well to try to talk me out of it. His only request, and it was understandable, was that I not fly to New York—his father had recently been killed in a tragic plane crash, and he couldn't bear the thought of the same thing happening to me.

And so it was that bright and early one Thursday morning in 1950 I boarded a train from Los Angeles to New York, feeling excited, hopeful, flattered, humbled—pretty much everything you can imagine other than afraid.

I couldn't afford a sleeper car, so I sat up for every minute of the three-day cross-country trip. Ah, youth. The Ford Agency had arranged for a room for me at the Barbizon Hotel for Women, and I headed straight there from the train station when I arrived on Sunday, slept all day and all night and was right on time for my Monday-morning appointment with Eileen Ford.

She was all business, a bit brusque and imperious, clearly not a woman who wanted to sit and chat for a while and then head on to lunch together. But after what seemed like only a few minutes, she called a photographer and said, "I have a new model," and just like that, I started working, less than an hour after I walked through the agency door.

In my first week I earned $350, which translates to about $3,500 today, and the jobs and the money and the excitement kept right on coming. I loved every second of it, from the endless, busy variety of the work to the skilled artistry of the people I worked with to the other models, many of whom became my closest friends—so much so that more than sixty years later, we still get together for lunches every chance we get. And more than sixty years later, we rarely have a conversation without devoting at least a few minutes to reminiscing about Eileen Ford, who died in 2014 at the age of ninety-two.

There's a reason this woman was a legend as a modeling agent. She had a very specific, instantaneous eye when it came to prospective clients. If she wanted you, as I discovered, she was on the phone in a heartbeat, booking your first job. If she didn't, the rejection was usually blunt and brutal, anything from "You need a nose job" to "Your teeth are yellow" to "You're fifteen pounds overweight." Once she signed you, she was almost pathologically protective, carefully screening everyone she sent her models to meet, enforcing strict curfews, dictating everything from social lives to diets to dermatologists to hairdressers to street wear to how much skin should or shouldn't be showing in any and all photo shoots. In many ways she was more controlling than your worst nightmare of a mother, but she wasn't about to let anything bad happen to her models, not on her watch! If you weren't willing to adhere to her clear, nonnegotiable rules, you'd be escorted straight to the door, no arguments and no second chances.

As far as I was concerned, she took great care of us, and her rules weren't all that unreasonable in exchange for the amazing careers we were being given in return. I did my first *Life* magazine cover, titled "Too Much Jewelry?," in 1952, and not for one moment do I believe that would have happened without the power of Eileen Ford propelling me through the door.

That *Life* magazine cover was shot by photographer extraordinaire Milton Greene, who was perhaps best known as Marilyn Monroe's photographer, business partner, and friend. I worked with Milton many times, and he and his darling, tiny wife Amy and I became good friends as well.

They invited me to their home in Connecticut for several weekend gatherings, and on one particular weekend Marilyn Monroe happened to be staying with them. I'm still trying to figure out whether or not I can say I met her.

It was a Sunday afternoon, and hours passed before Marilyn emerged from her suite on the second floor. I looked up to see her descending the stairs, presumably to come down and join the group.

Instead, she stopped on the landing, where she sat down in the corner and stayed there.

End of story.

Seriously, she never said a word, she just sat there on that landing with a rather blank, unwelcoming look on her face. I never saw anyone approach her, and I kind of lost track of her. Later I noticed she'd just disappeared, perhaps back to her room or who knows where.

I have no idea what was going on with her. I wrote it off to terrible shyness or insecurity and left it at that. Milton and Amy didn't seem to think a thing about it, and I wasn't about to ask them. It was none of my business, and frankly, I wasn't that interested.

So that was the perfectly lovely Sunday afternoon in Connecticut when I either did or didn't meet Marilyn Monroe. Your call.

And then, of course, there were the added bonuses of living in New York, a city I love, sharing a huge, wonderful apartment with a few of my friends and fellow models and being paid very generously to do work that exhilarated me and made me feel blessed every single day. My Minnesota friend Caroline Povell even came to New York and joined the Ford Agency as a model, and we privately marveled over and over again at where we two small-town Midwestern girls had ended up.

There's something about several women, even women who like each other as much as we did, living together under one roof that can get—shall we say?—a little edgy and competitive. Thankfully, we all ended up going our separate ways before any friendships were ruined, and I eventually found my way to a beautiful apartment of my own in Forest Hills, grateful for the peace, quiet, and privacy.

Just when it seemed as though life couldn't get much better, along came an amazing invention called television. Every family in America was buying one, which meant they needed shows to watch, which meant a whole new opportunity for advertisers, which meant a whole new world of possibilities for print models, runway models, and actresses.

Suddenly we were booking television commercials, delightedly opening refrigerator doors on camera, taking ecstatic sips of coffee, and gracefully waving our hands over shiny new Studebakers. The residual checks were fabulous, and I loved learning the skills of performing live on soundstages.

It's hard to picture now, but back then there were cigarette commercials everywhere, and three of us were booked to do them on the wildly popular *Perry Como Show*, which aired live every Monday, Wednesday, and Friday night. The commercial went like this: One model would put a cigarette to her lips, the next model would light a cigarette, and the third model would exhale smoke in a state of absolute rapture.

I had to learn how to smoke for those commercials, and since it's impossible to fake smoking, I was addicted in no time. I kept right on smoking and enjoying it until the news came out in about 1965 that it causes cancer, emphysema, a prematurely aging face (that may have been the one that pushed me over the edge), and God knows what else. Once again, "I'm not going to do that anymore" came to the rescue—I quit cold turkey and put that killer out of my life without a single relapse.

There was another popular series on the air at the time, the TV adaptation of a radio series called *The Aldrich Family*. I was there to shoot a small role as somebody or other's girlfriend. The fact that it was my first acting job was far overshadowed by the fact that somehow, on my first day, I managed to lose my balance and fall backward off the stage. Fortunately, a young man happened to be standing at the right place at the right time to catch me in his arms and save me from hitting the floor. My leg was bleeding badly. In fact, I still have the scar. While he bandaged me, he asked if I was okay, and I focused on my hero for the first time.

He was tall, dark, and handsome, with a confident, infectious smile and piercing eyes.

I assured him I was fine, just a little shaken up. Then I thanked him for catching me and introduced myself.

"Tippi Hedren," I said.

"Peter Griffith," he replied.

And just as I had with the first Peter in my life, my dear cat, I fell in love.

I was twenty-one when I met Peter Griffith. He was eighteen, a former child actor who'd appeared on Broadway, and we became inseparable from the moment we met. He was fun, he was very, very smart, and he was wonderfully supportive of my career. When we weren't going to dinners and parties and the theater in New York, we were visiting his charming parents on Long Island and his equally lovely relatives in Maryland. They had a gray horse I've never forgotten. I loved that horse and rode her every chance I got. But occasionally, for some reason, without warning, she'd decide she'd had quite enough of being ridden and throw me, and I'd go limping back to the stables brushing dirt off my jodhpurs, clinging to what little dignity I had left. I became the center of a lot of hilarious family stories for that—that mare would already be in the barn, settled into her stall, before I'd finally come dragging into view, and yet I never could bring myself to stop riding her.

A few months into my relationship with Peter I took a trip to Arizona for a Sears catalogue shoot. My old boyfriend Jimmy Lewis was going to school there, and we had a brief, sweet reunion. I loved seeing him again, but it erased any doubts I might have had that my mind and heart had moved on.

Peter and I had been together for about a year when we decided to get married. I was still living in my Forest Hills apartment, and we chose a nearby Lutheran church for our wedding. Everything about that day was perfect except that my sister Patty was too pregnant with the first of her five children to travel and take her place as my matron of honor, but Peter's sister Sally and my closest modeling friends made a gorgeous team of bridesmaids. I designed my virginal white knee-length wedding dress, I flew my parents in from California, and it meant the world to me to have Daddy walk me down the aisle and give me away.

It was 1952. I was twenty-two. Peter was nineteen. Somehow the fact that we were too young for this never entered our minds.

My career was thriving, between TV commercials and magazine covers for everyone from *Glamour* to *The Saturday Evening Post* and *Seventeen* magazine, and there were things I loved about being a wife.

We moved from my Forest Hills apartment to a great building at 81st and Park when the commute became too much of a grind, and I enjoyed making a home for us there. Peter loved horses, and of course so did I, so I decorated with that in mind, with horse-related artwork and forest-green decor. It was exciting to show off my minimal cooking skills at dinner parties for our friends and experience the novelty of socializing as Mr. and Mrs. Peter Griffith. I threw myself wholeheartedly into my new role of married woman, and I kept myself busy enough for a while to drown out the quiet feeling in me that something had changed, that for some reason being married didn't seem as special as dating.

Then the United States of America intervened. Peter joined the army, became an MP, and was sent off to the Korean War.

My self-sufficiency kicked right in, and instead of indulging in missing my husband, I appreciated my time alone, going where I wanted when I wanted, keeping my own hours, enjoying work and relaxing with my friends. I even bought a fabulous Morgan convertible, in red, my favorite color.

That car was a cop magnet. I lost track of the number of speeding tickets I had to pay off, and always did, by the way. Okay, maybe it had a little to do with the fact that Morgans weren't built to be slaves to speed limits, but still, how about some sympathy for the young blond woman who was just trying to break in her new car?

I'd been looking at apartments again and moved to a perfect one at 430 East 56th Street on the East River. There was a tennis club there, the Town Tennis Club. I didn't play tennis. I still don't. But I joined the club anyway, thinking it might be a nice, safe place where I could go by myself, meet new people, and make new friends.

I was right. Also members of the tennis club were an irresistible couple named Lillian (Lily) and Hubert (Hubie) Boskowitz. She called him Potsy. He called her Pussy-Mouse. (I didn't ask.) They were positively elegant. They owned a fantastic brownstone just off of Park Avenue, but they were so funny and down-to-earth that they put the names Potsy and Pussy-Mouse above their door. From the first day we met, Lily and Hubie took me under their very busy, very social wings. I met fascinating people through them, and on any given night they'd whisk me off to the opera or the theater or dinner or a party or an art gallery opening, always laughing, always having fun, always making me feel like family rather than a third wheel. We remained close friends until they died many, many years later, and I was so moved that when Lillian passed away, she left me two diamond bracelets she cherished.

Peter went on leave to Tokyo, and I met him there for a lovely couple of weeks together, during which he told me the oddest, most amazing story. He and some of his fellow MPs in Korea had ambushed an enemy tent, and once inside, they found several of my magazine covers pinned to the canvas walls. Peter said it was all he could do not to kill the tent's occupant and tear down those photos of me. What on earth are the odds?

And then, because I'd already gone halfway around the world traveling from New York to Japan, and I had the luxury of being able to afford it, I decided I might as well go the rest of the way and kept heading west.

I didn't think a thing about traveling from one country to another by myself, and had a glorious two months of exploring India, which was a fascinating assault on the senses, and Egypt, a place I'd always yearned to see. What a magnificent experience, to be in the presence of the Pyramids and the Sphinx and to almost literally feel antiquity in the earth itself, making you aware that you're a part of something timeless and far greater than yourself, a deep sense of being humbled and empowered at the same time.

Then it was on to a glorious time with Dr. Thomas Rees, his wife Nan, who was a fellow model, and some other friends in the South of France. Someone briefly introduced me to Senator John Kennedy on my first afternoon there, the operative word being "briefly." They exchanged a little small talk, including the fact that his wife Jackie was in Italy recovering from a broken ankle, and then we all went right on with our day.

I was in my hotel room early that same evening preparing to meet everyone for dinner when the phone rang. It was the concierge.

"Miss Hedren, Senator Kennedy asked me to tell you that he has a car waiting for you downstairs."

I took the phone away from my ear and gaped at it for a second before replying, "Please tell Senator Kennedy I already have plans for the evening, but thank you anyway."

I hung up and fumed. I was thoroughly disgusted with him. He was a representative of the United States government, for heaven's sake—a representative of our government who should have been in Italy taking care of his wife and her broken ankle, if you asked me. And I was offended that he thought, even for a moment, I might say yes to such an arrogant, presumptuous invitation. Logically, I knew it wasn't personal. It was strictly about genitalia, and the concierge was probably already on the phone with the next lucky candidate, who might easily say, "I'll be right down." But emotionally? How dare he?

I went right on with my evening, and I don't doubt for a moment that Senator Kennedy went right on with his.

The only glitch in an otherwise perfect trip was when I became very sick in Paris, with chest pains and shortness of breath and a persistent cough. A friend came to my hotel room to check on me and immediately rushed me to the hospital, where I was diagnosed with pleurisy.

It was a shock to have my life interrupted by a very real health problem. I've always taken great care of myself, and I was pretty sure that was supposed to count for something. I also wasn't born with the patience gene, so lying in a hospital room surrounded by concerned friends instead of having dinner with them at a café on the Seine was infuriating. The minute they let me out of there, I headed straight back to New York and back to work, partly because I'd missed it so much and partly because I was eager to prove to myself that whatever the hell pleurisy was, I'd beaten it, and I was still every bit as healthy as I'd earned the right to be.

Keeping a young marriage alive and well was hard enough without the added complication of a long separation of thousands of miles. When Peter came home from Korea, things felt different between us, but we did the best we knew how to do, and we were elated to learn at the end of 1956 that we were going to have a baby.

On August 9, 1957, I gave birth to the most extraordinary, most exquisite love of my life, our daughter, Melanie Griffith. I'd heard and read a thousand times that there's no love deeper and more unconditional than the love between a mother and her child, but I can honestly say I had no idea what those words even meant until they laid that baby girl across my chest when she was only a few moments old.

Shortly after I arrived in New York in 1950, I'd gone to lunch at the very exclusive Russian Tea Room. A woman was moving among the tables reading the patrons' tea leaves, and when she got to me, she studied the pattern of leaves in my teacup, looked into my eyes and said, "Ahhh! A daughter of great fortune!"

I had no idea what she was talking about at the time, and I'd given it little if any thought, but it came rushing back to me when I looked into our perfect newborn's eyes, and I still remember holding her close to me on the day she was born and whispering, "A daughter of great fortune." Then I held her in my arms and walked her over to the window of our room at Doctors Hospital in Manhattan to show her the East River and introduce her to her awesome hometown of New York City.

Melanie Griffith was and is my great fortune, my best friend, my love, my luckiest blessing in a life that's been filled with them.

I adored everything about being a mother.

Sadly, being a wife was becoming more and more difficult.

Peter and I had been social drinkers from the day we met, enjoying fine wine and champagne as much as the next person.

After Peter got out of the army, though, it was impossible not to notice that his drinking was gradually increasing, to the point where he was getting drunk several times a week. The charm I'd always found so irresistible about him eroded into an obnoxious, glassy-eyed carelessness when he'd had too much to drink, and the man I'd fallen in love with and married seemed to be slipping away.

Another problem, one that had actually existed unaddressed from the beginning of our marriage, was the fact that I was making significantly more money than Peter was. His acting career had withered and died in his midteens. He worked for an insurance company for a while and then got a job in commercial production, but he spent a lot of time unemployed.

I honestly didn't think a thing about being the primary breadwinner of the family. We had a secure, comfortable life I could afford, including a wonderful nanny named Josephine for our baby girl, and I'd never believed in relying on any man to take care of me when I'm perfectly capable of doing that myself.

But while we never had an actual conversation about it, it was obvious that Peter resented it. It weighed heavily on him that he couldn't compete with me salary-wise. He felt angry and emasculated to the point where he'd occasionally be snide and demeaning to me, and before long he found an easy, obvious, destructive way to overcompensate—he turned to other women.

It didn't take a rocket scientist to figure out that something was going on when he'd come home at all hours of the night or not come home at all, no matter how sincere his excuses sounded or how indignant he'd get that the thought of his being unfaithful could even enter my mind.

When I still cared, it devastated me. I felt betrayed, diminished, and insulted to my core that a man I'd loved as best I could would look elsewhere, as if my best wasn't enough, and then look me in the eye and lie to me over and over again. And as far as I was concerned, he wasn't just cheating on me, he was cheating on our baby daughter as well, choosing to be away from home more and more, when he could have been there with her. She deserved much more, and so did I.

Then when I stopped caring, when I hit my "I'm not going to do this anymore" wall, I kicked him out.

Peter moved in with his girlfriend.

I flew to Mexico and got a divorce.

He'd been absent so much toward the end that it was weeks before Melanie even asked, "Where's Daddy?"

Still, the timing could have been better. It was becoming more and more apparent that my ten-year modeling career was waning. The phone wasn't ringing as often, aspiring models in their late teens and early twenties were continuing to flood into New York City every day and creating excitement because they were pretty and new, and after two years of starting to feel like old news, I decided it was time for a change.

I packed up Melanie, our nanny Josephine, and our animals—our poodle puppy, kitten, and bunny—and moved back to Los Angeles, where Melanie could get to know her grandparents and I could regroup.

Three

I spent a very long time kicking myself for my years with Peter, thinking, "What a stupid marriage."

We were too young to have a clue what we were getting into, that's for sure. I looked back on the wedding ceremony, and that moment when we vowed to love, honor, and cherish each other "till death do us part," and wondered if we would have said "I do" so quickly if those words had been changed to "for the rest of your lives." That sounds so much longer and has so much more gravity than "till death do us part," don't you think? Peter was nineteen when we got married. I was twenty-two. Death? At that age? On such a pretty, happy day? Never heard of it.

There was that wonderful, inexplicable spark between us at the beginning, and the thrill of romance. I love romance. It's a perfect foundation for a healthy, exciting dating relationship. For a lifelong commitment? Not so much.

We had what we thought was a lot in common. We both loved socializing, going to the theater and dinner parties and great restaurants, and we both "cleaned up" well—we looked really good together. But when it came to the essence of who we were, our beliefs and priorities and work ethics and personalities, we had virtually nothing in common at all, and yet I'd walked up that aisle on my daddy's arm in 1952, thinking, "Yeah, this will work." What?

The day I stopped kicking myself and wondering how a smart woman like me could have made such a stupid mistake was the day a simple, undeniable fact hit me, with the help of a fascinating book called *The Other Side and Back* by Sylvia Browne: If I hadn't married Peter Griffith, there would be no Melanie. No one else on this planet but Peter could have cocreated this treasured daughter with me, who's completed my life since the day she was born. If my marriage to Peter was about nothing more than bringing Melanie into this world, then not only was that marriage not a stupid mistake, but it was a blessing.

Peter went on to form his own production company and to marry four more times. He died of emphysema in 2001, and it probably speaks volumes about his taste in women that all five of us wives went to his funeral in Texas and thoroughly enjoyed one another. We almost felt like sisters, and it was extraordinary, and very adult of us, come to think of it, that there was such a great camaraderie between us.

And until the day he died, Peter and Melanie adored each other. That made me happy, and I would never have tried to deny them that love or have interfered in their relationship in any way. How he and I came to feel about each other was beside the point. He was her father. My daddy and I loved each other to the moon and back, no matter how many miles separated us at any given time. I'll always cherish the fact that Melanie can say the same thing about her daddy, and that she's passed along the tradition. She has three children by her three different husbands, and when holidays and special occasions come along, everyone's invited, including ex-husbands, their spouses, and their other children—all of us connected, all of us part of the same extended family, petty resentments strictly prohibited.

One Thanksgiving, surrounded by all those dear people, Melanie asked me to say grace. I gave a prayer of gratitude for our love of each other that we shared with an amazing understanding.

I admire that daughter of mine so much for the open heart and open arms that are always there for anyone and everyone she's ever loved.

Melanie was four years old when she, her nanny Josephine, our sweet little menagerie, and I moved back to Los Angeles in 1961. Because financial planning is not my forte, I rented a beautiful, expensive house in Westwood, in keeping with the lifestyle we were accustomed to in New York. It was such a joy to give my daughter a safe, lovely place to grow up with our poodle and our cat and our bunny, and to watch her and my parents fall in love with one another, that on most days I could avoid thinking about the fact that my bank account was slowly ebbing away.

Commercials and occasional print work came along now and then, but there was no way around the reality that fashion models have a limited shelf life. I was in high, nonstop, glorious demand when I was in my twenties. But as my thirty-first birthday came and went, the flood of offers was slowing to a trickle. My huge stack of magazine covers and catalogues weren't going to pay the rent or transform me from what I'd been to what I'd become—a single mother with a high school education and no bankable skills to speak of. I should have learned how to type.

I had no idea what I was going to do.

Looking back, I'm as amazed as you might be at the incredible Cinderella pattern of my life. Opportunities I hadn't dreamed of or even thought about were handed to me on a silver platter, landed right in my lap out of nowhere, almost as if I'd planned them ahead of time, and it was my choice to either ignore them and let them go to waste or to pay attention and give them my best shot. "What shall I do now?" I'd ask, and the universe would say, "You're going to do this. Now make the most of it." A woman with a business card meeting my streetcar in Morningside, literally falling into the arms of the future husband who would cocreate my beautiful daughter. And then along came another glass slipper, with a note from God reading, "Okay, now you're going to do *this*."

It was Friday the thirteenth of October 1961.

My phone rang.

I answered it to hear, "Are you the girl in the Sego commercial?"

The Sego commercial? Yes, I'd done a commercial a few months earlier for a new meal replacement shake from Pet Milk called Sego. I hadn't given it another thought, other than being grateful for the paycheck and the residuals and wondering if it might be a little misleading to hire a hundred-pound model to sell a diet drink. Why would anyone be calling about that?

It seems a "well-known director" and his wife had been watching *The Today Show* that morning and happened to see the commercial. He'd promptly called the executives at Universal Studios, where he was under contract, and ordered them to "FIND THE GIRL."

Once we'd established that I was apparently "the girl," the caller wondered if I'd be available to meet with the director's agent at MCA the following Tuesday.

MCA was a huge, powerful agency. Of course I'd be available. But who was this "well-known director"?

The caller wouldn't tell me. He simply gave me the information for Tuesday's meeting and hung up.

I was dumbfounded. What in the world could this possibly be about, and who in the world could this director possibly be? He must be pretty important if he could order the executives at what was arguably the biggest studio in town to "find the girl" and they would jump to the task. Who *was* this man?

It was a fun, intriguing three days from that Friday to that Tuesday, trying to figure out who the mystery director might be, not to mention what he might want with me. I had a party at my house the night after the phone call, and my agent, Mort Viner, was there. He was with MCA as well, and he knew about the phone call, but even he wouldn't tell me who it was.

Countless scenarios played out in my mind, including the most likely one: A lot of models were also either actresses or aspiring actresses. This director might easily be assuming that I was one of those, find out that the thought of being an actress had never even been on my radar, thank me for my time, and send me right back home to sign up for typing classes. But whatever it was and whoever he was, I was excited and ready to play it out.

I was right on time for my meeting on Tuesday at MCA with superagent Lew Wasserman, head of MCA, who would buy and control Universal Studios a year later. He was tall and slender, with black-framed glasses and a readily accessible smile, and we exchanged a few pleasantries as we sat down together in his office.

Then he ended the mystery.

"Alfred Hitchcock wants to put you under contract."

I just stared at him, speechless, wondering if I'd heard him correctly. I also had to fight an urge to laugh—I'd been staring at walls covered with framed photos of Alfred Hitchcock in Wasserman's outer office while I waited for this meeting, and not once did it enter my mind that he might be the mysterious "well-known director" I'd been obsessing about all weekend.

I'd seen most if not all of Alfred Hitchcock's movies. He'd earned his status as an icon. He was brilliant. He was prolific—literally dozens of classic films, and he was conquering a whole new medium with his hit television series *Alfred Hitchcock Presents* and *The Alfred Hitchcock Hour*. This man wanted to put *me* under contract? From seeing me in a Sego commercial? And a contract for what? Was I dreaming?

Wasserman, in the meantime, was sliding some neatly typed paperwork to me across the desk.

"It's a straightforward, standard contract," he said. "Look it over, and if you agree to it and sign it, we'll set up a meeting for you and Hitch."

The only people who called Hitchcock "Alfred," he added parenthetically, were people who didn't know him. "Mr. Hitchcock" or "Hitch" were the only two choices when addressing him.

Everything was a dazed blur as I looked through the pages in front of me, but I did manage to register the words "$500 per week." Enough said. I signed on the dotted line above my typed name, and I was under contract to Alfred Hitchcock before I'd even met him.

Next thing I knew I was driving through the gate at Paramount Studios, and Hitchcock's secretary Peggy was showing me into his office. Whether or not he planned it this way I have no idea, but my first look at him was the famous profile that greeted his audiences every week at the beginning of his television show. He was shorter and even rounder than I was expecting, and he was remarkably unattractive. But from the moment he turned to welcome me, he couldn't have been more charming. He led me to a small table, where a lovely luncheon for two and an expensive bottle of red wine were waiting for us, and we spent a delightful hour together. He had a dry British wit and a fondness for spontaneously reciting very funny, slightly off-color limericks. We talked about travel and food and wine, and I was fully prepared to make it clear to him, when the subject inevitably came up, that I knew nothing about acting and had never acted a day in my life.

The subject of acting never came up. The subject of why in the world he wanted me under contract never came up. We simply ate, laughed, and had an enjoyable, stimulating social conversation. Then, after a pleasant good-bye, I thanked him and left, more curious than ever and still in shock over how dramatically my life had changed in just a few short hours. I didn't know why me. I didn't know what any of it was about or what promises I'd made in that contract I'd signed. All I knew was that I always kept my promises and that I had a generous, steady paycheck to look forward to. My little girl and I were going to be just fine.

Melanie, my parents, and I celebrated my incredible Alfred Hitchcock news over dinner that night. Melanie had been thriving ever since our move to California. She was extraordinarily pretty, smart, and strong-willed. She inherited my love of animals, but not the shyness I went through at her age—she was much more outgoing than I was, and I never had to wonder how she was feeling at any given moment. Whatever it was, good or bad, if she felt it, she openly, confidently expressed it. She was loving, affectionate, and sensitive, and she was my favorite sidekick. I probably treated her more like an adult than a child. Like most parents, in those hours before I go to sleep at night I find myself looking back at what I'd do differently now if I had the chance. That's one of them.

As we toasted my future with Hitchcock, my parents were thrilled for me. I don't think Melanie especially understood what was going on, she was just adorably thrilled because the rest of us were. Mom and Daddy didn't have a single doubt that whatever Hitchcock had in mind for me, I could do it and do it well. I still marvel at their unwavering belief in me. It was like having a hidden bank account I could draw from when my belief in myself was running low.

The studio system that was common practice during Hollywood's "golden age" was on its way out by the time I went under contract to Alfred Hitchcock, who'd moved to Universal by then. Actors under contract were no longer required to take classes in singing, dancing, diction, poise and movement, horseback riding, and countless other skills that would prepare them for a wider variety of roles and groom them for stardom. But I still had a lot to learn and a considerable amount of work to do to accomplish what was expected of me, and I loved every minute of it.

I was assigned a voice coach, not for singing (dear God), but for speaking effectively. It was fascinating—she taught me, for example, how to place my voice. Instead of placing it in the back of the throat, she said, I should place my voice at the lips. It sounded trivial, but once I started learning what she was talking about, I was surprised at what a difference it made.

I was also assigned to the brilliant, Academy Award–winning wardrobe designer Edith Head. From the first minute I stepped through the tall red double doors of her building on the Universal lot, I knew I was in the hands of the best of the best. Her eyes sparkled with a genius imagination behind her trademark round-rimmed glasses, and it's impossible to calculate the number of hours we spent together, usually laughing, while she created a glorious array of clothing for me, everything from ball gowns to cocktail dresses to pantsuits to skirt suits for me to wear on-screen and off, all under orders from Hitchcock. I knew a thing or two about fashion myself after all those years of modeling, so Edith and I spoke the same language, which made our working together even more meaningful. She began inviting me to cocktail parties and dinners at her home, and we developed a genuine friendship. More than fifty years later I still have and cherish some of the fabulous clothes Edith Head designed for me.

And then, of course, there was the little matter of acting lessons. Hitchcock had scheduled a screen test for me, a requirement for every contract player, I was sure, and he saw to it that I had the two best acting teachers in the business. I was taught by Alfred Hitchcock and his wife, Alma Reville.

Alma was an extraordinary woman. She was already an accomplished film editor when she and Hitchcock met, and she had an unbelievable ear for dialogue and eye for detail. Everyone on the Universal lot knew the story of Alma pointing out a moment in *Psycho* when you could see Janet Leigh breathing after she was killed, a moment Hitchcock had missed, and the scene was recut accordingly. Alma had an enormous, well-deserved influence over her husband while never trying to upstage him or even share a part of his spotlight. She was plain, quiet, stunningly gifted, and one of Hitchcock's most valuable underrated assets.

We usually met at their house in Bel Air, which he preferred over the more formal setting of his office, and Hitch and Alma gave me an education in acting beyond anything I could have dreamed of while getting me ready for my screen test. Technique was only the beginning. They also taught me how to break down a script, how to analyze a character, how to explore both the text and the subtext of a character's relationships with other players—it was a lot of hard, remarkable, mesmerizing work, and I enjoyed it as much as I needed it.

The screen test Hitch had devised for me would have been a challenge even for a seasoned actress. I'd be performing scenes from three of his classic films: *Rebecca*, *To Catch a Thief*, and *Notorious*. The lead female characters in those films were three very complex, different women, and I worked exhaustively on them, hoping that what I lacked in experience I could make up for in earnest dedication.

Edith Head did the breathtaking wardrobe. The best hair and makeup team on the lot was reserved for me. Hitch flew in veteran actor Martin Balsam from back east, fresh from his work on *Psycho*, to be my scene partner. Elaborate sets were built, and Hitch's entire film crew was scheduled to shoot the test in color. I was grateful for my years of modeling and commercial work—I might have been brand-new at this acting thing, but at least I knew my way around a soundstage.

It all seemed like a whole lot of trouble to go through for what was probably just preparation for a small part on his television series or something, but I was so naive that I assumed this was simply how screen tests were done, par for the course when you were put under contract.

Not until later did I find out that it was unprecedented at the time, the most expensive screen test on record, at a cost of about $25,000—just under $200,000 in today's money.

I was blown away, not only by the fact that Hitch would invest that much time, effort, and money to make me look good, but also that he had the power at Universal Studios to make it happen.

He showed me the finished product a couple of weeks later, and I was stunned by it. The production itself was exquisite, Edith Head's wardrobe was flawless, Martin Balsam was amazing, and I could see the value of every minute Hitch and Alma had spent coaching me. I was pretty damned good! I could do this! I could act!

A few days after the screen test, I was summoned to a private meeting in Hitchcock's office—not with Hitchcock, who was conspicuously absent, but with his attorney, a grim-looking man named Ed Henry. I couldn't imagine what this was about, but I could tell from his tepid greeting that this meeting was neither social nor friendly.

As soon as we sat down he got right to the point. "Miss Hedren, I need to talk with you about your past . . ."

What?

". . . particularly your life in New York."

"Oh, you mean my modeling career and the start of my commercial work?" I chimed in.

"No," he said, "I'm afraid it's much more serious than that." He cleared his throat and continued: "We've heard from a variety of sources that there's a problem with your reputation."

What?

I looked right at him. "I beg your pardon?"

"Well," he continued, looking right back at me, "we've heard that you were rather . . . available to men."

Now I was staring at him. I managed to keep my voice even, and I enunciated clearly to make sure he understood every word I was saying. "I have no idea what you're talking about," I said, "but if I am correct, and I think I am, because the hair on the back of my neck is beginning to bristle, I find your implication very insulting, and I won't dignify it with a response or even attempt to continue this conversation."

On which I stood and walked out and *slammed* the door behind me.

I never did find out what on earth prompted that ridiculous, offensive meeting. Not for one moment did I believe anyone, let alone a "variety of sources," had said any such thing, so maybe it was some test on Hitchcock's part to see how I'd react to essentially being accused of spending my years in New York as a prostitute. I didn't know what it was about, and a point finally came when I didn't care.

As it turned out, it wouldn't be the last time I would storm out of Hitchcock's office and slam the door behind me, but that would come much, much later.

One afternoon not long after that bizarre meeting, Hitchcock and I were alone in his office when he told me he'd thought of another screen test he wanted to do with me. This one involved martinis.

I would drink a real martini, he said, and answer "a provocative series of questions."

Then I would drink a second martini and answer those same questions.

Then a third and a fourth, presumably until I was so drunk that my answers would be as provocative as the questions.

He described the whole thing in enough cinematic detail that I could tell he'd thought about it a lot.

There was something creepy to me about the idea itself and the quiet excitement in his voice as he talked me through everything from what I'd be wearing to each and every move I'd make to each and every shot he had planned while, at his direction, I'd get completely wasted and slowly but surely lose all my inhibitions on camera.

I didn't know what to say or how to react, so I said nothing and didn't react at all. I got the feeling it disappointed him.

That second screen test never happened, and I put it, and my uneasiness about it, out of my mind.

There was a lot of talk around the studio about the next Hitchcock film. The screenplay was written by a writer named Evan Hunter. It was inspired by a short story by Daphne du Maurier, who wrote the magnificent novel *Rebecca* that Hitchcock had transformed into one of his greatest movies. The short story and Evan Hunter's screenplay were called *The Birds*.

Every actress on the lot was vying for the role of Melanie Daniels, the lead female character in the film. Hitchcock had his choice of leading ladies, with a track record that included A-list movie stars like Ingrid Bergman, Grace Kelly, Doris Day, Kim Novak, Eva Marie Saint, and Janet Leigh. I admit it, every once in a while I'd catch myself drifting into a fantasy about Hitch casting me in a small role in *The Birds*, but I knew I was getting way too far ahead of myself. He and Alma and I were spending an enormous amount of time together, and they'd never even mentioned that movie to me.

Rumors persisted about who might get the lucky nod to star in *The Birds*. It was one of the most pervasive questions buzzing around the Universal Studios lot in the spring of 1962, and no one including me would have guessed the answer, not in a million years.

About three weeks after I did my screen test with Martin Balsam, I was invited to join Hitch, Alma, and Lew Wasserman for dinner at Chasen's.

Chasen's was a legendary restaurant in West Hollywood, a favorite hangout for everyone who was anyone in show business, from the biggest stars to the top executives. Frank Sinatra, Marilyn Monroe, Gregory Peck, Jimmy Stewart, Cary Grant—you name it, they were there on any given night. Ronald Reagan proposed to Nancy Davis in the "Reagan booth" at Chasen's. Elizabeth Taylor famously had ten quarts of Chasen's chili shipped to her while she was filming *Cleopatra* in Italy, as if there were no good food to be found in Rome.

We, of course, were seated in the "Hitchcock booth." All heads in the crowded restaurant turned as I crossed the room. Not only was I a new face in town, but I seemed to be joining none other than Alfred Hitchcock and Lew Wasserman for dinner, which meant if I wasn't somebody already, I might be somebody very soon.

Shortly after our drinks arrived, Hitch turned to me and, without a word, handed me a small gift box from a famously exclusive store called Gump's in San Francisco.

I opened it and found myself staring at an exquisite, delicate pin—gold and seed pearls, crafted to depict three birds in flight. It was beautiful, but I couldn't imagine what the occasion was.

Hitch answered the question before I could ask it. "We want you to play Melanie Daniels in *The Birds*."

I was stunned. I'm sure I gasped.

After just sitting there silent and frozen in place for several seconds with tears welling up in my eyes, I looked across the table at Alma. She had tears in her eyes, too.

I looked at Lew. He even had a tear in his.

Finally I looked at Hitchcock. His eyes were dry. He just stared back at me—very, very pleased with himself.

Four

I couldn't wrap my head around what was happening to me. It felt as if one minute I was thinking of signing up for typing classes and the next I'd been thrust into the lead in an Alfred Hitchcock film. He'd worked with some of the most accomplished, talented actresses in the world. He could have hired anyone he wanted, and he wanted me, a woman who'd never even had a passing thought about becoming an actress. That this brilliant, iconic director had so much faith in me felt like an overwhelming responsibility, but it was incredibly motivating as well. Whatever brought all this on, I was prepared to do everything in my power to make sure that believing in me was a decision he'd never regret.

Apparently the executives at Universal Studios were as mystified as I was about why Hitchcock cast me. They'd been impressed by my screen test, but that didn't eliminate their biggest objection, which I couldn't argue with or do anything about: I was an unknown. The studio had high hopes for *The Birds*. It was their next Alfred Hitchcock film, their follow-up to the massively successful *Psycho*. They'd committed a whole lot of money to see to it that this movie would be the biggest box office hit it could possibly be. They felt they had the right to have a name on the marquee that would add to the audience's built-in Hitchcock excitement, not inspire them to stand outside the theater with their wallets still in their pockets, scratching their heads and saying, "Who the hell is Tippi Hedren?" The executives' opposition only added to the intense pressure I was already feeling, but Hitchcock never even flinched.

One day at the studio he became concerned that I was losing weight. I wasn't. I hadn't lost or gained an ounce since I was a teenager. But suddenly large baskets of bread and potatoes began appearing on my front doorstep with notes in them reading "Eat me." I didn't think much about it. True, it seemed a little controlling, and true, it was a little unnerving that someone had repeatedly been right outside my door without my knowing it, but paranoia has never been a part of who I am, and I had far too much on my mind to waste it on what was probably meant to be a harmless gesture.

Hitch's preparation for *The Birds* was exhaustive and meticulous. He worked very closely with Evan Hunter on the script and covered his office walls with graphs that outlined the rise and fall of every sequence in the film. He spent countless hours with his cinematographer Robert Burks, his photographic adviser Ub Iwerks, and his special effects expert Lawrence Hampton.

Bird trainer Ray Berwick was brought in to train the hundreds and hundreds of ravens and gulls. I remember him telling me that once he'd trained birds to peck someone on command, it was impossible to "untrain" them, so they'd spend the rest of their lives safe and happy in his massive aviary. I became great pals with Buddy, one of the ravens, and thanks to Ray, Buddy and I did some cute, wonderful tricks together to entertain the cast and crew off camera.

The Birds took six months to shoot. Between the trained birds, the mechanical birds, the composite photography, the animation, and the live action, it really was a masterpiece of filmmaking on Hitchcock's part. I was so intensely focused on holding up my end of it and doing my damnedest to rise to the extraordinary expertise of my castmates that I was barely aware of the technical artistry that was going on around me.

Rod Taylor, Jessica Tandy, Veronica Cartwright, and Suzanne Pleshette were all so wonderful to me, so supportive, and as time went by, so quietly sympathetic. Not once was anyone dismissive of me as the complete novice I was, or anything less than kind and embracing. We didn't socialize together off camera, partly because there was no time or energy left after long days of filming and partly because, unbeknownst to me, Hitchcock was too proprietary of "The Girl," as he referred to me behind my back, to allow it. In fact, as I eventually found out, he'd given an actual order, almost a threat, to Rod Taylor, and later to Sean Connery during *Marnie*: "Do not touch The Girl!" As irresistible as both those men were, I never let any romantic thoughts about them enter my mind anyway, and probably because of that, we became great friends. But "Do not touch The Girl"? Really?

In case you've never seen the film, or it was so long ago you've forgotten, *The Birds* is about a wealthy San Francisco socialite named Melanie Daniels (my character). She happens to meet a handsome, glib, rather cocky lawyer named Mitch Brenner (Rod Taylor) in a pet store in San Francisco. Before he leaves the store, he mentions in passing that his younger sister Cathy (Veronica Cartwright) is having a birthday. Melanie buys a pair of lovebirds for Cathy as an excuse to drive to Mitch's weekend home in Bodega Bay to deliver them and, of course, to see him again.

She's boating across the bay when, out of nowhere, a seagull swoops down to attack her, leaving her with a bleeding forehead.

Mitch, his sister Cathy and his mother Lydia (Jessica Tandy), who live in the house full-time, tend to her wound and invite her to stay for dinner. Cathy excitedly accepts the gift of the lovebirds, while Lydia treats Melanie with a cool, suspicious distance. As the evening proceeds, Melanie is convinced to stay for Cathy's birthday party the next afternoon.

She spends the night at the home of schoolteacher Annie Hayworth (Suzanne Pleshette), who was once romantically involved with Mitch. Annie tells Melanie not to take Lydia's apparent dislike of her personally. It seems that Lydia suffered a breakdown a few years earlier when her husband died, and she's mistrustful of any woman who might lure Mitch away from her and leave her abandoned.

The lives of everyone in Bodega Bay are turned upside down when, for no apparent reason, massive flocks of birds begin to viciously attack the residents. The children at Cathy's birthday party are attacked while playing in the yard. A huge flock of sparrows flies wildly down the chimney through the fireplace and into Mitch and Lydia's living room. A local farmer is killed by the birds, as is Annie, as she tries to protect the children from an attack on the schoolhouse.

Finally the birds surround Mitch's house, holding Melanie, Mitch, Cathy, and Lydia hostage. That night, during what seems to be a lull in the chaos, Melanie hears the unmistakable sound of a lot of fluttering wings coming from somewhere above her. She ends up climbing alone to the upstairs bedroom, where the birds quickly surround her and violently strike, trying to kill her, too. Mitch comes to her rescue.

She's desperately in need of medical attention. While the radio reports that the bird attacks are spreading to neighboring communities, Mitch, Melanie, Lydia, Cathy, and the lovebirds Melanie gave her ("They haven't harmed anyone") manage to escape the house and leave Bodega Bay while the birds seem to allow it—resting up, it's implied, to inflict more violent harm on the once-peaceful town.

On another level of the film, we learn that Melanie's mother abandoned her many years earlier, which makes Lydia's initial rejection of her sting all the more. Melanie's been looking for her mother ever since, and Lydia's eventual caring and compassion toward her gives her the emotional closure she's been yearning for.

I'll never forget asking Hitchcock while we painstakingly worked on the script and my performance, "Knowing what's happened to the farmer and Annie, knowing that the whole town's under attack and that the birds have surrounded the house, why in the world would I climb those stairs and go into that bedroom by myself?"

To which Hitch replied after careful thought, "Because I tell you to."

I've been complimented many times, by the way, about how beautifully I played the piano in *The Birds*. I do love a nice compliment, but I'm afraid I can't accept that one. Mom taught my sister Patty and me to play the piano when we were children. Patty became very good at it. I didn't. Trying to conquer the violin was all the musical challenge I cared to tackle. I remember thinking, "What's the point? No one's ever going to ask me to play the piano." Then, of course, there I sat at a piano on a soundstage, shooting a Hitchcock movie, being asked if I could play the piano.

No one minded that I couldn't, but it would have been nice if I could. At least I'd played enough and practiced enough that I knew what it would look like if I really was playing that song. I'll take credit for that, but nothing more.

It became a pattern I didn't really put together at first. Every time I'd be laughing and talking with a male member of the cast or crew, my next exchange with Hitchcock would be icy and a bit petulant. He might suddenly recite a particularly filthy, offensive limerick, or give me a terse, unnecessary criticism, especially when I was alone with him in the back of his limo, always looking directly at me to make sure I knew it was deliberate. At other times he'd launch into endless, pointless monologues, seemingly just to hear himself talk and remind me which of us was in charge. I'd refuse to react in any way and simply gaze out the window of that limo, thinking, "Get me out of here."

I couldn't avoid noticing when he began relentlessly staring at me on the set. Obviously there's nothing unusual about a director spending a lot of time looking at his actors. But this was an expressionless, unwavering stare, no matter where he was or what he was doing; even if he was talking to a group of people on the other side of the soundstage, his eyes would be fixed on me. The cast and crew noticed, too, and it made them as uncomfortable as it made me, but there didn't seem to be anything anyone could do about it. After one of our scenes together, Suzanne Pleshette pulled me aside and quietly whispered, "This is so sad, because I promise, making movies isn't always like this. I'm really sorry he's putting you through it."

I wasn't some naive fourteen-year-old girl. In ten years of modeling I'd learned how to deflect unwanted male attention. I'd never learned, though, how to deflect something like this.

One late afternoon I was in the back of the limo with Hitchcock as usual, going back to our hotel in Santa Rosa after a long day on the set. He was indulging in one of his monologues, and I was turned away from him, exhausted, looking out the window at nothing at all.

The limo was just pulling to a stop at the entrance to the hotel, which was swarming with guests and valets and some of our crew members, when with no warning, he threw himself on top of me and tried to kiss me.

Why he insisted on having an audience for that utterly disgusting encounter I'll never know, unless in some deranged fantasy he thought I might cooperate. He shouldn't have been one bit surprised that instead I screamed, "What?!" and then "Stop!," pushed him off of me, jumped out of the limo, and stormed into the hotel.

It was an awful, awful moment I'll always wish I could erase from my memory.

The next time I saw him was on the set. I dreaded seeing him again, but I wasn't about to give him the satisfaction of knowing how deeply he'd offended and affected me. Instead, I arrived all business and ready to work, as if nothing had happened.

We were shooting a scene in which Melanie takes refuge in a phone booth with birds crashing against it, trying to get at her. The phone booth had supposedly been equipped with shatterproof glass, and mechanical birds were suspended by wires far above it and some distance away so that they were traveling at very high speeds when they hit.

Mechanical birds number one and two went perfectly, crashing into the glass with identical sickening thuds. Mechanical bird number three, on the other hand, managed to shatter the "shatterproof" glass. Filming was suspended for the rest of the day while my dear makeup man Howard Smit spent hours with a pair of tweezers, picking tiny fragments of glass out of the left side of my face.

I've never accused Hitchcock of deliberately rigging that phone booth, and I'm not accusing him of it now. But a part of me did wonder if I was being punished for rejecting him and doing it so publicly.

One night toward the end of our shoot in Bodega Bay I was invited to join Hitch and Alma for dinner at our hotel in Santa Rosa. I couldn't think of an excuse to get out of it for the life of me, and since Alma was going to be there, I didn't try very hard. I liked her, and Hitchcock was always better behaved when she was around.

The evening was progressing perfectly well, and Hitchcock was at his dry-witted, entertaining best, until Alma excused herself to say hello to some people in the garden area outside the dining room. The moment she was gone Hitch segued into a story about directing Cary Grant and Grace Kelly in *To Catch a Thief*. It was such a seamless transition from the other stories he'd been telling that night that I didn't even see this coming—during a scene in which they were kissing, he said, he suddenly found himself getting aroused.

How's that for an image you could happily live without for the rest of your life? If there was more to that story, I have no idea what it was. I don't remember what I said or how I managed to accomplish it, but I was on my feet and out of there in a shot, wishing we could somehow be granted the power to un-hear things.

The production moved back to Universal Studios, back to Los Angeles, where I could finally be at home with my daughter again. She was my salvation, my reminder of sweet, innocent normalcy and of what really mattered in this world. I wasn't about to let her see the horrible emotional toll this movie was taking on me, so I did my best to be the mommy she loved and counted on, no matter what it took. She knew me so well that I'm not sure how successful I was at hiding my turmoil from her, but we never talked about it.

I couldn't tell her that I'd started seeing Hitchcock in the back of his limo driving past our house.

I couldn't tell her that I'd found out he was occasionally having me followed, and that he'd even had my handwriting analyzed.

I couldn't tell her that one day, in a relatively private corner of the soundstage, away from the set while we were shooting, he'd asked me to touch him, and I'd resisted the temptation to slap him and just turned and walked away.

In fact, I couldn't tell anyone. It was the early 1960s. Sexual harassment and stalking were terms that didn't exist back then. Besides, he was Alfred Hitchcock, one of Universal's superstars, and I was just a lucky little blond model he'd rescued from relative obscurity. Which one of us was more valuable to the studio, him or me?

I even introduced Melanie to Hitchcock one day. I was a little apprehensive about it. I didn't believe he would do anything to harm her in any way; I was just aware, as we all were, that he didn't really like children. But he was lovely with her and even presented her with her very own "Tippi Hedren" doll. For reasons I'll never understand, a story has gone around for decades that the doll, a replica of her mommy, was in a little casket when he gave it to her. That's completely untrue. The doll was in nothing but a beautiful gift box. It's that simple.

My behavior toward Hitchcock chilled to a polite, professional distance. I became skilled at getting out of being alone with him unless it was absolutely unavoidable. He was constantly asking me to have cocktails or dinner with him after work, and nine times out of ten I could escape it by lying about someplace I needed to be or an appointment I couldn't get out of, or by just telling him the truth—I needed and wanted to spend the evening with Melanie.

But from time to time his secretary Peggy would convince me to say yes. "Just one drink, Tippi. Where's the harm?" she would say, or "It's only dinner, then home you'll go to your little girl." Peggy was in an impossible position. She was sympathetic toward me, and always very kind. I was never sure how much she knew or didn't know, and I wasn't about to ask. But she was also very loyal to her boss, and she'd worked for Hitchcock for so long that she understood him, or at least she was sensitive to him and didn't want him hurt.

So on rare occasions I would have cocktails or dinner with Hitchcock. Sometimes Alma would join us. Sometimes she wouldn't. Whether she was there or not, he'd be on his best behavior, that charming, dry-witted man I'd met in his office that first day. I'd hold up my end of the conversation and perform my way through it, torn and in an impossible situation myself.

On one hand, I was loving making *The Birds*. I loved playing Melanie Daniels. I loved the work itself, and my castmates and coworkers, and the totally committed focus it required of me. I never lost sight of the incredible opportunity and responsibility I'd been given, and I treasured it. How dare Hitchcock inflict his apparent obsession on me like this, force this oppressive situation on me that I didn't ask for, didn't deserve, and did nothing to encourage, and run the risk of shattering the concentration on this movie I was fighting so hard to maintain?

At the same time, it was Hitchcock who'd given me this incredible opportunity in the first place. He was presenting me to Universal, as well as to the film industry and audiences in general, as someone I really wasn't—a full-fledged movie star. Because of him I was being given special treatment all over town, with invitations to every gala, every exclusive dinner and event. I was a movie star, not because I'd proven myself yet but because none other than Alfred Hitchcock said

I was. And he hadn't just given me this opportunity, he'd personally seen to it that I could take it and run with it. He'd literally taught me everything I knew about acting. He'd seen to it that the very best Universal Studios had to offer was at my disposal. He'd believed in me so much that he'd fought for me against all those executives who thought he was crazy for choosing me, a totally unknown novice, to star in this movie.

He also happened to be a brilliant, brilliant filmmaker.

I owed him.

I owed him 100 percent of the dedication, concentration, and talent I had to give to *The Birds*, and I owed him the professional respect any actor owed their director.

I didn't owe him my dignity, or an abandonment of the values I'd been taught as a child and believed in wholeheartedly. I didn't owe him my body or my soul.

I've always been much more independent than ambitious. To me, ambition implies wanting something so badly that you'll compromise yourself here and there along the way to get it. I don't have that in me. I never have and never will. I don't believe you can put a price on being able to look at yourself in the mirror and respect the person looking back at you.

So yes, there were many things I owed Alfred Hitchcock. I even owed him my refusal to let him break me, no matter how hard he tried.

And he wasn't done trying yet.

Everything was building toward the famous "bedroom scene," the scene in which Melanie (still inexplicably as far as I'm concerned) goes up the stairs alone, steps into the bedroom, closes the door, and suffers the most vicious on-camera attack by the birds in the whole film. Some critics and Hitchcock buffs have compared it to the legendary shower scene in *Psycho*.

Hitchcock had outlined it for me in great detail. It would be just me and a flock of relentless, homicidal mechanical birds. I'd have no way to escape, and I would end up on the floor, completely terrorized and almost mortally wounded.

He lied.

It was a Monday morning, the day we were shooting the bedroom scene, when our assistant director, my good friend James H. Brown, came to see me in my dressing room. Jim had always been wonderful to me, and we'd become friends. But for some reason, that morning he couldn't look at me. His eyes were all over the place—the floor, the ceiling, the walls, everywhere but on me, and he wasn't saying a word. We knew each other too well for this, and I finally broke the silence.

"Jim, what's going on? What's wrong?"

It was last thing in the world he wanted to say, so he just blurted it out to get it over with.

"The mechanical birds aren't working, so we're going to have to use live ones."

Then he bolted out the door.

It took me several seconds to pick my jaw up off the floor. They were using *live birds* for this final apocalyptic scene?! I trusted the expertise of our trainer Ray Berwick 100 percent, but not even the greatest trainer in the world could control every move an animal makes, especially when it's under stress.

Resigned and determined, I finished getting ready and walked out on the set to find a cage built around the bedroom door. All around the inside of the cage were huge cartons of ravens, doves, and a few pigeons. I refused to look at Hitchcock as I crossed the set to my mark inside the door and braced myself for whatever was in store for me.

I heard Hitchcock yell, "Action!" and right on cue, the handlers began hurling those live birds at me. It was brutal and ugly and relentless. Cary Grant, one of Hitch's favorite leading men, happened to be visiting the set that day and told me between takes, "You're the bravest woman I've ever seen." I was never frightened, I was just overwhelmed and in some form of shock, and I just kept saying to myself over and over again, "I won't let him break me. I won't let him break me."

The bedroom scene lasted about a minute in the final cut of *The Birds*.

Hitchcock spent five days filming it before he finally decided he had all he wanted.

On that Friday, the fifth and final day, when I arrived at the studio, on the verge of collapse, my dresser wrapped bands of fabric around me with small lengths of elastic attached to them. Then I put on my dress and she pulled the elastic through the tears in it. I lay down on the set in front of the door and stayed very still while they loosely tied the feet of a few of the trained birds to the elastic. By then I was barely coherent, not sure how much more of this I could possibly take.

"Action!" again, and I was pelted with still more live, screaming, frantic birds, while the birds that were tied to me began pecking me as they'd been trained to do. I was too focused on my own survival to notice, but I was told later that it was even more horrifying and heartbreaking for the crew to watch than the previous four days had been, and there wasn't a thing anyone but Hitchcock could do to put a stop to it.

It was midafternoon, after hours of filming, when the bird that was tied to my shoulder pecked me too close to my eye, and I finally snapped.

"I'm done," I said, with what little of my voice was left.

Hitchcock yelled, "Cut." The birds were untied from me, and I just sat there on the floor, unable to move, and began sobbing from sheer exhaustion.

Minutes passed before I looked up to discover that everyone had just left me there in the middle of that vast, silent soundstage, completely spent, empty, and alone.

Afterward, I met a doctor friend from New York in the Polo Lounge at the Beverly Hills Hotel, and he told me he'd never seen anyone so exhausted in his life. I wish I could say I spent that weekend taking care of Melanie, but I'm sure it was more a case of her taking care of me.

I fell sound asleep in the backyard while she was playing. She was worried about me because I hadn't moved in quite some time, and she shook me to try to wake me up and make sure I was okay. It startled me and I woke up flailing my arms, yelling, "No!" at the top of my lungs, before I fully came to and realized it was her and I was safe. It frightened my little five-year-old girl terribly. I held her for a long time, hating what all this must be doing to her.

I vaguely remembered waking up that Monday morning. I didn't remember driving to the studio or walking to my dressing room or lying down on the chaise. Then I was completely out cold. My makeup man Howard Smits couldn't wake me. My hairdresser Virginia Darcy couldn't wake me.

When I did wake up I was at home in bed, fully clothed, with no idea how I got there.

Our nanny Josephine called my doctor, who came to the house right away. Hitchcock showed up as well. After he examined me, my doctor turned to Hitchcock and told him I had to have the week off for some intensive rest.

"She can't," Hitchcock said. "We have nothing else to shoot but her."

To which my doctor incredulously replied, "What are you doing? Are you trying to kill her?"

I got the week off.

I spent that week either asleep or only semiconscious and so grateful that Melanie had Josephine and my parents to help when I was just plain physically incapable of it.

I was also mentally incapable of processing anything with any clarity at all, so I didn't even try. There was only one thing I knew with absolute clarity: My castmates, the crew, and I had worked too hard for too long for *The Birds* to go unfinished, and it all came down to me. I was sure they must be wondering when, or even if, I'd be back. It didn't matter that they'd seen it happen, what I'd been through, and they probably wouldn't have blamed me if I'd walked away. I could never and would never do that to them or to myself. It was a rough week for me as I recovered, but it had to have been a rough week for them, too.

So that next Monday morning, to make the statement I thought we all needed, I made an entrance. They opened the soundstage door to find me in my Edith Head finest, hair and makeup done to perfection, right arm extended with my raven pal Buddy perched on it. I marched in with Buddy to a deafening round of applause and cheering from the cast and crew, silently announcing, "I'm back. Let's finish this movie."

Hitchcock was there, but I can't tell you what his reaction was. I didn't so much as glance in his direction.

We did finish that movie, of course, and a festive, triumphant mood prevailed at the wrap party. We'd done it. It wasn't easy, to say the least, but we'd actually done it. I still remember that dear Suzanne Pleshette giving me an especially long hug that night. She was a good, supportive friend, and it meant the world to me.

I'll always be so grateful that Rod Taylor and I stayed in touch and that I saw him shortly before he died of a heart attack in early 2015. I went to his home in Beverly Hills, and he was so weak by then that he had to go up and down the stairs by sitting on each step one at a time as he went. He and his beautiful wife Carol and I sat at their kitchen table and had the loveliest visit. What a wonderful, handsome, virile man he was, and what a blessing that he was cast as my leading man on *The Birds* and was there for me in every way when I needed him.

I was proud and happy to publicize *The Birds* at every opportunity when it was released, and it was a nonstop whirlwind of press, galas, and awards shows. I was on Hitchcock's arm to walk the red carpet when *The Birds* was chosen to lead off the Cannes Film Festival, while Alma cheered from among the crowd behind the velvet ropes.

I was by his side for countless interviews.

I was at the Golden Globes and overwhelmed to win the award for Best Newcomer.

I was at the Academy Awards to cheer on Ub Iwerks, who was deservedly nominated for Best Visual Effects.

I was anywhere and everywhere the studio wanted me to be, and given A-list treatment by everyone in town.

It was a thrilling, amazing time. I never forgot for one moment that it was all happening because of Alfred Hitchcock, and I never forgot for one moment that I'd earned it. I didn't feel like a smoke-and-mirrors Hitchcock illusion anymore. I felt like a full-fledged movie star who'd worked hard for the privilege.

And once the excitement died down, I buckled up to prepare for what was coming next according to the ironclad contract I'd signed—my second Hitchcock movie, a film called *Marnie*.

Five

I'd actually first heard of *Marnie*, which was slated to be Hitchcock's next film, while we were still filming *The Birds*. Rod Taylor and I had just finished shooting the scene on the bluff in *The Birds* in which they talk about their respective mothers when Lew Wasserman arrived on the set and took me aside.

"Congratulations, Tippi," he said, with that wide, friendly smile of his. "You're going to be our Marnie."

Marnie was based on a Winston Graham novel of the same name, and Hitchcock had been working with writer Joseph Stefano on a screen adaptation since 1961. His intention was that Grace Kelly would play the title role. But by then she'd married Prince Rainier of

Monaco, and Her Serene Highness declined and retired from acting entirely, so Hitchcock tabled *Marnie* and focused on *The Birds* instead.

When *The Birds* was completed, work resumed on the *Marnie* script, first with Evan Hunter, who wrote *The Birds* screenplay, and then with writer Jay Presson Allen. In the meantime, actresses all over town, from Eva Marie Saint to Vera Miles and Claire Griswold, who were also under contract to Hitchcock, had been vying for the role of Marnie Edgar since the moment Grace Kelly turned it down.

I still remember Hitchcock, with a self-satisfied smile on his face, announcing to me one day, early in our filming of *The Birds*, that he'd put a new actress under contract.

I asked who it was.

"Claire Griswold," he said.

I was delighted. "Claire Griswold? I love Claire Griswold! We modeled in New York together!"

His face turned to stone, and after a quick, lethal glare at me, he turned his back and stormed away. It hadn't occurred to me until I saw his reaction that he'd expected me to fly into a jealous rage. Oh, please.

One day Claire, who'd done two episodes of *The Alfred Hitchcock Hour* by then, had a lunch with Hitchcock's secretary Peggy. Claire and her husband, Sydney Pollack, already had a beautiful son Steven, and she told Peggy that in the coming year they were hoping to expand their family. Peggy, in her usual impossible position of being sympathetic toward Hitchcock's actresses and loyal to her boss as well, explained to Claire that for the duration of her seven-year contractual commitment to Hitchcock, he would expect her to be immediately available for any role at any time—i.e., not pregnant, not giving birth, not needing to be home with a newborn. Not long after that, Mr. and Mrs. Sydney Pollack excitedly announced that they were expecting a second child.

The contract between Claire and Hitchcock was terminated, and Claire went right on with her life as a happy wife and mother of three.

Despite all the problems I'd had with Hitchcock's obsessive, often embarrassingly ardent, often cruel behavior toward me, I was quite excited to be cast as the lead in *Marnie*. I was still under contract, so turning it down wasn't an option anyway, but it was an extraordinary role, a psychological thriller that would present me with a spectacular acting challenge. God knows Hitchcock loved flawed, emotionally complex characters, and *Marnie* was filled with them.

I was determined to thoroughly and legitimately explore the internal journey of Margaret *Marnie* Edgar rather than playing her at face value as written, so in addition to studying the script, I spent a lot of hours with some skilled psychologists, asking them to explore that journey with me and describe Marnie's realistic reactions to what she's been through. I didn't want there to be a single false beat in my performance as I acted out her story:

When we first meet Marnie, she's just stolen $10,000 from her employer, tax consultant Sidney Strutt, whom she'd charmed into hiring her with no references and no traceable resume. She changes her identity and her appearance and leaves town. After a brief stop in Virginia to visit the stables where her beloved horse Florio is being boarded, she heads on to Baltimore to pay her mother Bernice a surprise visit. Bernice is more attentive to Jessie, a young neighbor girl, than she is to Marnie, but Marnie lovingly gives her money before she leaves.

Publisher Mark Rutland, a wealthy widower, has a business meeting with Sidney Strutt, who tells him about Marnie's recent theft. Mark remembers Marnie from a previous trip to Strutt's office.

Marnie applies for a secretarial job at Mark's publishing company, unaware that Mark knows who she is and what she's done. Mark, intrigued, hires her and begins taking her out. Marnie is plagued by nightmares and pathological fears of the color red and of thunderstorms.

Marnie's compulsive thievery recurs at Mark's office. She steals a large amount of money from the safe and disappears. Mark manages to track her down at the stables, where she's gone to see Florio. Rather than turning her over to the police, he blackmails her into marrying him.

It's on their honeymoon cruise that Mark learns of Marnie's pathological revulsion at being touched by a man. At first Mark is sympathetic, but he finally forces himself on her and has sex with her. The next morning when Mark wakes up to discover that she's not in their cabin, he searches the ship and pulls her out of the swimming pool, where she's attempting to commit suicide by drowning herself.

Lil, the sister of Mark's late wife, has wanted him ever since her sister passed away, and the news that Mark has actually married Marnie enrages her. Lil decides to create as much discomfort as possible for Marnie and invites Strutt to a party at Mark's house. Strutt recognizes Marnie, of course, and immediately wants to turn her in, but Mark stops him by threatening to take his business accounts elsewhere.

Another of Marnie's many lies to Mark is that her mother has died. Mark finds out that it's not true, and he hires a private investigator to track the woman down.

Marnie finally confesses to several more robberies in her past, and Mark promises to reimburse all her victims to keep her from being prosecuted.

She and Florio are invited to participate in a fox hunt. She's enjoying herself until the hounds corner the fox, which upsets her, and her panic is exacerbated when a fellow rider appears wearing a traditional red riding jacket. She urges Florio into a full, frightened gallop, causing him to fall while trying to jump over a fence and severely injure himself. Marnie has to mercifully shoot her beloved horse, after which she goes into a shock that seems to echo some incident from her past as she murmurs a compassionate "There. There now," over Florio's still, silent body.

Marnie catatonically goes to Mark's office, intending to rob him again and surprised to find that she can't bring herself to do it. Even when Mark finds her and dares her to go ahead and take the money, she backs away instead, leaving the money in the safe where she found it.

Mark decides it's time to take Marnie to see her mother in Baltimore. His private investigator unearthed the fact that Bernice was a prostitute when Marnie was a little girl, and he wants to confront her to see if the truth might help exorcise Marnie's demons. Bernice, in an angry effort to shut Mark up, attacks him, triggering the memory Marnie's been repressing since childhood: A drunken "client" of Bernice's, a sailor, tried to comfort Marnie when a thunderstorm frightened her. Bernice thought he was trying to molest her little girl and attacked him. To protect her mother, Marnie grabbed a fireplace poker and struck him. He died a very bloody death while the child Marnie stood over him and quietly murmured, "There. There now."

The restored memory of that horrible night elicits a confession from Bernice about Marnie's conception: She'd admired a boy's sweater, and he told her she could have it if she let him have sex with her. She let him, but he disappeared when she told him she was pregnant. "But I still got that old basketball sweater, and I got you, Marnie, and I wouldn't let them take you away from me. I promised God that if He'd let me keep you, I'd raise you different from myself—decent."

Marnie asks Bernice at the beginning of the film, "Why don't you love me, Mama? I've always wondered why you don't."

After Bernice's confession at the end, Marnie says, "You must have loved me, Mama. You must have loved me."

Bernice answers her, in tears, "Why, sugar pop, you're the only thing I ever did love."

Set free from the repressed memory that explains her pathological fears and behavior, Marnie asks Mark what she should do. He reassures her, promising he'll take care of her and defend her and stand by her. There's hope for all three of them as the film ends.

I just remembered something I haven't thought of in decades. Back in the days when everyone was asking each other, "Where were you when you heard that President Kennedy had been assassinated?" my answer was that Florio and I were on our way to a training session, getting ready for our scenes in *Marnie*.

The assassination hit everyone on that film like a horrible shock wave. It was all we talked about for days, and I never mentioned my very unattractive encounter with John Kennedy in the south of France a few years earlier. It was so trivial compared to the death of a president.

I think we were all grateful for the compelling, full-time, emotionally complicated distraction of making the next Alfred Hitchcock film.

The wonderful Louise Latham was cast as Bernice, Melody Thomas (now Melody Thomas Scott of *The Young and the Restless*) was hired to play Marnie as a little girl, Diane Baker was cast in the role of Lil, and to complete the embarrassment of riches, none other than Sean Connery signed on as my leading man Mark Rutland. As he had on *The Birds*, Hitchcock surrounded me with the most exquisite people, on-screen and off, and as he had with Rod Taylor on *The Birds*, he gave a nonnegotiable edict to Sean—"Do not touch The Girl."

In 2006 I had the profound honor of being a presenter the night that the American Film Institute celebrated Sean Connery's lifetime body of work. I was thrilled that they asked me, and I must say, I wore the most beautiful dress I'd ever seen in my life. At the after party I found Sean sitting alone for a moment and went over to sit beside him. He gave me the sweetest kiss on the cheek and said, "I wasn't able to do that when we were working together." (His gorgeous, tiny wife Micheline joined us moments later and wanted to steal that dress right off my body. I dared her to try it, and we laughed and hugged.)

I've been asked thousands of times if Sean and I were romantically involved during the time we shot *Marnie*. The answer is a simple no. Like Rod Taylor, he was gorgeous and wonderful and a dream come true as a leading man. We became great friends. But if anything had been going on between us off camera, when he wasn't busy practicing his golf swing, it would have shown in my eyes on camera, and a pathologically frigid Marnie Edgar looking at Mark Rutland with even a hint of a passionate connection would never have worked. Even our "love scene," for lack of a more accurate term, was as unromantic as could be, with cameras and lights and boom microphones and crew and Hitchcock just a few feet away, so I can honestly say I have no idea what it's really like to kiss Sean Connery.

I still remember Hitchcock telling me that he'd signed Sean Connery to be my leading man. I wondered out loud how I was supposed to play a frigid woman opposite Sean, of all people.

To which Hitchcock replied after a long pause, "It's called 'acting,' my dear."

The widespread belief at the studio was that Hitchcock had fired Evan Hunter from *Marnie* and hired Jay Presson Allen to write the script instead because Evan was very opposed to the scene in which Mark rapes Marnie on their wedding night. He thought it made Mark irretrievably unsympathetic. An equally widespread belief was that the rape was the scene that had driven Hitchcock to make *Marnie* in the first place, that a man taking his frigid, unattainable bride by force was Hitchcock's fantasy about me. I refused to let my mind wander into that possibility. I had a job to do and a performance to give. A whole lot of people were counting on me, and I was counting on myself. I couldn't afford to indulge in speculation.

I couldn't ignore the fact, though, that Hitchcock's behavior toward me was as obsessive and bizarre as ever, and it seemed to be escalating.

He had a life mask made of my face. My makeup man Bob Dawn put straws up my nose so I could breathe and covered my face with plaster for about fifteen minutes until it was dried enough to remove in one piece. Believe it or not, I didn't think much about it at the time. There were life masks of contract actors and actresses all over the walls of the makeup room. I had no idea until Bob told me much later that Hitchcock had my life mask made for no other reason than to keep it for himself and jealously guard it.

He had handwritten notes delivered to my house, accompanied by his favorite fine wines.

He had personalized stationery designed for me that, except for the name, obviously, was identical to his.

And then there was that beautiful, awful dressing room.

It was a huge, luxurious suite, with every convenience from a giant light-rimmed mirror in the makeup area where Bob Dawn could work on me in private, to a shampoo bowl and salon chair for my daily sessions with my hairdresser Virginia Darcy. Hitchcock designed it himself and had it painted French blue to coordinate with a decorator's dream collection of gorgeous French furniture. It "happened" to be located right next to Hitchcock's bungalow at Universal, and its most unnerving feature was a back door that led into an alley just a few yards from the door to his private office. He could come and go as he pleased without anyone seeing him, even if it was ostensibly for no other reason than to enjoy a glass of the wine or champagne that he kept in my refrigerator. I avoided that dressing room as much as possible while *Marnie* was in preproduction, but once we started filming, I'd have friends, Mom and Daddy, Melanie and Josephine, crew members, anyone and everyone I could think of meet me there—anything to keep my time alone with Hitchcock at a minimum. And not once did I ever open that back door.

Inevitably, though, sometimes it was just him and me, and it was usually the same excruciating dance. He would find some way to express his obsession with me, which he never referred to as an obsession, as if I owed it to him to reciprocate somehow. I would find some way to make it clear that his obsession wasn't reciprocated and never would be. He'd become cruel and petulant and then, within a few hours or a few days, start all over again.

One day he told me about a "recurring dream" of his, although it was obviously more of a fantasy. In this "dream" I was in his living room, surrounded by some kind of glow, and I told him I loved him and always would.

Then he added, "You're everything I've ever dreamed of, Tippi, you must know that. If it weren't for Alma . . ."

I could tell what was coming, and I'm sure I even warned him, "Don't."

"I love you," he said.

It literally turned my stomach. I managed to mutter something like "It was just a dream, Hitch," before I walked out of my dressing room in search of anything but time alone with him.

I was angry. I was in pain. I was anxious, and I was still utterly determined not to let Hitchcock ruin *Marnie* for me, the rest of the cast, and the crew, all of whom were working so hard despite tension on the set you could cut with a knife. It became my goal to get through it without a rift between Hitchcock and me that could never be healed. Looking back, though, that rift was inevitable. It wasn't a question of if, it was simply a matter of when.

I was even naive, or desperate, enough to hope that Hitchcock's intensity toward me might dissipate when the script called for Marnie to dye her hair to disguise herself when she is on the run after her first theft. One of Hitchcock's most memorable quotes was "Blondes make the best victims. They're like virgin snow that shows up the bloody footprints." I thought that maybe, just maybe, those few days when my hair was darker for filming would break his obsession, or at least give me a temporary reprieve from it.

In the end, all it did was make me even less recognizable to myself than I was already becoming. I knew I was slipping further and further inside myself, trying to hide from what was going on around me that I couldn't escape, and when even my reflection in the mirror seemed unfamiliar, I felt more lost than ever.

I'll never forget an incident that happened one afternoon at Universal. I was waiting for an elevator when Hitchcock's wife Alma approached me. She was a little awkward and reluctant, and all she said was "I'm so sorry you have to go through this."

So she knew. It surprised me, although I suspected that on some level or other, she'd had to tolerate it before, which I couldn't imagine. I didn't know whether to feel sorry for her or be angry with her.

"Alma, you could stop it," I replied. "You're the only one who could."

She just turned and walked away.

I had a similar hollow feeling when *Marnie* writer Jay Presson Allen and I were headed somewhere in the back of a limo, and out of nowhere she quietly asked, "Can't you love him just a little?"

I couldn't even come up with a reply to that. I just stared at her.

Making it even more awkward was the fact that during the filming of *Marnie*, Hitchcock had begun working with Jay on what he hoped would be their next film, the screen adaptation of a J. M. Barrie play called *Mary Rose*, in which I'd play the title character. It was an eerie ghost story in which Mary Rose's father takes her to an island when she's a little girl. She disappears, then reappears three weeks later unaware of having been gone. Years later, when Mary Rose is a young wife and mother, her husband takes her to that same island, where she disappears. Decades later she reappears, again unaware that she'd been gone and exactly the same age she was when she vanished. The second draft of the *Mary Rose* script had been completed, and I'd been hearing about it endlessly from Hitchcock. Our bizarre relationship finally detonated so completely that there was no coming back.

It started when I was being honored with *Photoplay*'s "most promising actress of the year" award. They wanted to present it to me on a Friday night on Johnny Carson's *Tonight Show*, which was filmed in New York in 1964. I was flattered and excited, especially when I checked my *Marnie* shooting schedule and discovered it shouldn't be a problem—I had that Friday off, so I could head to the airport when we finished on Thursday, be in New York for *The Tonight Show* to accept the award, fly home over the weekend and be back in plenty of time to work again on Monday.

There was no reason other than meanness and control for Hitchcock to refuse to let me take that trip, but that's exactly what he did. Not only did he refuse, but he picked up the phone, supposedly on my behalf, to decline the award and cancel my *Tonight Show* appearance.

I was furious, and I imagine *Photoplay* and *The Tonight Show* were, too, not with him but with me.

But the worst was still to come, just a couple of weeks later.

It was late afternoon. We'd finished filming for the day. I was alone in my dressing room when Hitchcock summoned me to his office. Things had been very tense between us after the New York fiasco, and while it was unavoidable to interact with him on the set, I could barely bring myself to look at him or speak to him.

I've never gone into detail about this, and I never will. I'll simply say that he suddenly grabbed me and put his hands on me. It was sexual, it was perverse, and it was ugly, and I couldn't have been more shocked and more repulsed. The harder I fought him, the more aggressive he became. Then he started adding threats, as if he could do anything to me that was worse than what he was trying to do at that moment.

He would scrap the whole *Mary Rose* project, he said.

I didn't care, I told him. In fact, "let me out of my contract."

He had no intention of it. "Besides," he added, "you have a young daughter and elderly parents to support."

"No one who loves me would want me to be this unhappy for any amount of money," I snapped.

Too bad. I still had two years to go on that contract, and he was going to make me honor it.

Then he looked directly into my eyes, his face red with rage, and promised, "I'll ruin your career."

I finally managed to push him off me once and for all and looked directly back at him. "Do what you have to do," I said, and I stormed out and slammed the door behind me.

I was shattered, but I wasn't remorseful, not for a single minute. I've made a lot of mistakes in my life. Refusing Hitchcock that horrible afternoon wasn't one of them. The next day poor Peggy Robertson, Hitchcock's secretary, had to come and tell me it would be best if I didn't come to the wrap party being planned for when filming was completed.

It was cruel and devastating, but I guess I wasn't surprised. The cast and crew were insulted on my behalf, and I also wasn't surprised to hear weeks later, once shooting was completed, that the party was a huge flop.

Hitchcock never spoke directly to me again. We were still filming *Marnie*, and he would give me directions and answer my questions only through intermediaries on the crew. In fact, to the best of my knowledge, he never spoke my name again. From that day forward, I was only "The Girl," nothing more. It made the atmosphere on the set unbearable, but no one blamed me for it, and I never blamed myself.

He also completely stopped caring about *Marnie*, to the point where he seemed to be sabotaging it. His legendary meticulous attention to every detail of every camera angle, every special effect, every technical aspect of his films eroded into apathetic sloppiness. And the campaign he'd been on since we started filming to convince anyone who'd listen that I was headed straight for an Oscar for my performance shifted into reverse. Now he was spreading cold, cruel insults about my performance to everyone from the Universal executives to his colleagues in the industry.

Despite Hitchcock's lobbying against me, Universal had every intention to submit me for an Oscar nomination when we finally wrapped *Marnie* and the executives saw the finished product. He blocked it. I was never submitted and never considered.

I immediately started getting offers for other films—the lead in *Bedtime Story* opposite David Niven and Marlon Brando; *Mirage* opposite Gregory Peck and Walter Matthau; and *Fahrenheit 451* opposite Oskar Werner, written by Hitchcock's friend François Truffaut, among others.

But Hitchcock still had me under contract for another two years, and to every producer and director and agent and screenwriter who called wanting to hire me, he had the same answer: "She's not available." The one that hurt me the most was *Fahrenheit 451*. I would love to have worked with François Truffaut. Hitchcock personally saw to it that it never happened, and I'm almost glad I didn't find out about that offer until later. It was tough enough to heal emotionally without the added anger and disappointment.

I knew Hitchcock was doing everything in his power to keep his promise to ruin my career. In many ways, he succeeded. I went on to make fifty films after *Marnie*, and I did episodes of several television series. But I was never offered another role as deep and challenging as the two I did for him, the two he chose me for out of nowhere and exhaustively prepared me for, before punishing me when, in his eyes, I paid him the ultimate insult of rejecting him.

I've made it my mission ever since to see to it that while Hitchcock may have ruined my career, I never gave him the power to ruin my life.

We never spoke again or had any further contact whatsoever. As far as I was concerned, there was no unfinished business between us, nothing more that needed to be said. I even felt a wave of sadness when he died on April 29, 1980.

It surprised everyone that I went to Hitchcock's funeral in Beverly Hills. I even had a floral arrangement designed in the shape of the iconic Hitchcock profile. I still have the frame.

I didn't speak at the funeral.

I was just there to honor his genius as a filmmaker and his contributions to the industry.

I was there to honor him personally as an unparalleled teacher and "star maker" who once believed in a former model who'd never acted a day in her life.

I'd already healed and moved on by the time Hitchcock died, far past anything I'd ever imagined for myself. So in the end, I was there to say, "Good-bye, and thank you, Hitch."

Six

Shortly after *Marnie* ended, in 1964, I married my second husband, Noel Marshall.

I know. What? Who?

Noel was my agent and manager. He'd also been helping me find a house to buy when I decided it was time to stop renting, so we were spending an enormous amount of time together. He had three young sons from a previous marriage, two of them a few years older than Melanie and the youngest exactly the same age, right down to having been born on the same day she was. Noel was incredibly impulsive, and he was ambitious, always full of plans and ideas, always busy, always on the move, always a great salesman.

He'd grown up on the tough South Side of Chicago, the oldest of twelve children, and he had a mind-boggling résumé. He'd spent one summer as a boy working at the St. Louis Zoo. He'd worked as a page at Chicago's NBC affiliate and directed episodes of the puppet show *Kukla, Fran and Ollie* as well as coverage of a national political convention. When he moved to Hollywood, he worked for Hughes Aircraft and Sears before setting up a commercial agency with his then-wife Jaye. Jaye got the agency as part of their divorce settlement, although they continued to work together off and on, and Noel went into the construction business—with no prior experience, mind you.

At that time in my life, he was also a much-needed distraction from Hitchcock. It was as hard to be preoccupied about Hitchcock with Noel around as it is to be preoccupied with your problems while zooming around on the craziest ride at an amusement park. And since everyone on the *Marnie* set knew I was getting married as soon as we wrapped that film, I'm sure I also deluded myself into thinking that when Hitchcock got wind of it, he might get discouraged enough to move on from his suffocating obsession with me. Looking back, I wonder if it might have actually intensified it instead. Who knows? I don't pretend to know what was going on in that man's mind, and even back then I didn't spend a lot of time trying to figure it out.

Wanting to escape someone you don't want to deal with is a really lame reason to get married. I was putting another barrier between Hitchcock and me. I wasn't in love with Noel Marshall, but I'm not sure I admitted that to myself when I made the commitment to marry him. I also think he knew I wasn't in love with him and wasn't about to let that stand in the way of a great idea like getting married and merging our lives together. When I say yes to something, I honor it, so when I said yes to Noel, I took the commitment seriously.

Just in case you think I'm exaggerating when I say Noel was incredibly impulsive about most things, our wedding was no exception. One Sunday afternoon we were sitting in the backyard of the charming home I'd bought on Knobhill Drive above Sherman Oaks, overlooking the San Fernando Valley. It had three different levels built into a hillside, complete with a beautiful private pool with a shaded patio. It was the first home I'd ever bought, I was proud of it, and I loved it there.

So there Noel and I sat, poolside, trying to decide where our wedding should be held, considering our guest list numbered about 250 people. We talked about hotels, we talked about churches, we talked about friends' houses, and then suddenly Noel said, "Why don't we just get married here?"

I looked at him as if he'd just grown a pair of antennae and patiently pointed out the obvious: "There isn't enough space here for 250 people."

He didn't bat an eye. "There can be. All we have to do is add two baths and two bedrooms and extend the living room. We'll just install a concrete pad over there, and . . . wait here." He suddenly went running off to the garage while I was still sitting there trying to picture some fraction of what he'd just blurted out off the top of his head. I hadn't begun to figure it out when he came running back carrying a sledgehammer, with which he began demolishing the wooden stairway that led from the yard twenty feet up to the street level.

Dissolve to a few weeks later, new rooms and extensions added, cutting it so close that we were pouring concrete with our own pumps the night before the wedding, concrete that wasn't completely set until about an hour before our guests arrived.

It turned out to be a perfect wedding. I wore a pale green lace wedding dress I designed myself, and we had a star-studded guest list. Everyone was well fed and well entertained, and to the best of my knowledge, no one knew that every few minutes I was glancing around at all the brand-new renovations, thinking, "Please, God, if it's going to collapse, don't let it happen until after everyone leaves."

Of course, by marrying Noel I'd now inherited three stepsons—Joel, John, and Jerry—while Noel had inherited a stepdaughter, my darling Melanie. We needed that extra space, and we hadn't even begun to imagine how much bigger our family was going to grow in the years to come.

Isn't it funny how sometimes that qualities we find so quirky and funny and interesting in our partners when the relationship is new become the qualities that are the first to drive us crazy after the newness wears off?

Noel's impulsiveness seemed so brave and exciting at first. "Oh, good, he's a *doer*," I'd say to myself in relief, since I'm not exactly known for sitting around eating bonbons either. He darted like a gnat from one new interest to another, from agent to construction to part-time agent to real estate development to . . . whatever came next. He was perpetually in search of a new challenge, another mountain to climb, another adventure to tackle. I began to look at every one of his new undertakings as the next unwitting target of his sledgehammer, and it got very, very tedious and very, very old.

But just as my first husband was worth it for giving me Melanie, the greatest treasure of my life, my second husband led me to my greatest passion, whether he meant to or not, and I'm eternally grateful.

I had a new husband, a new home to decorate, three new stepsons, a daughter who was growing more beautiful and strong-willed by the day, and, finally, a few new job offers when my Hitchcock contract expired and I was free to work again.

I waded back into acting with an episode of *Kraft Suspense Theatre* and an episode of the Ben Gazzara series *Run for Your Life* before an offer came to go to London for a movie called *A Countess from Hong Kong*, starring Marlon Brando and Sophia Loren, directed by none other than the legendary Charlie Chaplin. Who in their right mind would turn that down? And with a few exceptions here and there, I *am* a woman in her right mind.

It had been more than two years since *Marnie* was released, and it was obvious when I read the *Countess from Hong Kong* script that the Tippi Hedren "heat" in the industry had cooled down (thank you, Hitch). My part was a relatively small one, and my character didn't even appear until toward the end of the film. Still, no regrets. It was worth it, if only to work with Chaplin.

I found him to be an absolute genius. He wrote, produced, directed, and musically scored *A Countess from Hong Kong*, which made my head spin. What a stunningly talented man. Even more mesmerizing to me was the fact that before every scene, he would act out each of our parts to show us what he had in mind. Marlon Brando hated that—no one, not even Charlie Chaplin, was going to tell him how to perform a scene. I soaked it up with nothing short of fascinated delight.

Predictably, I'm sure, Marlon thought it would be a great idea for us to have an affair during filming. I made it clear right up front that I thought it would be a terrible idea, and there was nothing he could do or say to change my mind. It wasn't just that I was married to Noel by then. I also wasn't naive enough to think that after having known me for maybe about a minute and a half, Marlon had developed deep, meaningful feelings for me, and I had no interest in being his or anyone else's something-to-do-on-location. He was intense. God knows he was attractive. I would never claim that it wasn't kind of fun to be hit on by him. And to his credit, he took my quietly emphatic "No, we're not going to do that" for an answer and left it at that.

Sophia, on the other hand, was a joy, and we became good friends. She's even been here to visit me at Shambala. She remarried Carlo Ponti, Sr., during the shooting of *A Countess from Hong Kong*, and I'm so glad I got to know her during such an extraordinary time in her life.

Saying yes to a small part in that movie also led to the privilege of attending Charlie Chaplin's seventy-fifth birthday party, which was thrown on the *Countess from Hong Kong* set. The whole cast and crew attended, even Brando, who was never especially interested in socializing with the rest of us. I took ten-year-old Melanie as my date, and I have the most wonderful picture of Melanie, Sophia, and me at the celebration of that amazing man's life.

I'm the only actress ever to have been directed by both Alfred Hitchcock and Charlie Chaplin—both of them brilliantly creative directors, both of them meticulous perfectionists, both of them deservedly iconic. Sometimes it still makes me pause to catch my breath and say, "Really? *Me?*"

I had that same reaction to being given a star on the Hollywood Walk of Fame in 1973. My name among such superstars as Katharine Hepburn and Spencer Tracy and Gregory Peck and Fred Astaire and Lucille Ball and Elizabeth Taylor, and, of course, Alfred Hitchcock and Charlie Chaplin—people who'd committed their lives and their considerable talent to their show business careers, while I'd been handed an invitation to join them with no acting credentials whatsoever. I was so touched, and so honored, and I promise you, no one has ever been more appreciative than I was. Melanie was there to celebrate with me and our family and friends afterward in the historic Blossom Ballroom at the Hollywood Roosevelt Hotel, where the first Academy Awards ceremony was held, and she gave me my most unforgettable moment of the whole event when she told me she was proud of me.

I almost felt as if I'd stepped into someone else's life that day.

I'd been home from London and *A Countess from Hong Kong* for a few weeks when I got a call from an extraordinary man named Johnny Grant. Everyone knew and admired Johnny Grant. Not only was he the honorary mayor of Hollywood, but among countless other achievements, he was also an ambassador for the United Service Organizations, aka the USO, recruiting celebrities from all areas of show business and sports to visit our soldiers at war and at V.A. hospitals throughout the United States.

Johnny was calling with a remarkable question. He was organizing another of his many USO junkets to Vietnam. Would I be willing to go?

My answer wasn't just yes. It was, "Yes, I'd be honored."

A few weeks later I met my traveling companions Johnny Grant and Diane McBain at Camp Pendleton, a couple of hours south of Los Angeles, and we were off to Saigon. Diane and I became good friends, not only because we went on this trip together but also because she, like me, was a former teenage model who'd been "discovered" and gone on to an acting career. Neither of us had a clue what we'd signed on for with this trip to Vietnam. We just knew that whatever it was, it would pale in comparison to what was being asked of the men and women who were fighting day after day, night after night, in this ugly, unpopular war. If we could help prove to them that they hadn't been forgotten by their fellow Americans, and that we cared very much about them and deeply appreciated their service to our country, then by all means, sign us up.

We spent the first night in Saigon, where we appeared on a talk show hosted by a beautiful young Vietnamese actress named Kieu Chinh (pronounced "Ching"), who went on many years later to star in the hit movie *The Joy Luck Club*. It was traditional for her to welcome and interview all of us visiting celebrities on her show, televised throughout Vietnam. We were happy to oblige, and she was a lovely, gracious hostess, but we weren't there for publicity. We were there to visit our soldiers, and we were eager to get started.

Early the next morning we boarded a helicopter and headed off to one of the firebases, military encampments that provided artillery support to the infantry beyond the range of their base camps. The chopper flew very low over the trees so the enemy couldn't detect our location, and those rare moments when our nerves would fray and we'd wonder what the hell we thought we were doing vanished the instant we saw how much our being there meant to those brave GIs so far from home.

Every morning we were off to another firebase, and every morning we were greeted with the same incredible appreciation. We stayed in the most modest quarters, we ate lunches and dinners with the soldiers, and mostly we just sat and talked and hung out and listened to their stories—where they'd come from, the nightmares they'd been through, the lives and families they'd left behind and missed so much, and their dreams for when the war ended. I prayed for every single one of them every night after our long good-bye hugs.

It was a hard, gut-wrenching trip, and when Johnny called a few months later to ask if I'd go again, I said yes. I couldn't say no. I couldn't not go.

The second junket was with entertainer and comedian Joey Bishop and several others, and I discovered the hard way what an incredibly nice, patient group I was traveling with. We were about an hour into our drive from Los Angeles to Camp Pendleton when I suddenly, horribly realized I'd forgotten my passport. If they were tempted to just push me out of the car and keep driving, they never showed it. Instead, as we turned around to drive back to L.A. so I could retrieve my passport, because there was no other option, and I apologized eight or nine million times, they were much more gracious about it than I deserved.

(For the record, that kind of thing isn't typical of me. I might have had trouble convincing those particular traveling companions, but while I'm definitely a natural-born blonde, I've never been much of an airhead.)

Once we arrived in Vietnam, we were taken to a variety of remote locations by helicopters and C-130s to entertain the troops. We were well protected by armed soldiers and escort officers, and again, the reception we received everywhere we went was overwhelming. Those men and women were so grateful that they kept trying to give us patches from the sleeves of their uniforms, patches they'd earned, as if everything they were already giving us by serving in the military wasn't enough.

The hardest part of both those trips to Vietnam was visiting the base hospitals. We saw so many beautiful young GIs whose arms or legs had been shot off, whose injuries had left them blind or deaf for the rest of their lives, whose bodies spontaneously trembled from seizures in the wake of attacks that were more than their minds and nervous systems could handle. Every hospital bed was occupied by one indescribable, heartbreaking testament after another to the obscenity of war, and it made me feel inadequate that all I could think of to say to each of them was "What can I do for you? How can I help?"

We also landed in a jet on the massive aircraft carrier the USS *Enterprise* to visit our navy servicemen. I still have the solid metal object that's crucial to stopping the jets when they land. (I wish I'd written down the name of it when it was presented to me.) I use it as a paperweight and a powerful reminder of a tragic time in the history of the United States.

I did another televised interview with Kieu Chinh before we left, never dreaming that she and the Vietnamese people and I would become very important in each other's lives in the years to come.

I've kept in touch with a few of the soldiers I met on that unforgettable trip, particularly Tom O'Keeffe, 1st Infantry, Charlie Company, Cam Ranh Bay. He said to me once, "Tippi, you have no idea the danger that all of you were in when you came over. It was really complicated for us. We'd start four or five hours before you got there, including scanning the whole area by plane to make sure we knew where the enemy was, to make sure you'd be safe."

I've thought about that so often. He was right, I had no idea what all those GIs went through at the time to protect us, just as most of us have no idea of the brave, extraordinary efforts our armed forces go through every day, risking their lives to protect us and our country.

To every one of them, past, present, and future, from the bottom of a full, heavy, grateful heart that caught just a glimpse of those efforts on our behalf, thank you and God bless you for your service.

I hadn't been home long from my second trip to Vietnam when I was offered the lead in a film called *Satan's Harvest*. I was excited. Starring opposite George Montgomery was a lovely prospect, of course, and the script was fairly interesting, but mostly I was looking forward to shooting in South Africa, where I'd never been before. It would irreversibly, gloriously change my life.

It was 1969. We were on location, baking in the brutal Zimbabwe sun. I was sitting in my canvas chair under an umbrella, reviewing my lines for the scene we were about to shoot, when the Afrikaner assistant director announced, "Everyone please stand. The lion is coming through." My heart skipped. The king was approaching.

I imagine the thirty-some hot, sweaty filmmakers around me thought the same thing I did—*what?* But none of us questioned it, we simply stood as directed, including Noel, who was sitting beside me, as if we were about to recite the Pledge of Allegiance among the typical clutter of cameras, reflectors, lights, and booms.

Moments later a man appeared, moving toward us across the veldt. Beside him, impossibly graceful for his massive size, was a magnificent golden lion, his amber-brown mane like an aura around his proud head. The king of beasts indeed, I thought, pure royalty. East African tribes say that when a lion roars he's declaring, *"N'cht ya nani? Yangu! Yangu! YANGU!"* ("Whose land is this? This land is my land. Mine! Mine! MINE!") That's exactly how this creature approached us, surveying his kingdom vain and unchallenged.

I'd never been close to a lion before. Like most people, I'd seen them only at a distance at circuses and zoos. Like most people, I'd always been fascinated, in awe and deathly afraid of them, so it alarmed me when I realized that there was no rope or chain or restraint of any kind connecting this lion to the man beside him.

"Isn't he dangerous?" I asked the crew member who was standing nearby.

"Not as long as Ozzie is around," he replied.

Ozzie turned out to be trainer Ozzie Bristow. The lion was one of his big cats, Dandylion.

They arrived on the set, where Dandylion, purely in passing, playfully reached out a big paw to tap the cinematographer on the ankle, for which he received a disapproving chuck under the chin from Ozzie. They passed on through, Dandylion clearly finding the rest of us humans about as interesting as watching paint dry.

Dandylion and I were going to be working on this film together for several weeks, and I couldn't get to Ozzie fast enough to ask a million questions.

We were all asked to stand, he explained, because it's best for humans to be above the height of a lion. Below it, we become potential playthings. The games can easily lead to impromptu wrestling matches on the ground, and the smartest bet is on the lion.

The paw around the cinematographer's ankle? A common friendly greeting from a lion or tiger, Ozzie advised, and if the lion or tiger happens to be running as he or she is passing by, that greeting often results in the unceremonious upending of its recipient.

"What happens if he charges me?" I asked, still unable to take my eyes off this utterly majestic creature.

"Well, don't run, or he might tackle you," Ozzie warned in his soft-spoken Rhodesian accent. "And he weighs more'n forty stone." More than five hundred pounds. Good God.

Later that day Ozzie introduced us to Karma, an eighteen-month-old lion who thought he was still a cub. He was two hundred pounds of energy and silliness, as playful as a puppy and every bit as irresistible.

Ozzie injured his back a week later and had to take a few days off to rest. On the day he returned, I happened to be near the compound where the cats were kept, and I watched, moved almost to tears, when Dandylion and Karma spotted him and started jumping in the air, literally dancing in excitement as he went to hug them hello. They stood on their back paws and returned the hug, almost smothering him, making sweet, happy noises that sounded like "aa-oow, aa-oow."

When I told Ozzie how touched I was by that reunion, he grinned from ear to ear, as much in love with those cats as they were with him. But, he was quick to add, "Under certain circumstances, Dandylion could easily kill me tomorrow and never feel an instant of guilt." Basic instincts will always trump training and love at any given moment, he said, triggered by any number of things, including possessiveness over whatever they've decided is theirs, from food to a pile of leaves to a stepladder to a toy ball. After a vicious attack, they can quickly revert right back to being as sweet and gentle as before, with no remorse or conscience, as if they've done no harm at all.

Ozzie introduced me to his five cheetahs before I left that day. They were lithe, sleek, and exquisite, and unlike lions, they purred. Ozzie was only too happy to explain this. Cheetahs, lynxes, cougars, and domestic cats have a bony structure called the hyoid at the base of their tongues, a structure lions and tigers don't have, which allows them to purr.

My lifelong assumption that big cats were, in the end, nothing more than beautiful, vicious predators was starting to erode. They were infinitely complex creatures, far more extraordinary than I'd ever realized, and the more I learned about them, the more I wanted to learn.

Not long after, I had a few days off, so Noel and I took the opportunity to visit one of the fabled East African game preserves in Gorongosa, Mozambique's largest preserve. We rented a car and followed an open-air tour bus through the park, occasionally eavesdropping on the tour guide's lecture. It sounded a lot like the recorded ones I'd heard at countless zoos and wild animal preserves all over the world—"Cats have been around for forty million years . . . Lions are the only family-oriented big cats . . . Pride members hunt together, eat together, sleep together . . . express open affection"—until he added something like, "The largest pride of lions in Africa live in this house, the former home of a game warden until he was flooded out."

We'd stopped in front of an abandoned Portuguese-style house, and we couldn't stop gaping at it. There were lions everywhere. Some were reclining on the roof, looking back at us, unimpressed. Some were taking naps in the window frames. Two of them were relaxing in a dilapidated porch swing. One hilarious male was surveying his kingdom from a broken rocking chair, needing nothing more than a plantation hat, a glass of scotch on the rocks, and a cigar to complete the image.

Altogether, we were told, the pride that had overtaken the house consisted of thirty male and female lions and their cubs. We were mesmerized by them. They were barely interested in us. I have no idea how long we stood there taking in this unbelievable family portrait, but I do remember that as we reluctantly drove away, Noel said, "You know, we ought to make a movie about this."

Now, one of the most tedious things about many people in show business is their habit of viewing everything in the world through a filter of whether or not it has potential as their next project. "You know," they'll say, "we ought to make a [movie, sitcom, one-hour drama, play, cable show] about this [grocery store, car dealership, bicycle rental business, pottery class, cheerleading academy, travel agency]." It's endless, and only a tiny fraction of those bright ideas ever lead anywhere. When Noel blurted out that same tired cliché after the almost sacred sight we'd just witnessed, I'm sure I rolled my eyes.

I did mention that he was impulsive, right? In the five years since our wedding, he'd been in construction, he'd been a Realtor, he'd gone back into being a commercial agent as he was when I met him, and he was currently packaging film projects. Now he wanted to make a movie about a house full of lions? Based on what qualifications? I had a hunch he'd need more expertise than the handful of television shows he'd directed in Chicago.

As for me, my filmmaking expertise was limited to acting. Beyond that, I wouldn't even know where to start, although I certainly knew people who *would* know where to start, and to be fair, some very successful films started with flimsier ideas than this. But did I really want to star in a movie about a house full of lions? What would the story be? What would the film be *about*? No doubt about it, it was crazy.

Although, come to think of it, given a choice, I'd probably prefer working with live lions to working with live ravens.

I couldn't believe it. I was actually considering this.

We gave Ozzie the best laugh he'd had in months when we told him the bare bones of our idea over a gin and tonic in Zimbabwe.

"One lion, yes. Thirty? No." He chuckled and went on to outline just the tip of the iceberg when it came to working with wild animals on sets. Professional trainers, for example, usually double for the actors who are in scenes with those animals, complete with wigs and wardrobe and whatever else is required for them to resemble the actors closely enough for the required shots. The trainers aren't just there to protect the cast. They're also there to "handle" the animals on the set to get through the scenes in as few takes as possible—even the tamest, gentlest, most well-trained wild animals need to be professionally handled when shooting a movie. "So for thirty lions, imagine the number of trainers you'd need," he said, then threw back his head and laughed again.

We listened, I swear, and we respected his expertise. He was exactly right; this tiny glimmer of a film concept was insane. Noel and I weren't qualified to even think about taking it on. The whole thing was impractical everywhere we turned.

And yet we couldn't stop talking about it.

It was completely unlike me, but it was just exactly like Noel.

When filming was completed, we decided to do some sightseeing before we headed home. We went to Nairobi, on to the Mount Kenya Safari Club, which was owned by the late, great William Holden, and ended up in the Tanzanian Serengeti.

Have you ever visited a place for the very first time and found it to be achingly familiar, as if it's drawing you to it and won't let go? The Serengeti and its game preserves had that effect on me. It wasn't just the gently rolling green-gray landscape and the massive granite boulders defiantly presiding over seas of grass that completely engrossed me, it was also the animals, everywhere, so exquisite and so humbling—this land was theirs, and we were nothing more than honored spectators. Clouds of cawing birds, literally thousands of gazelles and impalas and giraffes, the nearby sounds of the hooves and high-pitched brays of zebra herds and the guttural rumble of lions when the sun set—the word "awe" doesn't begin to describe what stirred in me.

Looking back, I see it was only adding to the intensity of a perfect storm.

It spread the fire of my passion for animals that ignited when I was a little girl. Before my beloved cat Peter, there was Corky, a funny, frisky terrier mix I adored. He died of distemper because Mom and Daddy couldn't afford to have him vaccinated. I cried for weeks. After I left for New York to join the Ford Agency, Peter ran away from our home in Walnut Park and was never seen again. I hadn't been without animals since Melanie was born. Loving them was and is a part of who I am, and the thought of honoring that love on film for millions of people to see and share and maybe even learn from was becoming more and more irresistible.

Noel, in the meantime, had never shown any particular interest in animals, even during that boyhood summer job at the St. Louis Zoo. That was about the paycheck, not about the zoo. His passion was business. The art of the deal. Getting rich, crazy rich, one way or another, especially in Hollywood, where big money was everywhere, and if other people could make it, why couldn't he? If a movie about a house full of lions could help make that happen, then sure, he cared about lions.

We'd already agreed that we didn't want to make just another documentary about big cats. Those had been done over and over again, even by the late, great Walt Disney, who had the skill and the money to do them right. We wanted to tell a story, a story that would entertain and, at the same time, celebrate the connection between humans and animals.

We kept running ideas past each other that would satisfy that intention.

"What if," one of us would say, "the game warden who abandoned that house came back to find it full of lions?"

"What if he has a wife and kids?" the other one would chime in.

"What if we shoot it in the United States, and somehow . . ."

". . . all these animals escape from a local zoo and take over a family's house while they're away on vacation?"

"What if?"

"What if?"

The one what-if we never got around to was "What if we're in over our heads and need to give up this whole idea right now?"

By the time we got home we were pretty much obsessed. We

couldn't stop talking to anyone and everyone who'd sit and listen about that extraordinary pride of lions and our determination to make a film about them. Melanie, Joel, Jerry, and John were thrilled by the whole idea, whatever it was, and the possibility of turning it into a family project, while most of our friends and business contacts tried to find gentle ways to convince us we were out of our minds.

We didn't necessarily disagree, but that didn't mean we were giving up. We had too much momentum going to be reasonable. No matter what else was going on, I don't think an hour went by without one or the other of us saying, "You know what we could do?" and off we'd go into another discussion about this still unshaped, still imaginary film we'd begun referring to as *Lions*.

Then, as if we were getting a huge green light from the universe, I was offered a starring role in a movie called *Mister Kingstreet's War* with Rossano Brazzi and John Saxon—shooting in Africa. But wait, there's more. The script was about a married couple living on and managing a wildlife preserve that's being threatened by a war between Italian-owned Abyssinia and British Kenya.

I don't have to be hit over the head with a brick. Clearly Noel and I were supposed to keep moving forward with *Lions* and make it happen, and who am I to argue with the universe?

On every day off, every minute off, Noel and I visited preserves and talked to every lion expert we could find. The more we explored, the more we realized that filming *Lions* in the United States instead of Africa wouldn't just be practical, it would be a necessity. Very few domesticated lions even existed between the Tropic of Cancer and Cape Town, and we definitely needed domesticated animals for this project.

It also became imperative that we not just make *Lions* to entertain audiences. We also wanted and needed it to be a plea for wildlife protection around the world. We'd heard horror stories about poachers, some of whom used helicopter gunships to kill elephants. Wild leopards and tigers were almost extinct, thanks to the unconscionable, obscene "skin business." If even one hunter or poacher got the message "Please don't kill these magnificent thinking, feeling beings!" it would be worth everything we put into it, and maybe showing the potential of human/big-cat relationships would help get that point across next time someone thought about buying a leopard coat or a tiger area rug.

Noel started writing the script later that spring. Now called *Lions, Lions and More Lions*, the story line was about an American scientist who goes to study a pride of lions by living with them in a house much like the one we saw in Gorongosa. His family arrives to find that he's gone away for a few days, but offering them a surprising, scary welcome is the pride of lions, who've claimed the house as their own. So far we had no answer to the question "And then what?" We'd just established that I would play the scientist's wife, and Melanie, Jerry, and John would play their children. Joel wanted nothing to do with acting but volunteered his talents in art direction and set decoration. Noel would direct, and he and I would coproduce. Now if we could just find the right actor to play Hank, the scientist.

But first we had to gather our real stars, the whole reason we were determined to make this movie in the first place—cooperative big cats, *multiple* cooperative big cats. Without them we had no story and no film.

So we tackled the challenge of finding privately owned lions, putting them under contract and then teaching them just a few basic moves, *without the use of whips and chains*. That was a deal breaker. These animals would be taught through the Ozzie Bristow method of hugs, kisses, and soft words, or they wouldn't be taught at all. (We hadn't learned yet that certain lions, just like certain people, don't care to be hugged.)

Our first "casting session" took place at Africa, U.S.A., in the San Fernando Valley, a wildlife park owned and operated by veteran animal trainer Ralph Helfer. We weren't the first producers to bring their wild ideas to Ralph. Not even close. He'd heard it all, and he'd been asked every harebrained question Hollywood could dream up, from "Is it possible to train an elephant to sit in a jeep?" to "Do you happen to have an opera-singing parrot we could rent?"

Not only were we there to propose an equally wild idea, we'd actually decided that, for an even more spectacular film, we should increase the number of lions from thirty to fifty.

I didn't think it was possible, but he laughed even harder than Ozzie Bristow had.

"You can't force a bunch of adult lions to live together who don't even know each other," he told us between guffaws. "They're individuals. You're not talking about an African pride, you're talking about lions who are total strangers. They have to be introduced gradually. You have to let them see each other through a fence for a long time before you put them together, or they may kill each other or you. Even with gradual introductions, there may be fights you wouldn't believe. Have you ever seen a lion fight?"

No, we admitted, we hadn't, both of us feeling our brilliant project crumbling to dust.

It reignited again just as quickly when Ralph introduced me to Major, an incredibly gentle lion with a long film résumé of his own. I sat close beside him and rubbed my fingers into his thick mane, and I was rewarded with a wide, contented yawn.

"Ralph," I said as I luxuriated in my welcome proximity to this gorgeous creature, "isn't it possible that you're exaggerating? Look how gentle Major is."

"Major is twenty-five years old," he replied. I'd studied enough to know that in lion years, that meant Major was a sweet, docile guy in his eighties.

Okay. Point made. But still, there had to be a way to make our movie happen. We insisted on believing, just like every other producer with a great big dream and barely a clue what we were getting ourselves into.

Noel and I went to a New Year's Eve party to say good-bye to 1970 and ring in a happy, successful 1971.

We met a writer that night. His name was William Peter Blatty, and during a typical Hollywood cocktail party conversation, we told him about the film we were working on, and he told us about the novel he was working on.

"*Lions, Lions and More Lions*," we said.

"*The Exorcist*," he said.

On New Year's Day we watched the bowl games at Bill Blatty's house and talked more about our respective projects. *The Exorcist*, he told us, was a story about priests and demons and demonic possession. I remember thinking it sounded as if it might make a spectacular movie.

I doubt if either of us had even a fleeting intuition that spending January 1, 1971, at William Peter Blatty's house would end up having a profound impact on the filming of our lion story, and on our lives as well.

Seven

By the spring of 1971, after a lot of trial and error, Noel and I had learned, sometimes the hard way, that (a) more people than we ever imagined, all of whom knew one another, were busily buying, trading, and selling big cats, and (b) it wouldn't be practical to assemble our cast for *Lions* with other people's lions. We were going to have to create a pride of our own, fifty home-grown lions, because we'd said the word "fifty" so many times that this figure had become nonnegotiable, etched in stone. As for how we were going to keep or pay for that many big cats, not to mention where, we put those concerns in the "deal with that later" pile. Single-mindedness? Stubbornness? Headstrong determination? Sheer insanity? We didn't know, and we didn't stop to analyze it. Again, so typical of Noel and so atypical of me, but I was into it every bit as much as he was. In fact, I couldn't have been more excited or more driven.

Finally, one Saturday morning, we headed off to meet a man named Ron Oxley in a place called Soledad Canyon. We'd been referred to Ron by several "big-cat people," and Soledad Canyon was his suggestion. We'd never heard of it, and based on his directions, we got the general idea that it was pretty much to hell and gone, past towns we'd never heard of, like Canyon Country and Saugus, on the route we'd take if we were headed from Los Angeles to the Mojave Desert.

But we'd heard good things about Ron, and he added to the incentive by promising to introduce us to a lion named Neil, whom we could make friends with and even hug if we wanted. Enough said. Noel, thirteen-year-old Melanie, and I were on our way to Soledad Canyon.

"Soledad" in English means solitude, an apt name for the canyon we found ourselves driving through an hour later. The land was brown and rocky, with an occasional dusty driveway leading down to a small wooden house or a couple of single-wide trailers. The rare house numbers were virtually invisible, but we finally arrived at our destination, a modest cluster of cottonwood trees beside a stream and straight downhill from the main road. A rusty old mailbox bore the name Steve Martin—not the one you're thinking of, but an animal trainer who was getting into the business of supplying trained big cats to the television and film industry. His simple trailer home was surrounded by nothing more than some big cages, an expanse of sandy soil, and a pond.

Ron Oxley was waiting there to greet us. He was big, blond, and friendly, an animal trainer as well, with his own animal-rental business, and he boarded his menagerie of performers at Steve Martin's compound. Neil, Ron's lion, was the superstar of the group, with credits like *Daktari* and *The Illustrated Man*, but he'd aged his way past the ferocious roles he'd once played and was now quite docile . . . but still a lion, Ron reminded us as he led us to a picnic area beside the stream.

We had a brief coaching session before Ron formally introduced us to Neil.

"First of all, don't rush up to him," he said. "He doesn't know you, so be patient and let him come to you if he wants. He might brush against you. He might decide to take your arm or your shoulder into his mouth. If that happens, don't be afraid or pull away from him. He's not trying to hurt you, he's just getting acquainted. Don't turn your back to him, because he thinks it's funny to trip people from behind. If you run away from him or even move quickly, he'll think you want to play, and he doesn't know his own strength, so he plays pretty rough. You can pet him, but only if you make your scratches strong and firm, under his chin or in his mane, never on his face. Light scratches get on his nerves, like a fly or a gnat he'll try to swat away."

I doubt if he'd ever had a more rapt audience than the three of us. We all turned to silently stare at one another as Ron walked away, ready to be so obedient to those instructions that I'm surprised little halos didn't magically appear above our heads. No one wanted to keep that lion happy and comfortable more than we did.

A few minutes later Ron reappeared, walking beside his unleashed magnificent superstar Neil, golden brown and huge with a black mane. As advice goes, "Don't rush up to him" was right up there with "Don't leap in front of an oncoming train." Gee, no kidding. We stood there still as statues, openly gaping at this king of beasts who was elegantly approaching us.

Neil didn't find us even a fraction as riveting as we found him. Like Dandylion on the *Satan's Harvest* set, he didn't even glance at us, he simply ambled over to a tree, stood on his hind legs, put his front paws high up on the trunk, and did a full body stretch, showing off his nine-foot length from the tip of his tail to the end of his nose. That accomplished, he lay down on his stomach, paws extended in front of him as if to say, "Am I unbelievable or what?" And he was still ignoring us completely.

Once he'd made an entrance any seasoned entertainer would envy, Ron turned to me and said, "Go ahead, kneel down beside him."

I was thrilled. I slowly approached Neil, got down on my knees so close to him that I was almost enveloped in his mane, and began scratching him under the chin—firmly, as directed. No look yet, but no complaints either. I had butterflies in my stomach, from some mixture of awe, respect, and fear, flashing back to Ozzie's simple comment about his beloved Dandylion: "He loves me, but at any moment he could kill me." But my God, was it amazing to be nestled into that gigantic, stunning animal.

Then it was Melanie's turn. "Kneel down on the other side," Ron told her.

She did, with a look of awe I'm sure mirrored mine.

As soon as she'd settled in beside him, he suddenly turned his head toward her and took her whole right shoulder in his mouth. I was sitting right there, watching half of my daughter disappear into the fangs of a lion.

I froze, terrified. Melanie, on the other hand, young and immortal, started laughing, prompting me to almost scream at her, "For God's sake, hold still!"

It turned out Neil was just playing with her, and within moments he lost interest in Melanie's shoulder, opened his mouth into a wide, slightly bored yawn, and began staring almost contemplatively at a distant rock formation.

Melanie was still laughing with delight. Noel was watching Melanie, Neil, and me with the eye of a man who'd been appraising the potential of the last couple of minutes as a scene in *Lions, Lions and More Lions*. My heartbeat was gradually slowing to normal again as I left Neil's side and stood, still shaken.

Ron gave me a reassuring smile. "You know, to really get to know lions, you need to live with them for a while. How would you like me to bring Neil to your place for a visit?"

The verdict was swift and unanimous—it sounded like a fine idea to the three of us. And just like that, four or five days a week, we had a full-grown lion in our house.

Our home in Sherman Oaks was fairly secluded. Its two stories, built into a hillside, and its swimming pool and lanai were all enclosed by redwood fences and surrounded by large, healthy subtropical trees and plants. We were also tucked into the crook of an elbow curve on Knobhill Drive so that not even actress Karen Valentine, our neighbor directly across the street, had a clear view of our property. We were blissfully unaware of busy nearby streets like Beverly Glen and Ventura Boulevard, and they were blissfully unaware of us.

So on Sunday, May 2, 1971, when Ron brought a full-grown lion for his first visit to our house, it was discreet as could be. Ron parked his ordinary green van on the curve, looked up and down the street to make sure it was clear of traffic and pedestrians, and then quickly escorted Neil out of the van, down the short flight of steps, and right on through our front door. I already knew he was huge, but somehow he looked even more gigantic as he nonchalantly paused on the landing and looked down to survey the living room and then began casually exploring every room of the house as if he were a prospective buyer.

The one room that was off-limits was the room in which we'd safely sequestered Partner and Puss, my precious mutt and Melanie's treasured cat. We'd seen how docile Neil could be, but we didn't doubt for a minute that he might find Partner and Puss to be the two most irresistible members of our family for all the wrong reasons, and we weren't about to take any chances with their dear little lives.

Neil proceeded to the backyard to check out the pool, the lanai, and the redwood fence, and I watched in anxious silence as he decided to stand up on his hind legs and peer over the top of the fence to scan the Sherman Oaks hills. There was a vacant lot between us and our closest downhill neighbor, but I could still imagine that neighbor relaxing in her garden with an afternoon cup of coffee and looking up to see a giant lion staring down at her. I was greatly relieved when Neil decided there was nothing interesting out there and dropped to the ground again, with no phone call from the police asking if we happened to know anything about a reported lion in our yard.

His tour complete and only marginally intrigued, Neil headed into the living room to sprawl out on the floor for a nice nap while Ron told us more about his hard-won relationship with this beloved creature. It had taken years, he said, starting when Neil arrived from Africa as a young adult. Ron sat every day for hours at a time outside Neil's cage, and it was months before he even ventured inside.

Another month went by with Ron sitting quietly a few feet away, not forcing a thing, before Neil finally trusted him enough to approach him and make friends.

"So what are you saying?" Noel asked.

"I'm saying that you'll have to make a career out of establishing a film-ready relationship with an adult lion," Ron answered him. "If I were you, I'd get several cubs as soon as possible and start friendship routines and basic training right away."

I hadn't seen that coming. "You think we should get lion cubs? Where on earth would we keep lion cubs?"

"Right here in the house, where you can have constant contact with them," he said with an implied "duh" in his tone.

Noel responded without a second thought. "Sounds good to me. How about you, Tippi?"

I forced my eyes away from Neil, whom I hadn't stopped staring at, and scanned our expensive furniture, our custom-made draperies, and our treasured collection of mementos from all over the world.

Then I focused again on that sublime, magnificent creature, still sleeping safe and peaceful on my living room floor, and took a hard look at my priorities. That made the answer easy.

"Absolutely," I said. "Bring us some lion cubs."

Ron began the fairly lengthy networking process of finding us a couple of baby lions, and we began our education in the fine art of sharing our home with an adult one. Neil became a constant visitor, while Partner and Puss accepted the fact that when Ron's green van arrived, they'd be spending a few hours safely secured in a bedroom that was strictly off-limits to the houseguest they never met.

Neil was a fascinating, sometimes hilarious, sometimes alarming Lion Behavior instructor. We learned that when we were in the pool, Neil thought it was very funny to go to the edge of the water, wait for one of us to swim over to say hello, put his paw on top of that person's head, and firmly push down.

We learned that when he was thirsty, he'd alert us by going into the kitchen and standing up with his paws on the sink. We'd dutifully turn on the faucet for him, and just like a domestic cat, he'd slowly lap the running water from the underside of his tongue.

We learned that sometimes lions grimace, wrinkling their faces and baring their teeth. This makes the animal look ferocious, but it has nothing to do with anger. Instead, it turns out that lions do their most effective sniffing not through their noses but from two holes in the roof of their mouths, and grimacing is simply their way of accessing those two holes to get a better whiff of whatever they sensed in the air. Neil would grimace when he smelled something pungent or musky, from food or perfume to the scent of a nearby animal. Once we learned the difference between a grimace, called flehmen, and an angry threat, we found it impossible not to laugh when Neil would turn to us with that open-mouthed, goofy, wrinkly face.

We learned, inconveniently, that whether you want them to or not, lions roar. Sometimes it means something. Sometimes they just feel like it. A roaring session usually consists of about eight or ten roars before they've got it out of their system, followed by somewhere between two and ten bark-like sounds, the lion's way of essentially saying, "This conversation is now over."

Neil's first roaring session at our house came just after sunset one quiet evening while he was taking a stroll between the pool and the redwood fence. It came out of nowhere, and it echoed all through the hills. I immediately tensed up, nervous about the neighbors, and on about roar number two or three I turned to Ron in a bit of a panic and asked, "Any way to stop that?"

He grinned back with a shrug. "Not a chance."

On which comment, of course, my phone rang. The call was from a woman who lived about two hundred feet away, and her voice was quivering.

"Mrs. Marshall," she said a bit tentatively, "I keep hearing what I swear is a lion roaring, and it sounds as if it's coming from your backyard."

Without batting an eye I replied, "Yes, I heard that, too. I thought it sounded more like a motorcycle revving up."

She didn't seem completely convinced, but that certainly made a whole lot more sense than her lion explanation, and we hung up.

Thank you again for the acting lessons, Hitch.

I didn't learn until many years later how naive and stupid we were. I was so caught up in the thrill, the awe, the challenge, the passion, and the prospect of making our movie and sharing my life with these magnificent wild animals that my logic went right out the window.

We took countless pictures of Neil in our home to start some buzz about our great undertaking, all of them creating the illusion that Neil was actually living with us. The truth, of course, was that he never lived with us, never even spent the night in our house; nor did any adult wild cat. Most of those photos were staged, and not a single photo of Neil was taken without Ron being right there, just off camera. The picture that makes me cringe the most is a shot of Neil and Melanie side by side, "sound asleep" in Melanie's bed. In real life, that never happened and never would have, and I will always regret that we made it look as if wild cats can be trained into being predictable and harmless.

Eventually, a couple of decades later, I did everything in my power to make up for my stupidity. At the time, as the saying goes, I didn't know what I didn't know.

Our efforts at creating buzz were so successful that one day an editor at *Life* magazine called. He'd heard we were educating ourselves about big cats in preparation for a movie and that we actually had a full-grown lion in our house, and he wanted to do an article and photo essay about it. Our response, of course: "How soon can you be here?"

The day of the shoot arrived, and we were one excited household. After surveying the layout of our home, pool, and property, the *Life* photographer had decided he'd like to capture some Norman Rockwell shots of the Marshall family having a typical evening meal together, while our supposed "live-in" lion watched from his perch on the landing above the oval dining room table.

Our loyal, intrepid housekeeper, Emily Henderson, was on hand as always. She'd been an incredibly good sport about cooking and cleaning for us with the added complication of a four-hundred-pound wild cat in the house. The day I formally introduced them—yes, I actually said, "Emily, this is Neil"—I was braced for her to either run screaming from the house or freeze in panic-induced shock. Instead, she greeted him with a wide, beaming smile and not a trace of fear. She even happily posed for some "candid" shots with Neil in the kitchen, Neil lying in the middle of the floor while Emily stepped around him, preparing a meal as if he were just another routine occupational hazard.

Partner and Puss were safely secured in their room. Noel and the boys entertained Neil and Ron and photographer Mike Rougier. Emily, Melanie, and I prepared the broiled chicken, rice, vegetables, and salad and set a beautiful table with Wedgwood china, polished silver, candles, cut-glass stemware, and flowers. Then, after beautifying ourselves as well, Noel, Melanie, Joel, Jerry, and I sat down to eat, while John and Ron hid on the landing near Neil, John feeding Neil bits of chicken to keep him engaged right where he was.

The camera starting clicking away, taking shot after shot after shot of the Marshall family enjoying a typical evening meal while "their" lion raptly loomed above them. Unfortunately, Neil wasn't in as rapt a mood as any of us had hoped, so all the camera captured was shot after shot after shot of him looking away, looking around, looking anywhere but at us.

Thirty wasted shots later, while, unbeknownst to us, John ran out of Neil's chicken bits, the photographer told us all to relax for a minute or two while he reloaded the camera.

We did.

Neil didn't. Neil did what big cats do. In an instant, in one incredible, heart-stopping move, he leaped over the railing of the landing directly onto the dining room table to help himself to some broiled chicken, his right front paw ending up in the middle of my plate. The table teetered on two legs for a second and then tipped completely over in my direction, and next thing I knew, I had a lap full of food, broken Wedgwood, stemware, silverware, and flowers, while Neil gracefully bounded into the middle of the room to finish his entrée.

Too many years of modeling and acting, I guess—my immediate reaction was "Mike! Did you get that shot?" *Then* I joined my family in assessing the damage to our best dishes and stemware, our table, my clothes, and the rug, every square inch of which were decorated with rice, vegetables, salad, and beverage stains.

Mike Rougier informed me with disgust that no, he did not get that shot. He and the *Life* crew hurriedly packed up and left, cursing the day they were stuck with the assignment of capturing the Marshall family and their "pet lion" on film, I'm sure.

Fortunately, we discovered that a second camera, unmanned on a tripod, had tripped automatically and caught Neil in the middle of his leap from the landing to the table, headed straight for my plate.

For the record, none of this came as any surprise to Ron, and Neil was never reprimanded. Neil had behaved exactly as a big cat can be expected to behave, Ron pointed out, and trying to teach him counterintuitive manners like "don't go after food that's sitting right there in plain sight" would be an exercise in futility. The two of them simply disappeared into the green van and drove away, leaving our dinner party, our dining room, and my designer casual wear in ruins.

A week or so later we entertained several members of a BOAC (British Overseas Airways Corporation) public relations team. They were understandably anxious when Neil and Ron first arrived, emitting frightened little laughs from the backs of their throats and fiercely clinging to their British stoicism as best they could. After a few minutes, when it became clear that they weren't on Neil's menu for the evening, they relaxed, slowly but surely, into pure, fascinated awe.

Everything was going beautifully until later that night. Something terrifying happened that I'd heard about from Ron but never seen. With no warning and for no apparent reason, Neil suddenly became possessive, which is one of a big cat's most dangerous emotions, and the object of Neil's possessiveness was Ron. Maybe Ron had been paying too much attention to everyone else and not enough to him, and he didn't feel like sharing right then. There was no way to figure out the reason for Neil's sudden change in behavior, it just *happened*, and it made my blood run cold.

Neil and Ron and I were in the kitchen when, in a matter of seconds, Neil went from docile cat to ferocious cat. It started with a growl, from the depths of his soul, and quickly escalated. His tail began twitching, his bloodred mouth opened to bare his stark white canines, and his huge paw wildly batted the air. Ron instantly recognized what was happening and shouted at me, "Get out of here!"

I ran to the living room, slamming the kitchen door behind me. Noel and our guests were already on their feet, startled by the commotion. Scared and helpless, we stood there frozen in place and listened to the impossibly tense showdown.

My impulse was "That's not Neil. That's not the docile, easygoing Neil who's melted my heart." But of course the truth was, it *was* Neil, as inherently wild as he was lovable, and it was insanity to pretend otherwise.

Ron described the encounter to me the next day. He'd faced Neil down, less than three feet away from him, his arms raised to make himself as big and threatening as he could, and kept yelling, "No! No! Leave it! No!" He had to win. A trainer has to win that fight. If the big cat wins the fight, their relationship has to end, or the trainer will never be safe with that big cat again.

After about two minutes that felt like an hour, Ron managed to penetrate Neil's instinctive rage. Neil finally surrendered, tossing his head and mane, relaxing his mouth, and lowering his paw to the floor. His snarls softened to subdued muttering. Ron's arms dropped to his side, while we eavesdroppers in the living room heard the roars and the yelling subside and tentatively exhaled.

After a quick round of apologies, a thoroughly embarrassed Ron walked his lion to the van and drove away. As I closed the door behind them, I heard Ron, purely for stress relief and not because he thought it would do a bit of good, giving Neil the scolding you'd give a brat.

"What the hell were you thinking? Those are nice people! Why did you act like that in front of them?"

Once they were gone we poured our guests some nice strong drinks and toasted Ron's amazing, educated courage . . . and Neil, primal and complicated in that magnificent body like all the big cats and, in the end, the inspiration for a passionate commitment that will be with me the rest of my life.

God bless that brave BOAC PR group, too, who didn't hesitate to meet us a week later at Steve Martin's Soledad Canyon compound to work with Steve's two-year-old lion Boomer. Late in the afternoon Boomer was doing a photo shoot carrying a BOAC flight bag in his mouth. To demonstrate how unpredictable a lion's possessiveness can be, Boomer decided that bag was his. When the shoot was over, he stretched out on the ground, flight bag between his teeth, and settled in, refusing to move and daring anyone and everyone to even think about trying to take it away from him.

It took Ron and his trusty van to end that stalemate. He tied one end of a rope to Boomer and the other end to the bumper of his van and literally towed that lion, bag still firmly locked in his mouth, back to his quarters for the night.

The BOAC team wisely forfeited their flight bag.

Despite the difficulties that the BOAC team witnessed, we were becoming more comfortable around the grown lions, and it couldn't have come at a better time. After weeks of searching and networking on Ron's part and ours, we finally acquired our first lion cub.

A doctor in the upscale, wooded Mandeville Canyon area of Los Angeles, who foolishly believed it would be chic to have a big cat as a house pet, had adopted a three-month-old cub from an animal park. The cub, named Casey, had behaved exactly like a baby lion, growing at an alarming rate and having a high old rambunctious time destroying the doctor's house. He'd now been banished to the emptied-out guest house, where he lived alone, a very unhappy prisoner.

We were as excited to take that cub home as the doctor was to say good-bye to him. We drove home with me at the wheel and Melanie in the backseat with a very playful Casey, who spent the whole trip to Knobhill in her lap, gnawing on her hands and arms. He still had baby spots on his sides and legs, spots that typically disappear into a golden-amber adult coat at about nine months old or so. He also, of course, had paws the size of dinner plates, weighed about forty-five pounds, and was strong and adorable. It was love at first sight for all three of us.

It wasn't love at first sight for Partner and Puss. They'd tolerated their isolation when Neil was visiting, and now here came another furry intruder. Casey wasn't a physical threat to them yet, but at a foot tall, three feet long, and unpredictably zany, he was more of a handful than they cared to deal with. Their behavior toward him varied between avoidance and tolerance, and God bless them for everything they put up with over the years. As for Casey, he was perfectly content with all the attention he got from the new humans in his life, and if Partner and Puss didn't care to be part of his fan club—oh, well, their loss.

Ron Oxley was exactly right. To really learn about big cats, there's no substitute for living with them. From the moment we brought him home, Casey began giving us an education in Lions 101—what their various sounds and postures mean, just for starters. Even at three months, Casey made it very clear what mood he was in, and there was no doubt that this boy was going to live up to his title of "king of beasts" someday. He was very possessive of his nursing bottle, for example. He'd wrap his paws around it with an accompanying noise that sounded like "uh-*huh*, uh-*huh*," heartwarming as could be. Any attempt to take the bottle away and that sound would come from deep inside his body, just as Neil's adult guttural "uh-*huh*, uh-*huh*" was a signal of potential violence. Casey had an amazing "sound" vocabulary, from moans and grunts and growls to happy "aows" and hums. There was nothing haphazard about those noises—they all meant something, and part of our job was to learn to translate them.

Casey chose to sleep with Melanie in her bed, which she loved until the night I heard her let out a loud, piercing scream. I frantically ran into her room to find her clutching her thigh, in obvious excruciating pain. Casey was sitting on the end of the bed, looking up at me with the most innocent, angelic eyes I'd ever seen.

"He bit me!" she said in total shock.

"Why? What were you doing?" I asked her, almost as shocked as she was.

"Nothing! We weren't even playing. He was sitting there, and suddenly he just bit me."

Her skin was punctured and she was bleeding, although she and Casey were instantly friends again.

Two more lessons. Lesson number one: No matter where exotic cubs are being raised, their teeth are virtual petri dishes of bacteria, and antibiotics are essential if a bite punctures the skin. Lesson number two: If you live with big-cat cubs, being bitten is inevitable.

And we were just getting started.

One day I was driving up Knobhill just as Ron Oxley was driving down after a visit to the house. We stopped side by side, and he leaned out the window of his van with a huge grin on his face. "There's a present for you in your bathroom. You'd better go take a look."

I raced to the house and ran downstairs. There in my bathtub, curled up sound asleep on one of my sweaters, lay a tiny six-week-old cub—another excess baby from Lion Country Safari, where Casey had been born, it turned out. (Due to limitations on available space and money, zoos and animal parks often have to find alternative homes for big-cat cubs.)

I was cuddling our newest member of the family, a female Melanie named Needra, when Casey came ambling into the bathroom, took one look at this tiny lioness, and was so beside himself he nearly did backflips. Cubs desperately need companionship, and suddenly, here was a brand-new baby sister, just for him. They instantly became inseparable, playing together for the rest of the day until they wore themselves out and fell sound asleep beside each other.

By August of 1971, word was out that the crazy Marshall family in Sherman Oaks would provide a home for almost any healthy lion cub. Less than three weeks after Needra arrived, we had three more additions to our growing pride—Ike, Mike, and Trans. When they weren't running and wrestling with each other all over the house, they were playing with rubber dog toys we bought in the dim hope of distracting them from demolishing our furniture.

Another good lesson: Mike in particular thought tennis shoes were the best toy in the whole world. We found that enchanting, until we discovered the hard way that he found tennis shoes just as irresistible when someone happened to walk by wearing them.

Calls kept coming from everywhere to ask if we could please take another lion cub, or two, or three. A circus gave us Cindi, who had a broken leg no one had bothered to set, leaving her too crippled to be a desirable performer. Tiny Bridget, originally bought from a pet store, had been mistreated and arrived frightened and fidgety, tensing every time she saw a human. I wasn't sure I could handle a larger crouching, jumping demolition team than we already had, so I put out the word to friends that we'd be delighted to share the endless joys of raising baby lions.

One eager volunteer was Luanne Wells, wife of Frank Wells, who happened to be president of Warner Brothers Studios. Frank drove to the house and picked up five-pound spotted, blue-eyed Trans to take home to Luanne, and we couldn't have been happier—not about giving up Trans, but about the fact that at some point we were going to be looking for a studio to finance and release our movie. If Frank and Luanne fell in love with Trans between now and then, we just might have Warner Brothers in our hip pocket.

Even with all of us "supervising" them, even when we saw to it that the little lions spent as much time as possible in our fenced-in yard every day (praying all the while that our neighbors wouldn't notice), the cubs couldn't have been more destructive. Everything was a target for being torn to shreds, from pillows to our $3,000 sofa to the head of Emily's mop while she was trying to clean. Bedspreads were favorites for tugs-of-war. We'd been smart enough to stow away our art objects to keep them from smashing to the floor during wrestling matches, but for the most part, nothing that wasn't made of concrete survived that houseful of lion cubs.

None of it mattered in the end, though. I loved them, as did Noel and Melanie and the boys. They could melt my heart in the blink of an eye. One morning I was lying in bed, with little Needra curled up against my feet, sound asleep, when a loud sonic boom shook the house. She bolted awake, raced up my body to my shoulder, and buried her face in my neck, trembling. I held her close and whispered, "It's okay, Neenie, it's gone now, everything's fine."

I was hooked.

Incredibly, we managed to ignore the inevitable fact that in a few short years these cubs would be eight or nine feet long from their noses to the tips of their tails and weigh four or five hundred pounds. Our conversations about the future were limited to that "someday" when we'd begin shooting our film, with a cast of magnificent big cats we'd cherished since they were babies, big cats who, when they became adults, were capable of loving us one moment and killing us the next, without a second thought.

One day Luanne Wells called, apologetic but firm. Trans, now about three months old, was too incorrigible for them to handle, she said, and they were sorry, but they were going to have to return him to us.

"Of course," I said. "I completely understand."

I meant it. It didn't surprise me. Besides all the obvious challenges of raising a lion cub, Trans had shown signs from the beginning of being tougher than most, with a perpetual "I dare you" look in his eyes and in his stance. He'd be a handful, but I was perfectly happy to bring Trans home to rejoin the pride.

At the same time, though, my heart sank. So much for the big-cat love affair we'd hoped for between Trans and the president of Warner Brothers, and so much for that studio giving our movie a home and supplementing the funds we'd raised, which to date were still hovering right around zero dollars.

It was less than a week later. We were getting Trans settled back in and recovering from what felt like a huge setback to the film when, out of nowhere, I got a call from our pal William Peter Blatty. He'd finished his manuscript of *The Exorcist* and wondered if I'd mind reading it. Are you kidding? After hearing the bare bones of it at his house on New Year's Day, I couldn't wait.

I couldn't put it down. It was four a.m. when I read the last page of that book, and I excitedly woke Noel up.

"This is one of the most engrossing stories I've ever read," I told him. "If you don't sign Bill Blatty as a client, you're out of your mind." I knew beyond a doubt that *The Exorcist* was destined to be not only a bestselling book but a blockbuster movie as well.

Noel was continuing his career as an agent that summer, and he'd never heard me so excited about a book. Within days it was official—Noel was representing William Peter Blatty and his gripping novel about demons and priests. Included in the agreement was a clause stating that if and when *The Exorcist* became a movie, Noel would be the executive producer and guaranteed 15 percent of the profits.

Just like that, the hope that had ebbed away when Frank and Luanne Wells returned Trans to us with a resounding "No thank you!" came flooding back. It almost seemed like divine intervention. In exchange for all the big-cat cubs we were helping and everything they were putting us through, God was seeing to it that demons and priests would pay for our film.

Eight

It was inevitable. Disastrously inevitable.

One sunny October afternoon in 1971, our neighbor to the west was doing some gardening in her backyard when she looked up to see two lion cubs (probably Ike and Mike) peering over our fence at her, two big-eared tawny heads with amber eyes. From what I could understand of her semi-hysterical phone call, the cubs didn't try to jump over the fence into her yard or threaten her in any way. But this was the same woman who'd called a few months earlier to say she'd heard a lion roaring at my house. If I'd eased her suspicions at all with my "that was a motorcycle" story, the game was definitely over now. She'd actually seen not one lion but two, about the size of full-grown German shepherds, and she wasn't happy about it.

Sure enough, very early the next morning our doorbell woke us up. Noel answered it, fresh from bed, to find a uniformed Los Angeles County animal control officer standing there.

"Sir," the officer said politely, "I heard you have some lions living here."

In desperate need of a stall tactic, Noel managed to come up with "Excuse me, I'm not dressed. Let me get my bathrobe."

He closed the door and sprinted downstairs, grabbing his robe while he whispered to me, "Wake Melanie up. The two of you need to get those cubs over the back fence." As an afterthought he added, "But leave Bridget."

Cut to Melanie and me boosting the rear ends of five cubs over the fence into the vacant lot next door and then following them right on over. I can only imagine what it must have looked like to any neighbors who happened to be awake at that ungodly hour as the cubs began cavorting around the vacant lot while two blondes supervised them, shivering in the early morning chill, dressed in nightgowns and coats and sporting some seriously challenged bed hair.

Noel, in the meantime, took nervous little Bridget to the front door, holding her in both hands and extending her toward the officer with a remorseful "Here you go."

The officer looked at Noel, then at Bridget, then at Noel again.

"Forget it," he said, and he was gone.

We were living on borrowed time in that residential neighborhood. We'd known that since Neil's first visit; we just hadn't addressed it yet and figured out what to do about it.

One afternoon about two weeks later I heard Partner barking, upset, letting me know that something was wrong. I ran to check on him and discovered that someone had left a door open, and Casey was gone.

I dashed out the front door to look for him, pulling it closed behind me to keep everyone else inside where they belonged, and saw him standing in the middle of the street, deciding what he wanted to explore first. My heart was in my throat as I walked toward him, trying to appear calm so he wouldn't get alarmed and run. Then it hit me—I hadn't grabbed his lead, and without it I didn't stand a chance of bringing him home. I darted back to the front door. Of course I'd locked myself out. So I ran around to the side of the house, through the gate and up the stairs to the unlocked kitchen door, taking up precious time I couldn't afford.

Minutes later I was in the middle of the street, Casey's lead in hand but no Casey in sight. Ron's van was parked there. He'd gone with Noel to run an errand, leaving Neil behind in the van, and I said a brief prayer that Neil had not managed to escape, too, before I took a random guess and headed downhill toward the canyon road of Beverly Glen. It was five o'clock. Rush hour. Traffic was getting heavier by the minute, and countless hideous scenarios flashed through my mind as I began to run as fast as I could: Casey getting hit by a car; cars swerving to avoid him and causing a chain reaction of collisions; some poor elderly person having a heart attack at the sight of a lion the size of a well-fed cougar advancing toward them; some he-man hunter spotting him and immediately reaching for his rifle . . .

Finally I spotted Casey. He was in the middle of Knobhill, slowly but steadily approaching Beverly Glen. I yelled at him to stop, but he just glanced back at me with a quick "Oh, hi, Mom. We'll talk later. I'm busy" look and kept on going, while I grew more frantic by the second.

Suddenly I remembered an interesting fact about big cats that Ron

Oxley had told me one day. If they see a creature, including humans, who appears to be injured or infirm, they're apt to zero in on it. An eternity of genetic dictate tells them, "Investigate that! It's slowed down, so it may be food!"

I immediately affected an exaggerated limp and yelled at Casey again. He turned around to look, and this time he froze in place to stare, clearly intrigued. Still hobbling pitifully, I started back toward the house, making all kinds of deals with God if he would please just let this work.

To my amazement, it did. I glanced behind me and, sure enough, Casey wasn't just following me, he was stalking me, almost crouched to his belly as he crept along. It must have been an astonishing sight for the neighbors, but there was nothing I could do about it. I had to get this boy safely back to the house.

As soon as I saw that he was closing in on me, I took off at a dead run. He was tensed to jump me, not moving a muscle, when I stopped at Ron's van and, taking advantage of my motionless target, threw the lead around Casey's neck. The van began lurching wildly as Neil, accompanied by growling noises, tried to escape to see what on earth was going on out there.

At that instant I heard the phone ring. Let me guess—either the police or animal control, neither of whom I wanted showing up for a home visit at the moment. I tied Casey's lead to the bumper of the van and flew inside through the kitchen door.

It was just a friend calling. "I can't talk right now!" I yelled into the phone. "My lion's out!"

I was reaching to unlock the front door and retrieve Casey when the phone rang again. It was the same friend. "Tippi, I don't know what you're talking about. I could hear you perfectly. There's nothing wrong with your line."

Out of sheer relief, I was laughing as I untied our resident explorer and escorted him into the living room, where he settled in for a nice nap, exhausted from all that fun he'd had scaring the life out of me.

Miraculously, nothing happened until a couple of months later. I was on my knees doing a little gardening in front of the house on a bright, crisp morning when I looked up to see Bridget about ten feet away, beaming at me from the sidewalk.

I did my best to sound nonchalant, with a friendly "Hi, Bridget," while my stomach tightened into one huge knot. She strolled over to nuzzle my cheek, but before I could grab her, she trotted off to Knobhill Drive and loped away.

I had to make a split-second decision—run back into the house for a lead or chase her. This time I chose the latter. Bridget ran for about thirty yards, past Karen Valentine's driveway and up a wooden stairway that led to a hilltop house. I flew up the stairs two at a time and managed to get a firm grip on her tail.

Now what? Bridget was five months old now, too big for me to lift and probably too big for me to keep hold of her if I tried to drag her back down the stairs by the scruff of her neck.

I started yelling, "Help!" over and over, during which I noticed that part of the yard was enclosed by a chain-link fence. A perturbed-looking woman finally came out of the house to find me still holding on to Bridget's tail for dear life.

"Hi," I said inanely. "I hate to bother you, but would you mind if I put my cat in your yard while I make a quick call?"

She wasn't crazy about it, but said, "Sure," adding as I started pulling Bridget toward the chain-link enclosure, "I heard you had some cubs down there."

"I'm sure you did," I thought, feeling a noose tightening around all of our necks.

I called Emily from the woman's house, and a few minutes later she arrived with a lead and we walked Bridget home.

It was January 14, 1972, when the same animal control officer rang the doorbell. He was still polite, but there was no more stalling to retrieve a bathrobe, no more escaping over the back fence.

"You have twenty-four hours to get those lions off this property."

I tried to defend them. They weren't harming anyone or destroying anyone's property. They didn't bark, and they were strictly confined to our house and yard. Most of the time. They were still just sweet, funny babies, not even old enough to be dangerous yet.

He wasn't having it. "It's illegal to keep lions of any age within the city limits unless they're in a licensed zoo," he recited back to me.

Even if I'd had an argument to that, I was weeping too hard to offer it.

Noel came home a few minutes later, and we put in an emergency call to Steve Martin in Soledad Canyon, a call he'd actually been expecting sooner or later. Yes, of course, he'd be glad to board the six cubs for us.

We rounded them up the next morning and drove them to Steve's compound. It broke my heart to see them led away into confinement, but there was obviously no way around it. I went to Soledad Canyon every day for the next week to talk to them and nuzzle them and take them for walks by the river, missing them even more, I was sure, than they missed me and the only real home they'd ever known.

I honestly hadn't realized how natural our accumulation of baby lions had seemed to me, or how completely I'd lost my objectivity about them, until I had lunch one day with a good friend. She was excitedly telling me about a great surprise she'd just given her two teenage sons—she'd bought each of them a motorcycle.

I hate motorcycles. They're noisy, they're dangerous, and I cringe at the sight of them. I instantly blurted out, "How dare you do that? How dare you risk your children's lives by giving them motorcycles so they can ride off and kill themselves?"

She gave me a long, cool look and came back with an incredulous "You let your children live with wild animals and you're lecturing me about motorcycles?"

It was like a slap in the face, but I had no comeback.

And as fate would have it, these animals really were here to stay for us. A few weeks later, I returned home from a trip to find Noel there, greeting me with a smug smile I'd learned to recognize over the years. He'd done something he was very proud of without discussing it with me, and he couldn't wait to tell me.

I knew the drill. All I had to do was ask, "What's new?"

"Oh, nothing much," he said casually as he helped me carry my luggage to the bedroom. "I bought Steve Martin's acreage in Soledad Canyon while you were gone, but other than that—"

"You what?" I cut him off, in complete shock.

Noel's impulses were rarely driven by logic. By the time he explained this one, though, I had to hand it to him, it made perfect sense. We were currently paying Steve $25 per lion per day for our six cubs, and we planned to double or triple our animal population before we started filming *Lions, Lions, and More Lions*. We might as well be investing that same money in a mortgage.

But there was more.

"We'll use it for the movie location."

We still hadn't decided on the right location, but I was pretty sure it wasn't Soledad Canyon. "Noel," I pointed out, "there's nothing but desert out there. It's river bottomland, just sand and rocks and maybe three trees on forty acres. It looks nothing like African lion country."

"It will." He grinned, sure of himself as always.

In spite of myself, I started to get excited about the prospect of building our own compound in Soledad Canyon and bringing in all the animals we wanted. Lion movie or no lion movie, what a beautiful dream.

But first we had another movie to make, the movie I was starring in and Noel was producing, the movie I'd hurried home from my trip to shoot. It was called *The Harrad Experiment*, and it would costar veteran actor James Whitmore and a much-too-good-looking twenty-two-year-old hotshot named Don Johnson.

I'd never encouraged Melanie to become an actress. There were things about it I loved, of course, but there were also obviously things about it I would never wish on anyone, let alone a child. Following my parents' example when they raised me, I'd just given a free spirit her freedom and promised myself that I'd always be her most enthusiastic cheerleader and as unselfishly supportive as Mom and Daddy were.

I didn't think a thing about it when Melanie went with a girlfriend to an interview for work as an extra when she was around twelve. So I was really unprepared when Melanie called, beside herself with excitement, and announced, "Mom! I have an acting job!"

It seems the casting director of a Glenn Ford movie called *Smith!* had taken one look at Melanie's girlfriend and told her she was too old, then had turned to Melanie and said, "You're perfect."

I congratulated her and said something like "How great! Good for you!" just as my parents would have done. Then I hung up, reminded myself she was only working as an extra—this time—and that just because this news came as a shock didn't mean it was a bad idea for her to give acting a try if she decided she wanted to. She might be very good at it. She might enjoy it. If she didn't, she could walk away from it any time she wanted to pursue something else.

God knows she was pretty enough, and it was already apparent she was going to be a beautiful young woman. By the time she became a teenager she was as tall as I was, with long, slender legs and an air of total self-assurance I was just beginning to hope for when I was her age. She'd had a mind of her own all her life, which made her both a lot of fun and impossibly defiant depending on the situation, and she was maturing mentally and physically much more quickly than I knew how to handle. She was also becoming much more unpredictable—my childlike baby girl one day and a sullen, combative, secretive stranger the next. Mothers and daughters classically begin to have their toughest times together when daughters reach their early teens, and I wondered constantly if I'd made a mistake encouraging her to be quite so independent.

Melanie was fourteen when we began shooting *The Harrad Experiment*. Noel, the film's producer, suggested one day that we hire her as an extra.

"Sure, why not?" I said.

It changed everything.

As I look back on it, the subject matter of *The Harrad Experiment* is nothing short of ironic. The script was based on a novel of the same name, written by Robert Rimmer. It was about a fictional school called Harrad College, where students were taught sexuality and encouraged to experiment with their fellow students. It was a commentary on the sexual revolution of the late 1960s and early 1970s in the United States, and James Whitmore and I played the married couple who ran the school.

Don Johnson played one of our more, let's say, experimental students.

What I didn't realize was that this apparently wasn't just the case for the camera. I was oblivious and/or Don and Melanie were very, very discreet. When Melanie announced that they'd fallen in love, you could literally have knocked me over with a feather.

Don was eight years older than Melanie. He'd already been through two brief marriages, and he terrified me. He was handsome. His acting career was taking off. He was wild as a deer. There wasn't a trace of naiveté in him, and there was nothing about him that led me to believe he'd give a damn about my objections. I knew my daughter, my willful, headstrong daughter. If I'd tried to forbid her from seeing him or tried to talk her out of him, it would only have intensified her feelings for him and alienated her from me, and above all, I didn't want to lose her.

I hate admitting this, but it's true: As horrified and panic-stricken as I was, I had no idea what to do—not when she fell in love with him, and not when she moved in with him at the age of fifteen. I did have a serious talk with Don, needless to say. He was old enough to know better but too young and arrogant to be interested in what his beautiful new girlfriend's mom thought of him.

Many times over the subsequent years, I've wondered if Melanie felt I'd devoted so much attention to the big cats we were amassing that there wasn't enough left for her.

I've thought a thousand times how much easier the lions were to handle than my daughter was back then. There were no simple Ron Oxley rules like "When they do this, you do this"; "When they make this sound, they're telling you this"; and "When you need to discipline them, here's what works and what doesn't." It was the early 1970s, and help wasn't nearly as accessible as it is today. Therapy, rehab, programs for troubled teens, tough love, Dr. Phil—you name it, help was either rare or nonexistent in that era of sex, drugs, and rock and roll, and not for one moment do I believe Melanie would have cooperated, even if I'd exercised my right as the mother of a minor and forced her. If I'd tried to have Don prosecuted for statutory rape, I'm convinced to this day that my daughter would never have spoken to me again. As far as she was concerned, she was free, living happily with the man she adored, finishing Hollywood Professional School a year early, at the age of sixteen, booking acting jobs, and having a great time. What on earth was "troubled" about that?

I still remember standing at my kitchen sink on Knobhill one day in January of 1976 and answering the phone to hear my giddy eighteen-year-old daughter yell, "Mom, we're in Las Vegas and we just got married!" She was so excited, and I was so heartsick. My precious only child, much too young for all this to begin with, had her wedding without me, and she was headed for a world of hurt, I knew it.

The marriage was annulled after only a few months. Melanie's career was starting to take off by then, and she could afford a place of her own. From the day she moved out of our house at the age of fifteen, we've never lived together again.

Thank God, though, we were never estranged. There was an underlying distance between us for a while that neither of us knew how to talk about or mend, but—another thank God—we got through it, and we've been close ever since, probably more like best friends than like mother and daughter.

Of course, I'm well aware of the substance abuse problems she's struggled with, but that's a subject for her memoir, not mine. I'm sure she was genetically predisposed to addiction, since both her father and his father before him were alcoholics. I couldn't be more proud of her for continuing to fight that battle and for being so open about it. Melanie has never been shy or apologetic when it comes to expressing herself, so it's no surprise that when the press asks, she answers, unedited. I feel no moral superiority in the fact that I can't relate to addiction, with the exception of my years as a smoker, which ended as soon as I learned smoking could cause countless health problems. I've just been lucky enough to have a complete lack of curiosity about drugs and a healthy limit to my interest in alcohol, coming down, I guess, to the simple logic, "If you know it's not good for you, don't do it."

As for Don, to his credit, he sat me down many years after that nightmarish time in the 1970s and said, with utter sincerity, "I'm sorry I hurt you." I don't mind admitting that I used to wish I'd never even heard of a movie called *The Harrad Experiment*; if it hadn't been for that film, Melanie and Don might never have met, and life would have been so much easier.

After a lot of soul-searching and reading that book I mentioned earlier called *The Other Side and Back*, I don't wish that anymore. Without the journey Melanie and Don took together, there would be no Dakota Johnson, and I can't imagine my life without her. All three of Melanie's children are so precious to me. I love them so much and cherish my closeness to them. I'm even close to Don's son Jesse, by actress Patti D'Arbanville, thanks in large part to Melanie's inability to stop loving anyone she's ever loved, and her magnanimous, unselfish definition of the word "family."

Melanie Griffith is the great love of my life. It's an impossibility that I could love her more. That I could have loved her better will occasionally keep me awake at night for the rest of my life.

Nine

Meanwhile, back in Soledad Canyon . . .

Work was under way at our newly acquired lion complex. Noel, now sporting a "designer" hat, was busy building high chain-link fences to create spacious compounds for the big cats so they'd have ample room to do their exercising, marking, sleeping, rubbing, and just being lions. Using Noel's sketches, Ron Oxley was working on a model of the African Gorongosa house for the movie. Boomer, who'd finally lost interest in his infamous BOAC flight bag, had been an added bonus with our purchase of the property, making him our first official adult lion, and Noel had bought six more adult lions from an overcrowded animal park—Monte, Buddy, Scarface, Buggsy,

Suzy, and Jenny. They hadn't been treated well and had no reason to like humans, and we christened them the Wild Bunch.

Poor Bridget, our little Knobhill lioness, who'd already had her share of misfortune in her life, including abuse when she was an infant and being thrown thirty feet from a truck in a traffic accident on Soledad Canyon, was the first victim of the Wild Bunch. She'd spotted Jenny, the wildest of the group, in a compound by the pond and swum over to say hello. Cubs have a natural fascination with their elders, which, sadly, isn't always reciprocated—Jenny quickly dug under the compound fence and attacked.

Noel and I heard Bridget's terrified screams, ran to the pond, and lifted her out of the water. She was bleeding badly and more dead than alive, and I wrapped her in a towel and held her in my lap while we raced her to Dr. Martin Dinnes, a brilliant veterinarian who specialized in treating wild animals. Dr. Dinnes performed a three-and-a-half-hour operation on her, and the next day I took her home to Knobhill to recover. Dr. Dinnes believed that sick cats desperately need affection, so if that's what Bridget needed, that's exactly what she was going to get, whether the neighbors and animal control liked it or not. I drew the infection out of her sliced-up stomach four times a day, I gave her nonstop affection, and slowly but surely she fought her way back to normal.

At Bridget's expense, Noel and I had learned yet another valuable lesson. That attack wasn't Jenny's fault, it was ours. We had no business letting a cub wander around near strange adult cats, and we also had no business enclosing big cats inside fences without concrete bases that could keep them from digging their way out.

We needed a bigger staff in Soledad Canyon, sooner rather than later, and it was amazing how exactly the right people started showing up at exactly the right time.

Expert trainer Frank Tom, a stocky, personable Chinese Mexican, needed a home for his pet cougar and came to work for us to be near his beloved cat.

Sylvie Loboda signed on as one of the handlers. A tiny woman who talked baby talk to the animals, Sylvie was a veteran of a Mexican circus who, during her first performance, experienced an improvisational elephant taking her head into its mouth and trotting her around the ring. She kept right on working for that circus, and we decided if that wasn't enough to scare her off, Soledad Canyon might be just the place for her.

Joining the maintenance staff were our indispensable Liberato and Jesus Torres from Guadalajara, with a perpetual team of helpers at the ready, and Ben Sanders, who became boss of a five-man crew in charge of installing concrete bases for the fences and regularly tending and maintaining what had now become more than a mile of chain link.

The lion acquisitions kept on showing up almost weekly, a huge, belligerent cat named Togar among them. He arrived with a lioness named Alice from the San Francisco Zoo, and he'd been too tough and defiant for the zookeepers to handle. I was afraid of him from the first moment I laid eyes on him, but he was a playful, wonderful father with the more than thirty cubs he sired in Soledad Canyon.

Of course it had all started with the idea of telling a nice, interesting little story about a scientist and his family finding themselves sharing an African house with a pride of lions. So I was completely blindsided when Noel announced in the "by the way" tone he used when he was anticipating an argument from me, "We're getting a pair of tiger cubs."

"Yeah, that makes all the sense in the world," I shot back, "since you know as well as I do that *there are no tigers in Africa*. How are you planning to handle that in the script?"

"Beats me," he answered with a shrug and what I'm sure was supposed to be an adorable little smile.

Arguing about the tigers was pointless. Two six-week-old Siberians, Natasha and Ivan, were already on their way from the overpopulated Okanagan Game Preserve in British Columbia. Noel's vision for our movie was getting more expansive and expensive by the minute. In fact, the only animal I ever heard Noel turn down was a hippo, and even that was probably a close call. He revised the script from a zoologist studying a pride of lions to a zoologist studying a collection of big cats under one roof.

I admit it, though, I loved those little tigers from the moment they arrived. I settled them into the Knobhill home with Bridget, who had almost recovered from Jenny's violent attack on her. Our naiveté really did know no bounds. Our theory was that if six-month-old Bridget grew up with six-week-old Ivan and Natasha, the three of them would be perfectly happy to share the same compound when they grew up. That theory, of course, was based on our uneducated, preposterous assumption that, other than the obvious physical differences, all big cats are alike.

I was enchanted that Ivan and Natasha immediately began following me everywhere I went and insisted on being petted constantly, just like little lion cubs; but I quickly learned that while lion cubs love to be picked up and cuddled, tiger cubs want nothing to do with it and start screaming until they're put back on the ground. When I moved or rolled over during the night while sleeping with a lion cub, it would make quiet, contented little sounds and nestle even closer. When I did the same thing while sleeping with Ivan and Natasha, they scolded me with loud cries of complaint that clearly translated to "How dare you wake me up?"

From cubs to adults, tigers are edgier than lions. Their hearts even beat faster than lions' hearts do when they're at rest, so maybe that contributes to their being more high-strung. Tiger cubs love to play, but this activity can quickly escalate into combat, with their ears flattened back and their eyes almost glazed, and their genes dictate that they always finish a fight. We learned early on to end the contact and walk away.

From cubs to adults, tigers also happen to make the sweetest, most heart-melting "ff-fuff" sound through their nasal passages. That sound is kind of an all-purpose part of their vocabulary; it can mean hello or good-bye or how are you? It might even be just an expression of contentment while they lick the back of your hand. But again, unlike lions, who occasionally will enjoy sucking your fingers or your thumb, offering your fingers to a tiger is almost guaranteed to be a very, very bad idea unless you've been wanting to get rid of those fingers anyway.

Adult tigers seem to like people, but they're likely to lose interest in them quickly, too. I've looked into a tiger's eyes and wondered more than once who's in there at that particular moment—the friendly one or the distant one who might get aggressively unfriendly if I try to push my luck.

Ivan and Natasha also proved to be much more efficient at demolishing our home than our lion cubs, and at least twice as rambunctious. One day, in a desperate effort to calm them down, I turned on the television. Ivan didn't care. Natasha, on the other hand, walked right over and put her nose on the screen, which became a common practice. She'd then curl up on the couch or the bed to check out what I was watching. Her attention span left a little to be desired, but I appreciated any breaks I could get from the tiger cub insanity, no matter how brief.

The Knobhill house had become a way station for cubs en route to

Soledad Canyon so that they could get used to human contact while they were babies. I slept with them, I made sure to take them outside for bathroom breaks after every meal and nap, they were never confined and had full run of the house twenty-four hours a day, and I loved them . . . most of the time.

By late summer I'd taken Bridget, Ivan, and Natasha to the canyon and brought in Bacchus, another lion cub. Next came three four-month-old cubs—Peaches, Cherries, and Berries, the Fruit Salad trio—from the Texas Animal Preserve, courtesy of Dr. Marty Dinnes. I was making daily round trips from Sherman Oaks to Soledad Canyon, scooping up a few cubs at a time to bring home for a few days of socializing. It became the "new normal," and I did it without a second thought about the toll it was taking on me. The life I was living was self-imposed, after all, so I wasn't about to indulge in complaining or feeling sorry for myself until one week when, temporarily, I "hit the wall."

We'd adopted two desert tortoises, Samantha and Charlie. (More inaccurate "atmosphere" for the movie, I guess.) They lived in the backyard on Knobhill, and in many ways they were ideal pets—no barking, no roaring, no shedding, and certainly no chance that neighbors would see their little heads peering at them over the top of the fence. They were about the size of dinner platters and weighed less than twenty pounds apiece, and they were infinitely fascinating and fun.

I came home one day from some very chic luncheon to find Charlie alone in the backyard. I started looking around for Samantha, getting more and more frantic by the moment, and finally spotted her, helplessly submerged at the bottom of the swimming pool. Chanel suit, Valentino heels, and all, I leaped into that pool and rescued her. She survived, thank God, but it was a frightening several minutes for poor Samantha, Charlie, and me. (By the way, a friend of mine offered to keep the tortoises in her garage for me for a few days when I had to go out of town. When I got home and hurried over to pick them up, my friend told me that, sadly, while I was gone, her children had accidentally left the garage door open and Samantha and Charlie hadn't been seen since. We never found them. If you happened to find a couple of desert tortoises wandering around Sherman Oaks in the 1970s and were kind enough to take them home, I hope you had very happy lives together and let Charlie hibernate for the winter in your guest bathroom, as he insisted on doing in ours.)

Less than a week after the dramatic Samantha rescue, and the demise of a suit and pair of heels that is beside the point, I came back from my daily trip to Soledad Canyon to discover Peaches, Cherries, and Berries, aka the Texas Fruit Salad, in the process of pulling our king-size mattress out the sliding glass door, apparently thinking it would look much better on the patio. In the meantime, the mattress cover had been torn off; the mattress was full of holes as large as frying pans; and the bedroom drapes had been ripped from the traverse rods and were hanging at a pitiful half-mast after what was clearly a very enthusiastic tug-of-war. It looked as if a tornado had touched down in the house while I was gone and destroyed everything in its path before it disappeared again.

The cubs scattered like a small gang of young vandals as I stood there yelling at them, and within moments, once the initial shock wore off, I lost it. I burst into tears and couldn't stop crying from exhaustion, frustration, and a lightning-bolt awareness that I was in *way* over my head. We didn't own these precious animals. They owned us, and it wasn't their fault. They'd been shuffled from place to place with no say in the matter whatsoever, and no guarantee that they'd be taken care of and treated well. Again, *it wasn't their fault*.

But suddenly, at that moment, I wanted nothing more to do with them, nothing more to do with this stupid, ill-conceived movie, and most of all, nothing more to do with my crazy "We should make a film about those lions" husband. I wasn't exactly thrilled with myself, either. At no point had there been a gun to my head. At no point had I said no, let alone, "Absolutely not." If I really wanted someone to blame for this insanity, I could simply step to the nearest mirror.

Our dear housekeeper Emily had been upstairs vacuuming and hadn't heard the demolition derby going on beneath her. She walked in to find me sobbing and, incredibly, didn't even seem to notice the path of destruction around me but instead headed straight over to put her arms around me.

"Don't cry," she said, gently patting my back to comfort me. "Those little lions are going to pay you back."

It was exactly what I needed to hear at that exact moment, having nothing to do with money. "Those little lions" had already paid me back in more ways than I could count, touching my soul so deeply that I couldn't imagine my life without them.

Financially? That remained to be seen. There were days when *Lions, Lions, and More Lions* seemed like a dream as distant as Jupiter. But then the movie *The Exorcist* opened and turned out to be a blockbuster, breaking box office records at theaters all over the world, with Noel's "executive producer" on-screen credit and his promise from William Peter Blatty of 15 percent of the profits. It would realistically take a few years for those profits to show up in our bank account, but at least we were relieved of the stress of wondering where the money was going to come from to make our lion film.

Emily was right. "Those little lions" weren't just worth it, they were priceless. She and I took a deep breath and started restoring order to the house, but not before I went to find and hug the Texas Trio and promise they'd never have to be afraid of me again.

Though I didn't realize it at the time, the timing was probably perfect for me to get a phone call from Dr. Larry Ward.

Dr. Ward had met Noel a year or two earlier and asked if I'd be interested in working with a relatively new organization he'd founded called Food for the Hungry. FH, as it came to be known, was an international, evangelically based relief organization inspired by Psalms 146:7: "He upholds the cause of the oppressed and gives food to the hungry." Since that very first introduction, I was instantly interested in helping, with fundraising and anything else I could do for the incredibly worthy cause.

My first trip with Food for the Hungry had been focused on providing food, medical supplies, and financial aid to the impoverished survivors of the horrible, bloody Indo-Pakistani War, and I had joined Dr. Ward to help bring relief to newly liberated Bangladesh. As would also be the case on trips to come, I expected the situation to be heartbreaking, but there was no way to prepare for the heartbreak of the issue we took on. Among the victims of that war were civilian women who'd been brutally raped by rebel soldiers. Their tragedy was compounded by the fact that in their culture, rape victims were ostracized by their families, friends, and communities, as if they were now somehow unclean and unworthy to be a part of acceptable society. It was an outrage, but it was what it was. There was no time to try to enlighten the culture or debate the social insanity of victimizing the victims. It was an honor to work hard side by side with Dr. Ward and the other volunteers, finding refuge for those women, as well as medical doctors and psychologists, to get them through this unspeakably tragic time in their lives. Anything we did to help, even as little as it sometimes felt, was gratifying work.

Which was why I was so grateful to receive Dr. Ward's second call. As he told me, Food for the Hungry was headed to Guatemala to help the survivors of a series of devastating earthquakes there and he wanted to know if I could come along. When he asked me if I was, by any chance, available to go on that mission with them, what else was there to say but *yes*. And again, *thank you, God!*

There were plenty of skilled, wonderful people in Soledad Canyon to take care of the animals while I was gone. I was suddenly feeling very foolish for being so upset about cleaning up after a few rambunctious lion cubs when those poor earthquake victims were going through *real* devastation. I didn't just want to help them, I had to.

Next thing I knew I was in a DC-3 transport plane with four or five other volunteers, flying over Mexico en route to Guatemala. There were no seats. We sat on the floor, surrounding a huge pile of medical supplies strapped onto the floor of the plane's body. We were all preoccupied with thoughts of the tragedies we were about to face when the DC-3 flew into a horrible rainstorm and began lurching violently around in the stomach-turning turbulence of the dark, angry clouds. Before long we heard the pilot yell, "I've got to land this plane!"

It was nighttime. The plane dropped below the clouds, and it was immediately apparent that the storm had knocked out the electricity in whatever civilization might be below us. There was nothing but pitch-blackness down there for as far as the eye could see. Somehow the pilot was able to detect a small town and began circling and circling above it, prompting one of the most amazing sights I've ever seen.

I can only guess that the townspeople had heard planes in distress before under these same circumstances. If not, they were the most spontaneously resourceful people on the planet. While the DC-3 continued circling, it seemed as if everyone in that town who owned a car drove out into the nearby countryside, formed two rows of cars facing each other, about a hundred and fifty feet apart, turned on their lights, and created a runway for us. I saw it with my own eyes and I still can't quite believe it. We landed safely, and there's no doubt about it, we owed our lives to those anonymous heroes.

Impossible as it seems, the trip became even more unbelievable from there.

Our pilot was so sick and so shaken from that emergency landing that he couldn't continue with the trip and had to be transported back to the United States.

We volunteers had regrouped in the belly of the plane after the pilot had departed and were sitting there wondering what could possibly happen next when we got our answer, exactly the last thing any of us expected.

The copilot boarded the plane again, scanned us for a moment, and then announced, "Okay, Tippi, I can't do this alone. Come with me. I'm going to teach you how to fly a DC-3."

What?!

He disappeared into the cockpit. I took a beat to recover from the shock, glanced around at my fellow passengers, saw surprised smiles on their faces and some confident thumbs-ups, and headed for the cockpit to learn how to fly.

I don't have words to describe what a thrilling, challenging, unforgettable experience it was, or what a brave, patient man our copilot was.

He taught me how to read the clouds, including rotor clouds and standing lenticular clouds, which could contain dangerous wind shears. He taught me the basics: what each of the instruments on the instrument panel does and how to read them. It all fascinated me. That education continued hour after hour, day after day, while we flew from one destination to the next, dropping off supplies and volunteers. Somehow, maybe because we were so needed and were doing such important work, I was never frightened, not for a minute, and there was only one "yikes" moment I remember—we were flying along on a bright, clear day when the former copilot, now the pilot, stood up, said, "Take over, will you, Tippi? I'm going back for coffee," and left the cockpit.

Yes, I did it. I flew that DC-3 all by myself. It was one hell of a workout, and an accomplishment I'll always look back on with utter amazement.

I still have my logbook from that once-in-a-lifetime adventure locked away in my safe, and I'm proud and grateful to say that my work with Food for the Hungry was just getting started.

I arrived back in Soledad Canyon early one morning to learn that some time during the night Ivan and Natasha had disappeared. In fact, the prevailing theory was that they'd been stolen. A frantic search of the grounds was under way, but there wasn't a trace of the two babies, and we were all heartsick.

It had never occurred to any of us that we needed to worry about someone stealing our animals. Who in their right mind would run the risk of climbing the fences of a preserve filled with some of the most lethal predators in the world? On the other hand, who said the culprit would be someone in their right mind?

The search of the grounds expanded to all of Soledad Canyon while I called every airline at every airport in California asking if anyone was trying to ship or had shipped a pair of tiger cubs. We posted flyers everywhere and put ads in all the local papers. We questioned every member of the staff to ask if they'd seen anything, heard anything, suspected anything or anyone? One helper, a young man none of us knew very well, happened to be a no-show that day and was immediately added to the short suspect list.

Finally, the next day, after an anxious, sleepless night, I got an anonymous call telling me there were two tiger cubs in a silo on an abandoned farm a few miles away. We raced over to that farm, and there in the silo were Ivan and Natasha, frightened and hungry but unharmed and almost as thrilled to see us as we were to see them.

The tiger thief turned out to be the young helper who'd been playing hooky from the compound since the cubs disappeared. It seems he'd had too many beers after work and made the brilliant, drunken decision that it would be awesome to drive around in his pickup with the cubs in the truck bed and show them off. When the night was over and he'd sobered up a little, it occurred to him that it might not have been that great an idea after all, but he was too afraid to get caught bringing the little tigers back to their home, so instead, he just abandoned them.

He lucked out in two ways—we decided not to press charges, and he never had the misfortune to cross paths with me again, or any of the rest of us who loved Ivan and Natasha and couldn't bear to imagine what they'd been through so that some drunken idiot could spend a few hours getting a little extra attention at their expense.

Days later, with all the animals safe, sound and back where they belonged, we gathered in the canyon to greet Noel's latest acquisition from the Okanagan preserve, not another addition to the pride of lions or a new member of the tiger family, but Noel's idea of what filmmakers call "atmosphere."

Enter Timbo, a massive ten-thousand-pound African bull elephant.

Between the cubs and the adults, about twenty-five cats were living in Soledad Canyon when Timbo arrived. The minute he walked down the ramp of the trailer truck I wanted to be his close friend. This amazing colossus had been captured in Africa when he was six months old and taken to the Frankfurt Zoo. From there it was on to New York, where he was acquired by the Canadian animal park who sold him to us. He'd never performed in circuses, but he knew a few tricks that he was always happy to show off.

Timbo's new home was a barn that had been constructed at the west end of the property. He could walk along the riverbank beyond it for several miles beyond the barn for exercise and then return for his daily bath in the pond. Steve Martin, who'd never worked with elephants before and wanted the experience, took on the job of training him, a particularly important job since, when a pachyderm becomes accustomed to the voice of its trainer, it will ignore any and all commands from anyone else.

Timbo fascinated me, but he made me nervous, too. Steve knew very little about elephants in general and Timbo in particular, and I knew even less. About a month after he arrived, I rode him up the riverbank for a couple of miles. He became curious about this "thing" on his back and reached backward with his trunk to investigate, which resulted in the very odd sensation of having moist elephant "nostrils" examining my face.

To solve that problem I started riding closer to his shoulders than to his ears, doing the splits on top of him with my knees bent. It wasn't exactly comfortable, so I kept adjusting my position on subsequent outings and finally learned to ride him lying down, or standing up and balancing myself while we trundled along by the river.

It was clear from the beginning that Timbo loved human contact, and it was our pleasure to make sure he had it. We all pampered him and saw to it that his love of sweets and a case or two of beer were satisfied. I visited him often, whether I was planning to ride him or not, and always brought him carrots and apples, partly just because I wanted to spend time with him and partly because, for all I knew, he and I might be doing scenes together in a movie whose progress slowly but surely seemed to be moving forward.

One day I stopped by for a quick hello on my way to somewhere else and hadn't brought any of Timbo's usual treats. He was a little indignant about that, reaching out his trunk to see if maybe I had carrots or apples or sweets hidden on me and going through my pockets. The only thing he found that seemed to interest him was a pack of Clorets gum, and I aimed to please—if he thought he might like Clorets, he was more than welcome to give them a try. I put several of them in my hand and held them out to him.

He quickly swept them up with his trunk, put them in his mouth, and began to chew. It was instant euphoria. His cheeks puffed in and out, his eyes slowly closed, and he started making little contentment noises, clearly wondering where I'd been hiding this food of the gods for all this time. I'd never seen anything send him into such rapture before, and I never visited him again without a generous supply of Clorets on hand—a whole lot easier to lug to his barn than bushels of apples and carrots, too, so it worked out perfectly for both of us.

Construction had begun on the two-story "African house," the house the movie's scientist and his family would share with a collection of somewhere around fifty big cats. Fourteen telephone poles were sunk into the ground to make it sturdy enough to support their movement throughout the stairway and half-dozen rooms where we'd film the interiors, and Liberato and his crew tackled building that mega-substantial movie set as if they'd built a thousand of them before.

We had compounds full of animals, and the primary set was under way, but the "park" itself was still looking pretty sparse. The only other buildings were Timbo's barn, Steve Martin's house trailer, and a few other sheds for storing tools and food. So Noel began planting cottonwoods and Mozambique-looking shrubs. Sod was being put down in large specific areas, and there were plans to dam the pond and turn it into a lake. With every passing day our acreage was looking less and less like Soledad Canyon and more and more like Africa.

Once the transformation was under way, I started to visualize not just our film set but a very special studio we could rent out for animal features and TV movies, complete with soundstages, editing rooms, a commissary, and apartments for cast members who didn't want to make the relatively long commute from Los Angeles every day.

So many dreams, so little money. But we'd deal with that later, and how could we feel anything less than optimistic, with *The Exorcist* continuing to be such a record-breaking success?

In fact, the first cub born in our compounds, the offspring of Togar and Alice, was immediately named Billy, in honor of William Peter Blatty, whose movie was going to make our own movie dreams come true.

Billy was precious and appeared to be in good health, so it was inexplicable when, five days after his birth, Alice abandoned him, jumping to the roof of her house, sprawling out on her belly, and refusing to even acknowledge her newborn's presence. A lioness will often reject her cub or even destroy it if she thinks something is wrong with it or if she's unable to feed it. Billy seemed to be perfectly healthy, so we decided that either she couldn't produce the milk he needed or that she just plain wanted nothing to do with him for reasons we'd never understand.

Whatever caused this rejection, that poor baby began crying loudly for his mother, high-pitched cries that echoed through the canyon and broke our hearts, his eyes still closed and his little spotted head jerking around in search of her warmth.

Liberato and I stood watching them—Billy helpless and lost, Alice on her roof staring apathetically off into the distance as if she were thinking, "Baby? What baby? I don't know nuthin' about no baby."

"We have to help that cub," he said.

"You're damned right we do," I told him, and I knew we needed to do it soon. If Billy kept up those ear-shattering, squawling, pleading shrieks, Alice might get tired of it and hurt him.

So early that afternoon, with Liberato watching from just outside the chain link, I eased into Alice's compound, keeping my eyes on her every second, swept Billy into my arms, and backed slowly out through the high gate, knowing her maternal instincts might kick in at any moment and she could come roaring toward me to retrieve her cub. Instead, not once, not even when I picked up and walked away with the only baby she'd ever had, did she so much as glance in my direction.

As soon as I could, I began trying to bottle-feed him, but he refused the nipple and kept screaming. In a panic, I drove him to Dr. Marty Dinnes, who had no more luck giving the little lion a bottle than I'd had. Finally he said, "He'll have to be tube-fed."

I'd never been anywhere near a five-day-old cub before, let alone tube-fed one. I watched every detail of everything Marty did, fighting back my squeamishness, and I shuddered at Marty's instruction: "Be very careful not to hit his windpipe when you insert the tube. Even a few drops of fluid in his windpipe will cause him to come down with pneumonia in less than an hour, and there's no way to treat it."

Marty inserted the prepared tube into that tiny body, making it look easy, and within moments he'd fed Billy two or three ounces of formula. Squeamish? Too bad. Nervous? Get over it. If that's what I needed to do to save this cub's life, that's exactly what I'd do. I could at least give him a better chance than he'd been given by his own mother.

I took the spotted-head, petal-eared handful of fur back to Knobhill and got to work. I began feeding him every two hours, around the clock, setting an alarm during the night. My hand shook every time I stuck that tube down Billy's throat, terrified of getting fluid in his windpipe. Flying a DC-3 was a walk in the park compared to this, and acting and soundstages and photo shoots seemed like some imaginary past in someone else's life.

Finally, after three anxious, sleepless days, I tried offering him a bottle again, fitted with a preemie nipple, and he started nursing, happy and content. The relief was overwhelming. He'd lie belly-down on my lap, his head toward my knees while I held the bottle horizontally and found his little mouth with the nipple and, with my other hand, make sure to touch his side so he'd feel he was being snuggled while he was feeding. At night he'd sleep on my pillow or cuddle up close beside me, making that "aa-aow"/"Where are you?" sound even though I was right there, needing constant reassurance thanks to Alice abandoning him.

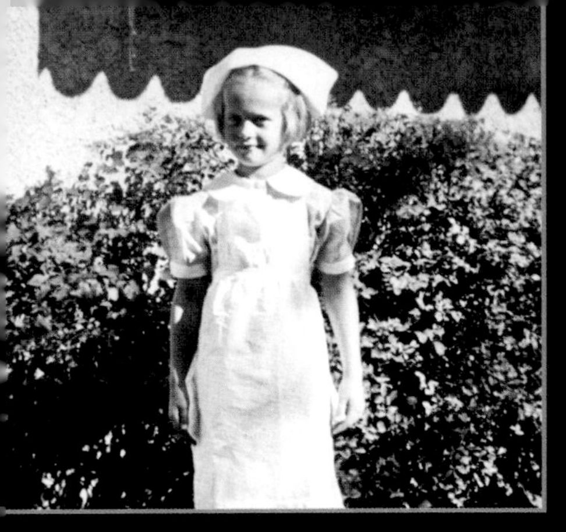

Playing nurse in my yard as a child. *(Courtesy of the author)*

Me and my first canine pal, Corky, at home in Minnesota. *(Courtesy of the author)*

The first Peter in my life, my beloved cat. *(Courtesy of the author)*

In my cap and gown after graduating from Huntington Park High School! One goal completed! *(Courtesy of the author)*

Love you, mom.
(Courtesy of author)

We didn't realize it at the time, but Peter and I were so young to be getting married at nineteen and twenty-two. *(Courtesy of the author)*

Two of my early modeling photos. *(Courtesy of Wynn Hammer)*

I was absolutely stunned when Hitchcock asked me to play the role of Melanie Daniels in *The Birds*. *(Courtesy of NBCUniversal)*

Here I am promoting *The Birds* all over the world! *(Courtesy of NBCUniversal)*

My dad could not stop smiling when he and my mom visited the set of *The Birds. (Courtesy of NBCUniversal)*

I am so glad Melanie had my parents while I was shooting *The Birds* and *Marnie*. I felt sorry being away from her. *(Courtesy of NBCUniversal)*

Like Rod Taylor in *The Birds*, Sean Connery was a wonderful dream-come-true to work with in *Marnie*. *(Courtesy of NBCUniversal)*

When my friend Johnny Grant asked if I would be willing to go visit servicemen in Vietnam, my answer wasn't just yes. It was yes, I'd be honored. *(Courtesy of the author)*

The Vietnamese refugees I helped integrate were some of the bravest, kindest women I have ever met. I soon discovered they loved my nails, and asked my manicurist Dusty to come teach them. *(Courtesy of the author)*

My charity work led me around the world and brought me great pleasure. *(Courtesy of Bill Dow Photography)*

Noelle was special to us from the beginning. Unlike other cubs, she loved to be cuddled. *(Courtesy of the author)*

We loved watching Noelle grow up into a big and beautiful tigon. One minute after this shot, she had me on the floor. *(Courtesy of Bill Dow Photography)*

The one thing about *Roar* we never discussed was the possibility of scrapping the whole thing. *(Courtesy of Bill Dow Photography)*

We decided we needed to make a spectacular promo for *Roar* in which I would escape from our house, but trip on a fallen log over our lake. Here I am two seconds before Cherries charged at me. *(Courtesy of Bill Dow Photography)*

Friends who knew me well weren't too surprised when I asked if I could stop by with my cheetah. *(Courtesy of Bill Dow Photography)*

This little cub, Anton, went on to mate with our beloved tigon, Noelle. *(Courtesy of Bill Dow Photography)*

This massive, ten-thousand-pound African bull elephant, Timbo, was Noel's idea of what filmmakers call "atmosphere." *(Courtesy of Bill Dow Photography)*

I knew I couldn't live with myself unless I took action to prevent some of the harmful breeding-for-profit practices happening in the U.S. *(Courtesy of Bill Dow Photography)*

I love when my soon-to-be-famous granddaughter, Dakota Johnson, visits Shambala. *(Courtesy of Bill Dow Photography)*

Our wonderful Shambala monthly safaris are fun and a great fund-raising opportunity. You won't see any big cats in silly costumes here! *(Courtesy of Bill Dow Photography)*

It's such fun growing older with my wonderful daughter by my side. Here, she and Antonio joined me at a Roar Foundation fundraiser. *(Courtesy of Bill Dow Photography)*

Hitchcock stopped speaking to me directly and only referred to me as The Girl during the last few weeks of shooting *Marnie*. This HBO film depicted my frayed relationship with him. *(Courtesy of Bill Dow Photography)*

I needed help blowing out so many candles when I turned seventy-five! *(Courtesy of Bill Dow Photography)*

I am so happy to receive this honor surrounded by so much love. Now I have to let people walk all over me! *(Courtesy of Bill Dow Photography)*

My darling Dakota Johnson was the best thing to come out of Melanie's marriage to Don Johnson. *(Courtesy of Bill Dow Photography)*

My daily meditation is a long walk through the footpaths of Shambala's forty acres. *(Courtesy of Bill Dow Photography)*

The only thing that I am sure of is that Shambala is where I belong. *(Courtesy of Bill Dow Photography)*

Two days after accepting the bottle, Billy opened his beautiful blue eyes to start checking out this world he'd been born into. A week or so later, when he was able to focus, I was the first human imprinted in his brain. As soon as he could track with his eyes, he'd seek out my thumb to suck as a substitute nipple, licking it with a little tongue that was already rough, on its way to being as coarse as a rasp when he became an adult.

At the ripe old age of three weeks, Billy had gained three pounds and was getting steadier on his paws by the day. He was adorably affectionate, standing up to put his paws on my leg so he could closely supervise while I prepared his bottle, and he was very playful. When I'd offer him his bottle, for example, he'd bat it away four or five times and then suddenly grab it with both paws and hungrily empty it in the blink of an eye. When he finished his bottle on my lap, I'd put him over my shoulder and burp him, after which he'd fall sound asleep.

It was perfectly natural, then, that a point came when, as far as Billy was concerned, I was his mom. Unlike our other cubs, who were always happy to see me but much more attached to each other and whatever they happened to be playing with or destroying at the moment, he needed to be with me all the time. He'd follow me from room to room, and when I'd sit down he'd jump up into my lap and softly rub his face against mine, the affectionate way lions greet and mark each other as "theirs." For a couple of months, when I had to leave the house, I took him with me in a square picnic basket I transformed into a portable baby lion bed. He became my sidekick everywhere I went, from meetings to interviews to visits with friends to the supermarket—even one day to a luncheon at a very exclusive restaurant.

The maître d', impeccable as always in his tuxedo, gave me his usual friendly greeting. Then, nodding toward my picnic basket and purely making conversation, he asked, "What have you got there, Miss Hedren?"

"A lion," I said, and he laughed and escorted me to my table.

As I left, I stopped to thank him and say good-bye and, with a smile, I opened the lid of the basket just far enough for him to see the sleeping cub inside. He was as enchanted as he was surprised, and I enjoyed knowing that I'd given him a great story to tell his family and friends over dinner that night.

In some ways Billy was a very typical little lion, rambunctious and destructive, stalking and pouncing on pillows, plants, Jerry's tennis shoes, tablecloths, bedspreads. Everything in his Knobhill world was a potential toy as far as he was concerned, and nothing was off-limits. I couldn't ignore the inevitable fact that someday he'd be a full-grown five-hundred-pound adult, so I started teaching him the meaning of inconvenient words like "No!" and "Leave it!" Neither of us particularly enjoyed introducing boundaries into that sweet boy's life, but a woman and her lion had to do what a woman and her lion had to do.

That, of course, included making Billy aware that there were more creatures on this earth than just two-legged humans—his own kind existed here, too. He was about three months old when I started driving him to Soledad Canyon for playdates with the other cubs, praying every mile of the way that they'd accept him. To my relief, he and Igor, another new tiger cub, instantly became great pals. They playfully pounced on each other, growling and snarling with mock ferocity as they rolled around together until they wore themselves out and curled up for a nap. It became a joyful errand to deliver Billy to his daily romp with Igor and drive him, or sometimes both of them, back to Knobhill several hours later. He quickly learned to love those playdates and the car ride there and back, and the instant he heard me pick up my keys in the morning he'd race to the front door, ready and eager for the adventure.

Finally, when he was nine months old, almost four feet long and weighing about a hundred pounds, it was time for him to graduate from Knobhill and go to the canyon to live. I talked to him all the way there, tears streaming down my face, assuring him in "Mommy talk" that he was going to be so happy in his new home and so well taken care of, and that we wouldn't even have to miss each other because I'd be coming to visit him every single day.

Billy settled in with Igor, lion cubs Cookie and Needra, and six other young cats. I watched him and Igor joyfully reunite, and stayed to make sure he and the other cubs got peacefully acquainted. Then I drove home alone, in tears again, not one bit ashamed of the maternal instincts that were spilling out of me for that little lion I'd been so close to since he was five days old. I knew it wasn't good-bye, it was just "see you tomorrow," but the Knobhill house seemed very empty when I got home.

In the meantime, Noel had been hard at work on the film script. We'd changed the title out of necessity—*Lions, Lions, and More Lions* no longer really fit, *and Lions, Lions, and More Lions . . . and Some Tigers . . . and an Elephant . . . and Who Knows What Else?* didn't really roll off the tongue.

We were now calling it *Roar*, and not a day went by when we weren't excitedly talking about it and planning for it and celebrating the continued overwhelming success of *The Exorcist*. Noel's share of the projected profits were going to allow us to make one hell of a movie, and we were so grateful, both for ourselves and for this growing population of wild animals who were depending on us to take care of them.

Then the bottom dropped out, thanks to news we could never have imagined, news so unthinkable it took days for it to even sink in.

There would be no *Exorcist* money coming our way.

Not one dime. Not ever.

Ten

It still astonishes me all these decades later.

Noel, for all his impulsiveness and slickness, was not a stupid man, so I'll never understand how he let this happen.

The deal he made for the film rights to the book of *The Exorcist* was, at the time, the highest-priced film rights deal ever made in this business. He wrote up a contract between him and William Peter Blatty confirming Noel's commission, executive producer credit, and 15 percent profit-sharing guarantee. He presented the contract to Bill Blatty, who orally agreed and initialed it in the upper right-hand corner *but never signed it.*

Yes, we'd pinned all our hopes for the funding of *Roar* on an unsigned contract. Technically, legally, Bill Blatty was claiming he didn't owe Noel one red cent from the profits on his blockbuster movie.

Morally? Don't get me started.

Noel immediately started looking for the best litigation attorney in the business.

I was at a party many years later and felt a tap on my shoulder. I turned around to find Bill Blatty standing there with a big smile on his face, greeting me with a friendly "Hi, Tippi!"

I walked away without saying a word. To my credit, I resisted the impulse to throw my wine in his face.

With not a single cent paid, we desperately needed money, not only for *Roar* but also for the weekly expenses of our growing population of four-legged cast members. Noel was on the phone and at meetings every day in search of backers. It became routine for me to make lunches on Knobhill and drive them out to Soledad Canyon to entertain potential investors and give them a tour of the compounds, hoping they'd be so enchanted with the animals, the African house, and what we were trying to accomplish that they'd be unable to resist reaching for their checkbooks. As anyone in this business will confirm, raising money for an independent film, let alone the million dollars we needed, is a slow, tedious roller coaster with no guarantee of success, and it can be painfully discouraging.

Fighting depression was a challenge, but I dealt with it by remembering a Christmas many, many, many years earlier, back home in Minnesota. Daddy had been through more health problems, and there was very little money for Christmas presents. My gift that year was a can of pineapple, my favorite fruit.

I know how to live broke. In fact I'm living proof that things can turn around, and that you really can be content and broke at the same time. So we kept calling and meeting and serving lunches. In the meantime, we had no business taking in more animals, but we did it anyway.

We heard through the big-cat network that a cheetah was available in San Diego. Noel and I had been fascinated by Ozzie Bristow's cheetahs in Africa, and we couldn't resist. The cast of *Roar* had already expanded beyond lions anyway, so why not write in a cheetah while we were at it? They were almost extinct in the wild by then, and it would be an honor to help one who needed a home.

His name was Pharaoh. He was an adult, probably three or four years old, a hundred and twenty pounds, larger than usual for the breed. His two owners worked all day, five days a week, so with the exception of long walks on weekends, he spent most of his time on a twenty-foot chain attached to his harness—particularly sad for the fastest land animal on earth, and one of the most elegant and dignified.

Noel retrieved the wire cutters as soon as we brought Pharaoh home to Knobhill. The instant we snipped off his harness and its padlock, he let out a loud "ohhhh" sound that was unmistakable relief. He was free from his shackles for the first time in years. I can't imagine what it must have felt like to him, but that sound brought tears to my eyes.

I took him for a tour of the house and the yard. He was especially interested in the mirror-smooth pool, walking over to peer at it very closely. A little too closely, it turned out—he promptly slipped over the edge and fell in. It was stupid, and he knew it. He was so embarrassed he wouldn't look at me when he scrambled back out and shook himself. Dripping wet, his body was almost shockingly thin, but the black lines on his face—"tears" from his eyes to his mouth, and extensions at the corners of his eyes—were so distinct and such gorgeous facets of his natural markings that they looked as if he'd found a really great brand of waterproof eyeliner.

Our relationship was off to an awkward start, so that night, when he sprawled out on the bed, I sat down beside him for a nice talk. While I was sitting there, I decided to take a peek at the dewclaw hidden on the back of the ankle of his front leg. I started gently parting the fur covering the dewclaw and was instantly rewarded with a karate chop to the face. That dewclaw I'd planned to inspect raked across my right cheek, leaving a permanent hairline scar.

Okay. Too friendly too soon. Got it.

Pharaoh's vast vocabulary was brand-new to me and unlike a lion's or a tiger's way of communicating. His "happy" sound was a distinct chirp. His "hungry" sound was a low, throaty vibration. His "stay away" warning sound, accompanied by the tensing up of his body, was a high two-pitched hum. He used that during our first few days together when I'd come too close to him while he was eating, and I'd immediately back off. But after a week or so, after we'd established that I wasn't interested in stealing his food, he ignored me and went right on eating, and eventually I was able to feed him by hand, as long as I kept my palm perfectly flat and didn't accidentally let a finger or two seem like part of the meal.

I was more than willing to leave his meals alone, but as it turned out, he wasn't willing to do the same for me. The family sat down to a lovely dinner of linguine and clams one night, and Pharaoh, whose head was the same height as our dining room table, gracefully walked up and cleaned off my plate in one lightning-fast gulp. Everyone else scrambled into the kitchen holding their plates above their heads while Pharaoh and I had a useless talk about manners and about my surprise at a cheetah being even remotely interested in seafood and pasta.

The time came to introduce Pharaoh to Soledad Canyon and the other big cats who would be his neighbors one of these days. I was excited for him, knowing he'd spent most of his life with no one but humans and hoping he'd be exhilarated to discover a whole new world of friends with four legs.

Sadly, it terrified him. His eyes widened and he began trembling at the sights and sounds of the lions and tigers, and no amount of comforting and reassurance could calm him down. The poor guy couldn't get back to Knobhill quickly enough, and Noel and I agreed that if we decided to use Pharaoh in *Roar*, it would have to be a scene that didn't include any other big cats.

Pharaoh was fascinated with items around the house. He would walk over to anything from a framed photo on the coffee table to the clock on my nightstand to a napkin holder in the kitchen and study them endlessly, with a refreshing lack of interest in destroying them. I got curious to know how he'd react in places other than home that would be free of lions and tigers.

A friend of mine owned a dress shop less than a mile away, and I called to ask if there were a lot of customers around.

"Only a few at the moment," she said. "Why?"

"I was wondering if I could stop by with my cheetah."

She knew me well, so this question didn't catch her completely off guard. At least I wasn't asking if I could bring in an adult lion or those three crazy-destructive Texas tiger cubs. I wouldn't describe her "Sure" as enthusiastic, but it wasn't an "Absolutely not" either, and Pharaoh and I were off to our first boutique together.

He was spectacular. Once my friend and her customers caught on that they weren't in danger, they couldn't take their eyes off him. He was too busy browsing to pay any attention to them. He wasn't especially interested in the clothes; with his dignified elegance he was definitely a tuxedo man or nothing at all. The displays of hats, scarves, and costume jewelry, on the other hand, fascinated him, and he was in no hurry to leave.

Bolstered by the success of that excursion, I called my friends at California Jewelsmith in Beverly Hills, who thought Pharaoh might be an attention-getting change of pace from their usual clientele. They were right. He behaved like a perfect gentleman, customers were mesmerized by him, and he was so intrigued by the array of exquisite watches, bracelets, diamonds, emeralds, and gold chains that I almost expected him to ask to borrow my credit card.

He even lay quietly at my feet while my dear manicurist Dusty Butera tended to my nails, and it took a lot of self-restraint for her not to give his nails a quick coat or two of polish while she was at it.

This gorgeous creature definitely needed a scene or two with humans in *Roar*, that was for sure. And believe me, it occurred to me more than once while we were on our tour of upscale retailers to turn to the clients who were especially intrigued by him and say, "Want to invest in a movie?" I resisted the temptation, but only because I would have felt too tacky soliciting money from my friends' customers.

It's always been my habit after I've been away from home for a few hours to walk in the door, find any and all animals I'm living with, say hello, give them hugs, and ask if I missed anything while I was gone.

One late afternoon I came home, greeted Puss (Partner was staying in Soledad Canyon at the time), and started looking for Pharaoh. He was nowhere to be found—not in the house, not in the yard, not up and down Knobhill, and (thank God) not at the bottom of the pool.

There was no one to ask. Noel and the boys were out doing whatever, and it was Emily's day off. I searched some more. Still nothing. Oh, God, not again.

In that same horrible panic I'd been through before with Casey and Bridget, I grabbed the phone and started with a call to the pound. No Pharaoh. I moved on to calls to the neighbors, one of whom said, "We saw him walking down the street about a half hour ago. We tried to call you—"

"Which way?" I cut them off, frantic.

They told me, and I grabbed Pharaoh's lead, leaped in the car, and started driving the narrow, winding hillside streets. It was rush hour again, of course, with traffic building up on any number of the routes he might decide to explore, and there I was, trying to track down the fastest land animal on earth. He could have been miles away by now . . . or hit by a car . . . or shot. I felt as lost as he was.

After an hour of no luck I headed home again, hoping against hope that maybe he'd found his way back to Knobhill. He hadn't.

I called the pound again. To my shock and relief, animal control had Pharaoh in custody. Someone had notified the police that there was a "wild cat" sitting in a vacant lot at a very busy intersection less than a mile from our house. Two squad cars had responded and found Pharaoh. The officers stepped cautiously out of their cars with their guns drawn and were approaching him, taking aim, when one of them said, "Look, he's got a collar. That's someone's pet. Don't shoot."

Pharaoh's sightseeing expedition had come within seconds of costing him his life, and I let him stay in jail overnight before I gratefully picked him up and brought him home.

Rarely did a day, or even an hour, go by when we weren't thinking about and talking about *Roar.* Beyond the oppressive fact that we had no money, there were plenty of other problems to deal with.

For one thing, we still had no leading man for the central role of Hank, the Gorongosa zoologist. Even worse, there was no way around the fact that no actor in his right mind would have agreed to do it. Not even the amazingly physical Sean Connery would have or should have taken on a film involving one unrehearsed scene after another of grappling with live lions and tigers, no matter how supposedly well trained they were. Hollywood's superb array of stunt men were out of the question, too, unless we could find one who'd be willing to live with and get to know the big cats, and have the big cats get to know him, too. This wasn't a job for a stranger. This was a job for a man with a lot of unique skills and familiarity with the population of Soledad Canyon.

In the end, there was no way around it—this was a job for Noel. Our producer, art director, landscape architect, big-cat handler, writer, and director was going to have to add "star" to his list of credits on this movie.

The rest of the cast was already assembled, of course. I'd play Madeline, the zoologist's wife, and John, Jerry, and Melanie would play our teenage children. Third son Joel was in his second year at UCLA by then, majoring in art. He'd be a huge help behind the scenes, with his skills in carpentry, landscaping, set design, and electronics.

We were well aware that we'd be facing a lot of criticism, from both inside and outside the industry, for putting our children in danger by having them work so closely with wild cats, and we had more than one long discussion with them about it. We assured them that if they wanted out, we'd understand completely. Making the movie would be hard enough without all the inevitable negative feedback to deal with. We made all three of them well aware of the risks, and all three of them came to the same conclusion—they knew the risks, they knew the cats and how to interact with them as safely as anyone could, and they loved the cats. As for the criticism, if it didn't bother us, it wouldn't bother them. "Count us in," they said, and we promised each of them a percentage of the profits, please, God, *on paper, not just initialed but signed.*

The one thing about *Roar* we never discussed, even if we privately thought it from time to time, was the possibility of coming to our senses and scrapping the whole idea. There were countless arguments against going ahead with this movie, but there were about eighty reasons to refuse to give up—about eighty big cats and our sweet elephant Timbo—who were counting on us to feed them and love them and keep them as safe as humanly possible, and finding still more new homes for them after all so many of them had been through, sending them off to God knows where to have God knows what happen to them, was unthinkable to me.

We didn't just want to make this movie, we *had* to make this movie, if not for us, for them.

What we really needed, we decided, was to make a great promo, some spectacular footage Noel could show to Paramount or Citibank or overseas investors. We didn't have a script for anyone to read, since much of what was written was and always would be an outline that depended on plenty of lion and tiger improvising. We didn't have a "bankable" male lead. We didn't have risqué bedroom scenes or aliens or special effects. We didn't even have much of a story line for the film, or any way to explain the impact of human/big-cat interaction to corporate minds.

But we could show them.

The test scene we decided on was kind of a chase by our lake in which I would be running from a herd of lions and tigers, headed for a big log that had fallen over the water. I would fall on the log, and the twenty or so big cats would either step or jump over me on their way to the other side of the lake.

We rented dual Cinerama cameras and handpicked the lions and tigers who'd be chasing me, including my pals Casey, Billy, Igor, Boomer, and Needra, and we assembled a group of handlers to position themselves nearby, just off camera. Noel thought a rehearsal would be a good idea, so once all the people, animals, and equipment were in place and he yelled, "Action!" I took off running.

My fall onto the log went well, and the cats were doing a perfect job of stepping and gracefully hopping over me, single file, not even seeming to notice I was there.

But then along came Cherries, one of the Texas Fruit Salad trio that had tried to destroy the Knobhill house. She was almost two years old now and weighed two hundred pounds. She slowly walked across me, and unlike the cats who'd preceded her, she looked down as if to say, "Well, well, well. Who have we here?" and started batting my head with her paw. She was getting a little aggressive, and I yelled at her, "Stop!" and "Leave it!"

For a minute or two it seemed to work. She stopped swatting me and proceeded to the end of the log. I was watching every move she made, so I saw her reach the end of the log, I saw her turn around and look back at me, and I saw her eyes narrow.

I knew I was in trouble, and I yelled at the handlers, "Stay with me, guys!" But before they could make a single move toward the log, Cherries was charging hard at me, and then she was on me. She put her front paws on my shoulders to pin me down and took the back half of my head in her mouth. I don't have words to describe the sound echoing inside my head as her teeth scraped against my skull, but it haunted me for a long time.

In a matter of seconds Noel raced onto the log, grabbed Cherries by the scruff of her neck, and pulled her off me. As soon as she released me, I raised my head, and I can still see her face just inches from mine, her skin pulled back, her mouth wide open with some of my blood on the fur around it, her teeth glistening. I was terrified, and in such shock that I felt very little pain.

I was bleeding badly, down my face and into my eyes. Everything seemed to be happening in slow motion, including a moment I still remember with crystal clarity that makes no more sense to me under the circumstances than it will to you: I spotted a torn-off piece of one of my long fingernails on the log a few inches away, and I hurriedly grabbed it and slipped it into my shirt pocket so that Dusty could glue it back on when I saw her at my standing appointment the following Monday.

I held a bloody towel to the back of my head while a friend rushed me to the Sherman Oaks Hospital, to a doctor who knew me and didn't need an explanation for why and how I'd been bitten by a lion. After he examined me, he announced, "We're going to have to shave your head."

"Not a chance," I snapped back. "I'm filming."

He was a little surprised, clearly not accustomed to patients disagreeing with him. But he finally admitted that perhaps the lacerations weren't that deep after all, so he simply cleaned me up, secured the wounds with butterfly clamps, gave me a tetanus shot, and sent me off to Knobhill with an antibiotic.

I remember insisting that we stop for ice cream on our way home. I needed a hot fudge sundae, with nuts. The shock hadn't worn off yet, I guess, but I'm also sure the hurt little girl in me needed to be comforted.

I didn't realize until that night how angry I was—angry at Cherries for attacking me, angry at Noel for putting me in a position to be attacked, angry at myself for agreeing to be part of this harebrained mess in the first place. I vented it at Noel.

"Today was the most frightening thing that has ever happened to me," I quietly growled at him. "It's never going to happen again, do you understand?"

He sighed, pretty rattled himself. "Okay, we'll cancel the promo shoot."

"Like hell. We're doing the promo shoot. We have to," I reminded him. "But not with Cherries."

We reconvened at the lake the next day and filmed the log scene while Cherries stayed in her compound. All the cats behaved perfectly, and the footage we screened the following night was spectacular, exactly what we needed to excite investors into believing what we did—that one way or another, *Roar* had to be made.

Life seemed to shift into fast-forward once that promo was finished and ready for Noel to start showing it to "money men" all over the world.

We acquired Cleopatra, our first of several leopards, who became very attached to Noel during her temporary stay at Knobhill with Pharaoh and charged me one day in a jealous rage over "her man." She lunged into my arms and bit me on the shoulder. It was just a "warning shot"—she barely broke the skin. Leopards are expert tree climbers, and from the day she moved to Soledad Canyon I never walked the grounds without looking up into the thick branches and leaves of the cottonwoods when the leopards were out of their compounds, knowing that Cleo would love nothing more than to pounce down on the slutty "other woman" in Noel's life.

Another love triangle in the canyon took us completely by surprise. My precious Billy, the "bottle baby" I raised when his mother rejected him, began ferociously charging anyone who came near me when he and I were spending time together. From Noel to sweet, tiny Sylvie to our elephant handler Jeff, Billy was instinctively compelled to protect me from them, raising up on his hind legs, claws out, teeth bared, firing off chest-deep machine-gun growls that were unmistakable warnings to the intruders to stay away from me. Once they backed off, he'd rush straight back to pace back and forth in front of me and push me farther away from these supposed threats. It broke Billy's heart and mine that I could never spend time with him again unless we were completely alone in his compound. How could he possibly understand that protecting me was unacceptable behavior? And when I was nowhere around, he was as sweet and friendly as ever to Noel, Sylvie, Jeff, and everyone else in the canyon.

Sophia Loren came to visit Soledad Canyon. It was wonderful to see her again, and she couldn't wait to meet the animals. We took lots of photos as I walked her around among the compounds while we caught up with each other's lives. Taking some pictures of Sophia and Timbo and me was a must—she and I both decided that there weren't enough shots floating around in the press of Sophia Loren with an elephant. She set down her bag and her notebook on a rock off camera for the pictures, and when she was ready to leave she retrieved her purse but couldn't find her notebook anywhere, until we both noticed that Timbo was chomping on something. He raised his trunk and opened his mouth, and there it was, the metal spiral and the wet little ball of paper that used to be Sophia's calendar and the addresses and phone numbers of everyone she'd ever known. She was an incredibly good sport about it, and we agreed that at least she had a great story to tell when people said, "Of course I'll give you my address and phone number again, but what happened to your notebook?"

Several months later I lost my beloved Pharaoh. It was impossible to figure out exactly how long he'd been ill—he instinctively knew not to appear infirm in front of the other big cats, so he'd done his best to look as if everything was fine. But finally I could see that he was beginning to shrink and that the glint in his eyes was fading. Once he'd stopped eating and drinking and the veterinarians in Los Angeles had told me his kidneys and other organs were deteriorating, I drove him to the University of California at Davis, near Sacramento, in my opinion the finest veterinary school in the country. Dr. Murray Fowler, the head of vet medicine there, did all he could, but Pharaoh died three days later. I made the long drive home with Pharaoh's body, alone and grief-stricken.

Pharaoh was the first of our adult cats to die. There would be more, of course, and we'd lost some cubs over the years. Every death devastated me and sent me into a depression, no matter how many times I told myself that it was a natural part of this life I'd chosen. The loss of any thinking, feeling creature capable of love, wild or domestic, is a loss of a little bit of purity and perfection on this earth, a loss none of us can easily afford or take lightly.

To this day, when death comes to our animals in the canyon, we bury them here on the property, with tears and dignity. I have a special loathing for taxidermy, and for those who display "trophies" of animals they've killed, as if they take pride in something so obscene.

I'd just returned from a trip with Food for the Hungry in the wake of a devastating hurricane in Honduras when Noel was bitten on the hand by Hudu, one of our lions, during a training session in the African house where the lions and tigers were learning to mingle together.

We rushed him to the Sherman Oaks Hospital. The doctor on duty treated the wound and insisted that it had to be sewn up. Noel argued, explaining that we'd had some experience with this kind of thing and we'd learned that a wound from cat teeth should be left open to drain and heal. But the doctor insisted, sutured Noel's wound, and sent him home.

By midnight he was in agony, with red lines extending from his hand all the way up the full length of his arm. By one a.m. we were at St. John's Health Center in Santa Monica. The diagnosis: advanced blood poisoning. Within another twelve hours Noel was in critical condition and near death. He pulled through and wasn't released until three weeks later, under strict orders to continue his medication for another two weeks.

From then on we avoided suture-happy doctors, kept puncture wounds open, suffered through the antibiotics, and let our bodies' natural healing process do the rest.

We were coming closer and closer to the brink of total financial devastation as the weekly expense of housing and maintaining the animals continued to grow. But somehow, as broke as we were, we never considered giving up, and we couldn't bring ourselves to stop welcoming new arrivals to our menagerie. Our lions, tigers, elephant, leopards, and panthers (actually leopards in black coats rather than spotted ones) were joined by a few cougars. Cougars are classified as a "game animal" in California, so captivity was the only safe place left for them, and at that point, what difference could a few more mouths to feed possibly make?

I'm sure it goes without saying that by now the thought of any animal being killed for its skin or its tusks was utterly abhorrent to me, so when I started gathering the most valuable belongings I owned to take to the pawnshop, the first to go was the fur coat Alfred Hitchcock had given me. That and my wedding ring and some other jewelry bought some food for our menagerie, but of course we'd soon need more.

We put our two rental houses in Beverly Hills on the market, along with some land we owned in Newhall, while Noel kept showing the *Roar* promo to anyone and everyone who'd stand still long enough to watch it.

Somehow, the more desperate we got, the more determined we got, and we were coming up with more ideas of things to sell and more ideas of potential investors when early one morning the phone rang.

It wasn't a studio, calling to offer a generous check and the facilities to make our movie.

It wasn't the big-cat network in need of housing for more abandoned animals.

It was Dr. Larry Ward of Food for the Hungry. They were on their way to Vietnam. The war had ended, and there were scores of "boat people" in desperate trouble.

Could I possibly come help?

All things considered, I was a bit torn for a second. Then again, I couldn't turn them down.

"I'll be there," I said, and with that I started a whole new chapter of my life, long before the one I was living had ended.

Eleven

The Australian navy provided the battleship *Akuna* to Food for the Hungry for our tour of the South China Sea searching for Vietnamese refugees, lost and desperate, with no idea where to turn and nothing left but their decrepit boats. For six weeks we looked for those poor men, women, and children, brought them on board, and gave them food and fresh clothing and a warm place to rest for a while. Then, because of international law, we had no choice but to put them back in their boats, guide them toward safe places to land, and pray for them.

Food for the Hungry had acquired a huge abandoned tuberculosis sanitarium in Weimar, California, near Sacramento, so we were able to provide housing for many, many Vietnamese women who found their way to the United States. They weren't welcomed in this country, as if they'd had anything at all to do with a war that decimated their homeland and their lives, and they were some of the bravest, most inspiring women I've ever met. They didn't want to be a burden here, they wanted to work. They wanted to contribute. They wanted to earn our acceptance and respect.

Over a period of time we helped integrate them into the United States. We helped them learn English, get their driver's licenses, and find American sponsors. I brought in typists and seamstresses to help them develop skills that could lead to steady jobs, and you've never seen a more devoted, grateful group of students, especially when most of them started expressing a common interest—they *loved* my nails!

In fact, they were so fascinated with my long, manicured nails that I called Dusty and asked if she'd consider making the round trip from Los Angeles to Weimar once a week to teach these women manicuring skills. She said she'd be happy to. I knew she would. So every week, here came Dusty, and she taught them everything they needed to know, with an emphasis on the paper-wrapped Juliette Manicures that were popular before acrylics came along. When they finished Dusty's course, we rented buses to send them to beauty school in Sacramento to get their cosmetology licenses—all in English, by the way.

Out of our first group of about sixty women, twenty-five went on to get their licenses and open their own businesses. If you've ever wondered where the billion-dollar Vietnamese manicure/pedicure salon industry in this country got its start, now you know. Dusty and I are so proud to have been a part of it, and we're still in touch with some of our thriving, successful graduates, many of whose children have gone on to become doctors, lawyers, and CEOs thanks to the educations their mothers were able to afford.

Several of the husbands got involved, too. They discovered when going to pick up supplies for their wives that they were having to go to four or five different shops to find everything on their lists, so they created consolidated, incredibly successful beauty supply stores that carried everything from nail files to pedicure chairs.

It was thrilling to become a part of these families' lives. I got to know and love so many of them, and there aren't words to express my admiration for their strength, their dignity, and their refusal to let losing everything, including their homeland, stand in their way. They went on to organize the Vietnamese-American Nail Association, with salons throughout North America, and I was honored to be presented with a Humanitarian Award in Washington, D.C., for work with the "boat people" that brought me nothing but joy and some cherished lifelong friendships. I may have planted the seed of the Vietnamese nail salon industry, and I'll proudly take a bow for that, but it's the hard work, dedication and skill of those amazing men and women who nourished that seed into the huge success it is today.

Kieu Chinh, hostess of the television talk show so many of us appeared on during our USO visits to Vietnam, tracked me down in Weimar one day. She was crying on the phone, and I asked what was wrong.

"I've contacted all these celebrities I worked with, and no one will help me get to America."

I could hear the fear in her voice, and I wasn't having it. "Dry your tears," I told her. "You'll be here tomorrow."

Food for the Hungry made it possible to keep that promise.

She arrived with nothing, so she came to stay with me on Knobhill.

She and I happened to wear the same size clothes, and I was happy to share my wardrobe with her and to find her an agent, although there were very few roles available at the time. She went on to get a job with the Catholic charities helping Vietnamese refugees, cofounded the Vietnam Children's Fund, which built schools in her homeland, and became as popular an actress here in the United States as she was in Asia. I love and admire her so much.

I was in Sacramento when the call came from Noel. He was sobbing. I'd never heard or seen him cry before.

"Needra's died," he said. "You have to come home."

I flew back to Los Angeles that day, in tears myself, to learn that our lioness Samantha had died as well, of unknown causes. We called in experts from UCLA and UC Davis, who gave us the horrible news that we'd been invaded by a virus. It had killed Samantha and Needra, and by the time it ran its course four months later, we'd lost fourteen of our lions and tigers. Because there was no way to specifically identify it, other than to note that it didn't affect the leopards and cougars and that it was probably airborne, there was no way to vaccinate our animals against it. All we could do was pray that it never, ever happen again.

The hits just kept on coming. Around that same time, we also managed to survive a flood and a very real threat of fire in the canyon. Our elephant trainer quit, leaving Timbo depressed, with no one to take him on his regular walks. We had to make the sad decision to sell the Knobhill house, with all its amazing memories, and move into one of the three trailers we'd installed on the Soledad Canyon property. We were on a serious downhill slide, and I truly believe the only things that kept us going were our unconditional love for those animals and the occasional flickering hope that when life got that bad, it had nowhere to go but up.

Some marriages make it through crises stronger than ever. Ours wasn't one of those marriages. We spent almost no time together, and we had little or no social life. I went to family gatherings alone and found myself preferring it that way. The relentless anxiety everywhere we turned was causing us to turn our angry frustration toward each other. I'm not sure we even realized it then, but our marriage was beginning to disintegrate.

Life started its subtle upswing one Sunday morning with a knock at the door. I answered it to find a tall, red-haired, friendly-looking young man standing there.

"Hi, Mrs. Marshall. My name is Tim Cooney, and I hear you need an elephant trainer."

If he hadn't been a total stranger, I would have hugged him.

Tim, it turned out, had been a trainer with the circus but was burned out on all that traveling. That same day he started working for us, sitting in the barn with Timbo, talking to him, reading, feeding him, just hanging out and getting acquainted for hours and hours every day. After three weeks they began taking their exercise walks again, and the joy came back into our elephant's eyes.

Our animals were healthy again after that virus dealt us those fourteen devastating losses, and the family began growing again, first with a couple of tigers named Panda Bear and Singh Singh and then, over the next several weeks, with ten beautiful little lion cubs. Birth felt like a promising sign, like hope, like a reminder that there really is a future.

And then, on a Monday morning, Noel called with news so incredible that I kept making him repeat it because I couldn't believe I was hearing him correctly:

The British entertainment company EMI had committed to investing half a million dollars in *Roar*, and a Tokyo producer named Banjiro Uemura was putting up another half million.

I was so weak with relief and happiness that I literally fell into the chair behind me. Five years of dreaming, planning, praying, grieving, sacrificing, meetings, lunches, phone calls, and just remembering to breathe had finally paid off. What difference did some hocked jewels and a few houses make when all was said and done? We finally had the money we needed to get *Roar* under way, and we could start filming in about a month. All we had to do was gather a crew and rent lights, cameras, and sound equipment, and this is Hollywood—if you've got the bank account, anything and anyone you could possibly need to make a movie are always just a phone call and a few miles away.

Big cats, of course, have their own agendas and couldn't care less whether or not you're busy relearning how to exhale.

Less than two weeks after we got the incredible news about EMI and Banjiro Uemura, Luna, a four-year-old lion, decided to take advantage of a slightly ajar perimeter gate and go strolling off toward the railroad tracks and the northern mountains.

All of us went into emergency, drop-everything search mode. We had to find her, *fast*. It wasn't just that she was one of ours and we loved her. We'd also discovered that there was no affordable way for us to carry insurance that would cover wandering big cats. If Luna attacked an animal or a person, we could easily be wiped out in a heartbeat. She wasn't a "Knobhill graduate," so none of us really knew what she might do if confronted while she was out on her own.

We were out all night, picking our way through rattlesnake terrain, spreading out behind trackers who were following her distinctive paw prints, hoping our flashlights would catch the glow of her almond-shaped eyes in the darkness. She was nowhere to be found.

By midday the next day there were about twenty of us involved in the search, most of us carrying walkie-talkies. We weren't about to notify the authorities, which would have led to the arrival of press and TV crews, some of them in helicopters, compounding an already potentially dangerous situation.

We were also very aware of another frightening possibility—some of the residents in the area were proud, chest-beating, he-man hunters. If they got wind of a lion on the loose in their vicinity, they would have grabbed their rifles and fired up their four-wheelers in a race to hunt down poor Luna and mount her stuffed head above their fireplace.

We had to guard against any of them eavesdropping on our walkie-talkie citizen-band radio communications so they wouldn't catch on to what we were searching for or where she might be located. We worked out a code, "Perfect Location," as an alert to the rest of the search parties that Luna had been found.

The helicopter we hired scanned the land from overhead while the ground crew swelled to more than forty people. By nightfall of the second day we were frantic, knowing that a lion on the loose for three days with no food is a walking, desperate, five-hundred-pound killing machine.

The second night came and went, and I was on high alert for the crackle of a walkie-talkie or a call from a neighbor saying, "Are you by any chance missing a lion?" The stress was unbearable. My sister Patty was visiting from Oregon, and she was right by my side as the sun rose on another day of no news.

Finally, midmorning of the third day, the receiver I was manning in the CB station suddenly buzzed to life, and a voice came through to announce, "I've found the Perfect Location."

Just as suddenly, the voice faded away before the searcher could identify himself or tell us where he was. I started frantically pushing all the switches on the receiver without a clue what any of them did, during which I collapsed into an uncontrollable fit of giggles—three nightmarish days, two sleepless nights, thousands of dollars for helicopter rental, Luna, by the grace of God, had finally been found, and I had no idea where, thanks to a couple of dead fifty-cent batteries.

Moments later a handler raced in to announce Luna's location—she was under the road bridge, maybe three football fields away but still on our property. Noel and I had speculated that if one of the tigers were missing, they'd probably wander miles and miles away, but Luna, being a lion, would probably stay close to home. Sure enough, there she was, contentedly curled up in the cool, lush foliage by the river, camouflaged beneath the bridge and perfectly safe.

We were getting a truck ready to go retrieve her when Noel stepped up and said, "Don't bother, I'll just walk her down."

He knelt beside the bridge where he and Luna could see each other and coaxed her with a simple "Come on, Luna, let's go home."

Having put us through quite enough drama for two and a half days, Luna anticlimactically strolled with Noel back to her compound, where her roommates ran to surround her with noises I swear sounded a lot like "So, tell us all about it. Where did you go? What did you do? Did you bring us anything?"

It was a disruption, to say the least, but we were relieved to have her back so that we could return to focusing on the film. I loved every minute of preproduction. It was exciting, stimulating, and involving. Between that and the animals and my ongoing work with the Vietnamese refugees, I woke up every single morning with a purpose, and to this day, that's my idea of a life worth living.

Our "studio" in Soledad Canyon would never have been confused with Universal or Paramount. It was no-frills, but it worked. Noel had done a superb job of transforming the property into acres that looked like East Africa. The African house on the edge of the lake was ready for filming. The plywood support buildings—the camera, machine, and electrical shops; the editing rooms; the wardrobe space; and the kitchen/commissary to feed a hundred people—were finished. The animal support buildings, including the animal hospital and medication refrigerator, were up and running. The parking lot was transformed, just in case, into a paramedic helicopter pad. We lucked out and found an electrician who also happened to be a licensed paramedic, so we were as ready as we could possibly be for every eventuality.

Our cinematographer was Jan de Bont, who'd worked on such foreign hits as *Keetje Tippel* and *Max Havelaar* and was nominated for the German film *Turkish Delight*. He and his beautiful wife Monique van de Van, star of *Keetje Tippel* and *Turkish Delight*, lived in the mobile home up the road from ours, which made Jan available on a moment's notice and gave him a three-minute commute to work on foot.

For still photography we hired a quiet, talented darkroom employee named Bill Dow, who'd printed scores of photos for Food for the Hungry. It didn't bother us in the least that he'd never worked on a film set in his life or that he'd never taken still shots of big cats. He had exactly the right temperament to learn on the job and do whatever needed to be done without so much as glancing at a clock, and all these years later he's a dear, cherished friend.

We were a nonunion shoot, which made the experienced professionalism of our camera, lighting, and sound people even more amazing. Our production manager, Charles "Chuck" Sloan, had an impressive television résumé, with the added bonus that he'd helped raise some of our big cats. With only a handful of exceptions, like our pigtailed Frank Tom, the crew had never been within miles of a big cat before.

A local girl named Alexandra Newman had come on board many months earlier to do routine chores with the animals. She arrived with no experience but ended up becoming a qualified vet technician. After demonstrating a natural affinity for the tigers and leopards, Alex became closely involved with the jaguars, the most dangerous animals in the world as far as I'm concerned, exquisitely beautiful and completely unpredictable.

Alex had loved and bottle-fed our two jaguars, Patricia and Henry, since they were infants. The three of them had a warm, comfortable friendship until one day, without warning, while Alex was changing the straw in his den, Henry suddenly decided he didn't really like her after all. All black-velvet 175 pounds of him crouched and then sprang at her in one raging lunge. She managed to keep from being seriously mauled by holding up a small chain-link screen in front of her while she quickly escaped. From that day on, Henry reacted with sheer viciousness every time he saw her, even at a distance, and like me with Cherries, Alex would never go near him again.

We never did get to the bottom of what prompted Henry to turn like that on someone he'd known and been fond of since he was a cub, but in case his sister Patricia was as much of a ticking time bomb as he was, we gave both of the jaguars to a trusted, well-maintained zoo. Alex and I both sighed with relief as we saw their transport truck disappear down the canyon road.

We obviously needed a strong, reliable, smart, and fearless team of handlers, and we'd recruited a few of them from the maintenance and fencing crews around the property. Darryl Sides, for example, became not just a recruit but graduated to foreman of our handlers when I saw him scale a fourteen-foot-tall chain-link fence in two lightning-fast upward reaches, as if there were a monkey in his recent lineage, to rescue a maintenance man who'd accidentally strayed into the lake compound.

Mike Vollman had left a Midwestern carnival, come home to California, and joined our fence crew. Within a couple of weeks he was an apprentice handler and went on to become a skilled handler and trainer.

Noel recruited Rick Glassey and Steve Miller, who'd been working in Marine World's Tiger Moat as trainers, to be bit players in water and attack scenes. Their experience had taught them that tigers can start out having a great time with sparring matches in the water and then instantly escalate into deadly fights, and casting even the most willing actors and actresses for those minor parts was out of the question.

Our animal cast now numbered 132 big cats, one elephant, three aoudad sheep, and a collection of ostriches, flamingos, marabou, storks, and black swans for background. The birds were Joel's exclusive responsibility. He wanted no part of the big cats, but he loved those birds, and since he was our set dresser in general, it made perfect sense that he would "dress" the outdoor sets as impeccably as he dressed the indoor ones.

And then, of course, there was our human cast. Noel, our leading man, writer, director, producer, etc., etc., etc., made up for his lack of acting experience with his experience with our animals.

I did triple-duty as actress/coproducer/costumer. It took four days of shopping to assemble the cast wardrobe, and usually shopping for clothes pre-filming is a fun, exciting adventure. Unfortunately, there would be no gowns and tuxedoes and fabulous shoes and handbags for *Roar.* We were strictly going for a drab, practical, wash-and-wear look, or as I came to think of it while I shopped, the "polar opposite of Edith Head" wardrobe.

Jerry Marshall, son Jerry in the film, had done a few TV commercials.

John Marshall, son John in the film, had some acting experience on TV episodes and commercials.

My cherished Melanie Griffith, daughter Melanie in *Roar*, was in the process of building an extraordinary acting career. She was awesomely talented, awesomely beautiful, and sometimes awesomely impossible for me to figure out.

Our only other principal actor, playing the role of Hank's/Noel's assistant zoologist, was Kyalo (pronounced "Chaalo") Mativo, an authentic African from the Kamba tribe in Kitui Province, Kenya. His mother gave birth to him on a dirt road while walking home with a bundle of thatching grass on her head. He was on a four-year film scholarship at UCLA, had written and directed for the Voice of Kenya TV station, and had acted in a couple of short German films. Kyalo was deathly afraid of the big cats, so he bravely embraced the role but instantly vanished from the set the moment his scenes were over.

Finally the night before filming arrived.

If I'd been acting the next day I would have been studying my lines, worrying about getting enough sleep and how my face and hair and wardrobe would look.

But Noel was starting with some staged lion fights. I wouldn't be needed on camera.

I took a long, peaceful walk that evening. I stopped at each compound and at the elephant barn to say hello, preoccupied with what was about to happen and what it had taken to get here.

We had months of dealing with live lions and tigers ahead of us, with no idea how they'd behave with the excitement of so much equipment and so many unfamiliar people around them. A lot of the big cats would be interacting with each other for the first time. So many things could go wrong, with no way of preparing for them beyond what we'd already done, no way of predicting . . . and so many scenes involved my precious daughter being no more than an arm's length away from harm. John and Jerry, too, of course, but Melanie . . .

We'd been told for years by big-cat experts that we were out of our minds, that there were perfectly good reasons no one had ever taken on a film like this before. Were we arrogant or delusional to believe that we could and should be the first, that we had some special kind of expertise or luck or magic? Who exactly did we think we were to risk all these lives—our crew's, our animals', ours, and most of all, our children's—for what really amounted to nothing more than a very, very expensive home movie?

What were we thinking?

What if those experts were right?

What if this film really *was* too dangerous to make?

Twelve

"Roll film."

With those two simple words, words we'd worked toward for six long years, *Roar* was officially under way. It seemed as if there should be band music and balloons and confetti, but instead there was just an awareness of all the money that was on the line: EMI's, Banjiro Uemura's, almost a million dollars of our own, a San Diego investor's—the list of people who were counting on us went on and on. We had to make this work, in spite of the fact that the only thing we could predict about making this movie was the absolute unpredictability of our real, four-legged stars.

Less than a week into filming Casey, of all lions, bit Noel in the hand. It was a serious puncture, piercing Noel's palm, and we were off to Palmdale Hospital. It wasn't a rage bite on Casey's part, it was pure frustration and confusion from all the unfamiliar activity going on around him. Our fault, not his.

Noel's wound was treated and he hurried back to Soledad Canyon, intending to get back to the set to pick up where filming left off, but the pain from the spreading infection made it impossible. With our director and male lead unable to work, we had to shut down for a week.

Almost since the beginning of filmmaking, crews have used small sandbags to anchor the bases of lights, reflectors, cameras, and other equipment that have to remain perfectly stationary while an outdoor scene is shot. No problem. We were prepared with a generous supply of small canvas bags filled with sand. What was a problem, which we couldn't have anticipated in a million years, was that some of the lions decided to become wildly possessive of the sandbags, dragging them on camera in the middle of scenes and fiercely defending them from anyone who dared to come within fifty feet of their treasured bag of sand. If reshoots weren't so expensive, we might have found it hilarious.

A week after Noel's latest hospital trip, Casey got into a fight with Tongaru, one of our most notorious bullies, apparently a battle for dominance over the film crew, Soledad Canyon, and the universe in general. Everyone instantly stopped what they were doing, terrified. Even the handlers froze in place. A fight between two grown lions is one of the loudest, scariest, ugliest phenomena in the animal world. They typically start by circling each other, heads slightly cocked to the side, making piercing eye contact. Then one or both of them rise on their hind legs, "arms" outstretched, to make themselves appear as huge and intimidating as possible, manes seeming to stand on end and framing wide-open bloodred mouths, canines bared. Their growls and roars come from deep in their bellies, rumbling and metallic-sounding, sending ice up the spine of the witnesses. They lower themselves to stalk and circle each other again, almost in slow motion, before one of them lunges, sharp claws ready to impale the other, and a fierce skirmish begins, with each of them trying to pin their opponent to the ground and sink their teeth into their opponent's throat. This frantic scuffle to stay on top and keep from being pinned is accompanied by a lot of vicious biting, clawing, screaming, and rumbling—sights and sounds that haunt anyone unfortunate enough to be nearby when they happen. There's nothing you can do but watch, hold your breath, and pray that neither of them will be seriously injured, which they seldom are. Only someone with a death wish would try to separate them.

It probably lasted a few minutes at most, but it seemed like hours. Tongaru won, and poor Casey retreated, his feelings more damaged than his body, thank God.

I still don't know if it was that sudden violent outburst, or if it had just been building for a long time, but shortly after the Tongaru vs. Casey heavyweight championship match, Melanie sat me down and said, "Mom, I don't want to come out of this with half a face." She was pulling out of *Roar.*

I didn't blame her. Not one bit. I was probably even a little relieved. Whether she was afraid for her face, which could have been disfigured in the blink of an eye and destroyed her acting career, or for her life, I didn't want my girl afraid, especially not for a film she was involved in only because of me. I didn't try for one second to try to change her mind, as if that would have been possible anyway. Neither did Noel, John, and Jerry. We hadn't shot any of Melanie's scenes yet, so we could replace her—not easily, since her replacement would need to have the guts to work with big cats and the agent and parents who'd even allow it. But this is a town full of young actresses who would do almost anything to be in a film, probably even the "almost anything" this role would require.

We ended up hiring a young, courageous actress named Patsy Nedd, who'd been a friend of Melanie's since childhood. We knew her, we liked her, and she and Melanie had played with the lion cubs together on Knobhill. That hardly made her an expert on big-cat behavior, but she was unafraid and willing to learn, and we were lucky to have her.

Two weeks later we were shooting a sequence in which the terrified family flees to a rowboat to escape from the wild cats.

Our intrepid Jan de Bont decided he wanted a pit dug so that he could stand in the pit with his main camera lens on the same level as the surface of the lake. Then he'd pull the camera back and have the cats jump over him as they rushed to attack us. Noel insisted that Jan and his assistant wear football helmets, for obvious reasons, which they agreed to, so one of our prop guys drove into town to buy helmets while a few of the guys dug a pit to Jan's specifications.

A green tarp was retrieved to put over the pit, with some shrubbery around it to help camouflage it. Jan, in his helmet, climbed into the pit with his camera, under the tarp, but just before Noel announced, "Roll film," Jan discovered that the helmet prevented him from getting to the eyepiece of the camera, so he removed it.

Cameras were rolling when along came Cherries, my old nemesis, who looked down to see this mysterious round object moving around under the tarp. What fun for any cat, and especially for her! No one had loved pouncing on moving toes under blankets more than Cherries when she lived on Knobhill, or had a greater time playing with bowling balls in her compound. She froze in place for less than a second to watch what was now Jan's unprotected head protruding from beneath the tarp, and then she pounced.

In less time than it took to say it, Cherries grabbed Jan's head in her mouth and ripped off his scalp from the nape of his neck to his hairline, all in one piece, literally peeling his head.

I saw it happen and screamed . . . which is exactly what the scene we were shooting called for me to do, so for several awful seconds everyone thought I was acting. No one caught on until I finally started yelling, at the top of my lungs, "Jan is hurt! Jan is hurt!"

A frantic race to the emergency room and a hundred and twenty stitches later, Jan's scalp was reattached. We were all so relieved and so heartsick.

His assistant had just started that day. When we got the news that Jan was miraculously going to be okay, he turned to me, still deeply shaken, and said, "Tippi, look, I have to quit. Take my day's pay and buy that poor son of a bitch some flowers."

Jan was obviously in the same grip of *Roar* fever that had infected Noel and me years earlier and wouldn't let go—to our absolute amazement, that tough, brave, determined man was back on the job three weeks later, despite his wife Monique's understandable reluctance to let him anywhere near the set again. He knew he was capturing some unprecedented footage of big cats, and he wasn't about to give up.

Unfortunately, the rest of the crew didn't share the obsession. They'd seen Noel injured the first week of filming. They'd seen the ferocious fight between Casey and Tongaru. They'd seen Jan scalped and rushed off to what was becoming known as the "Noel Marshall *Roar* Wing" at the Palmdale Hospital. One of them said to me, "Am I scared? You're damned right I'm scared."

They held a meeting and resigned en masse.

d. We'd completed twenty-six days of filming, t rolling again until March, when winter would East Africa set in the canyon would be lush and instead of brown and bare. We celebrated the holiday in our Levitt mobile home by the river, with our choir of big cats caroling us as the sun rose.

I was pouring myself a cup of coffee one morning when Noel quietly announced, "Melanie's coming back to work."

I couldn't believe my ears. She and I had talked many times since she left *Roar* in October, and she hadn't mentioned a word about it. She'd made three movies since then—*The Star Maker* with Rock Hudson, *She's in the Army Now*, where she met her future husband Steven Bauer, and *The Garden*, a low-budget Israeli film.

But unbeknownst to me, Noel had called and talked to her about coming back, and she agreed.

I instantly picked up the phone. I was thrilled, but nothing had significantly changed on the set. We'd learned a little more about handling the cats during filming since we started, but there were still plenty of risks for everyone involved. On one hand, I'd silently hoped she'd come back, because I missed her terribly. On the other hand, while I would have rushed a machine-gun nest to protect her, there was nothing predictable about the cats other than their unpredictability, and I wouldn't have asked her in a million years.

"Are you sure?" I asked her, my voice trembling a little.

"I'm sure," she said. She was emphatic and absolute as always. I was so happy and so apprehensive.

We started filming again, and Melanie was most certainly back. She'd bought a small house in Malibu Beach by then and made the two-and-a-half-hour commute to Soledad Canyon every day. She was great fun to have around, with her amazing sense of humor and her uncanny talent for doing impressions, including an especially hilarious one of Marlon Brando, and she and our reassembled crew got along beautifully.

Patsy Nedd had done a wonderful job of replacing Melanie, but her scenes had to be reshot when Melanie stepped back in.

It was worth every dime, having nothing to do with Patsy and everything to do with the family being together again.

Now if we could all just get through this movie in one piece before we ran out of money.

Animals, being animals, couldn't be less concerned about schedules and tight budgets. We knew that from the beginning, of course, but isn't it interesting what a huge difference there can be between knowing something and actually dealing with it when it happens?

There was a "simple" scene that involved Nikki and Gregory, two Siberian tigers with the attention spans of a couple of gnats, riding in the backseat of a cut-down 1937 Chevrolet driven by Noel and Kyalo. That shouldn't take long, right? But between getting the tigers accustomed to the Chevy, teaching them to sit in the backseat and reassuring them that there was nothing threatening about the engine starting and the Chevy moving so they'd stop leaping out of the car, we spent seven weeks—*seven weeks*—filming it.

One of the key scenes in *Roar* involved Togar, with his reputation for ferocity, chasing the family around the second-story balcony that wrapped all the way around the African house. I remember suggesting to Noel that we use one of the more docile lions instead, but no, "That scene needs Togar," he insisted.

Togar was going to be on the loose for a while, so special precautions were taken to make sure he didn't get bored and either head downstairs to destroy the first floor or come blasting out of the house and run away. The fence crew wrapped chain link all the way around the balconies, and wire mesh was installed across the upper stairwell. An elevator was rigged to lift Togar, in his cage, to the second floor, and wait for his cue.

Cameras were ready. The handlers were alerted. Togar was in his cage in the elevator, poised to come charging out, fiercely bellowing in a homicidal rage. Melanie, John, Jerry, and I were in position, braced to shriek with terror at the sight of him and run for our lives.

"Roll film."

The cage was thrown open.

Togar stepped out of the elevator without a peep, let alone a bellow, looked around, yawned, strolled over to a corner, and sprawled out for a nap in the sun.

Togar was demoted to "extra" status for other scenes and replaced by the reliably ferocious Tongaru, who came through for us, after many, many hours of waiting, regrouping, and wrangling the scene's new star.

And then there was the sequence for which Jan de Bont had sacrificed his scalp months earlier, the sequence in which the lions would chase us around the lake until, frantic, we came across an old rowboat, at that point our only possible means of escape. "And the family rows around the lake," the *Roar* script said—one sentence that took months, off and on, to film.

Big cats are born with the love of the chase. When an animal, four-legged or two-legged, runs, big cats are guaranteed to run after them and show off their expertise at open-field tackling. So the chase scenes went beautifully, as did the scene in which Melanie, John, and I leaped into the rowboat and pushed off, John sitting with his back to the bow and Melanie and I facing forward. Once we were out on the lake, no matter where the bow was aimed, the lions followed us along the shore, waiting for us to come back, disembark, and run so we could do that fun chase thing again.

The idea of the scene was that we were so terrified and paddling so frantically that none of us noticed that instead of escaping, we were actually running aground. The moment the boat touched land, we would find ourselves surrounded by a large welcoming party of big, hungry cats and shove off again.

We ran aground.

The lions gathered around us.

We screamed and proceeded to shove off again.

But one of the lions had a better idea. Instead of letting us head out onto the lake again, he reached out his huge paw and, the instant the boat started to reverse its way off shore, gripped the bow and pulled us right back to dry land so we could run and play some more.

The camera was filming while, for fourteen takes in a row, we ran aground in that rowboat into the midst of a waiting circle of cats, screamed in terror, shoved off, and got dragged onshore again by a lion with a mind of his own and no respect whatsoever for the cost of fourteen failed attempts to shoot a scene.

That lion, by the way, was—who else?—Tongaru.

Through it all, we were anxiously awaiting word from EMI about the possibility of future financing. We'd sent them some footage that we thought was spectacular, and it wasn't easy to keep filming, mostly on credit, while holding our collective breath. The silence from across the pond was deafening.

More cubs kept arriving, too, which was joyful and overwhelming at the same time. I couldn't possibly help raise them all while coproducing and acting in this very complicated movie. Alice, the infamous worst mother in the canyon, rejected four more of her surviving cubs, and they had to be bottle-fed. The rest of the cubs, in addition to needing constant love and close proximity to humans, needed careful watching as well, for such danger signs as listlessness, dullness in their eyes, loss of appetite, and fever, and I just plain couldn't do it. So through the grace of God, I managed to find surrogates who rose above and beyond the call of duty.

Leo Lobsenz, director of the Elsa Wild Animal Appeal, named in honor of Elsa of *Born Free* fame, was one of our heroes. He not only stepped in as a substitute father for several of the cubs but also took them to Elsa fundraising events, to Los Angeles area schools, and to the Braille Institute, where blind children had the time of their lives petting the cubs and playing with them.

Actor Gardner McKay, who'd owned his share of lions, raised many of the cubs.

Pat Breshears, mother of John's girlfriend Lin, became an expert in the care and feeding of cubs and also supervised a half-dozen other human moms.

One of them, an artist named Penny Bishonden, became the cubs' best friend, and eventually an expert trainer and vet tech in Soledad Canyon. Penny had wonderful instincts about her "foster children's" need for play and the joy of discovery. One day, for example, she placed a skateboard on her angled driveway. Within moments a cub, with no coaching whatsoever, walked over to the skateboard, sniffed it, mounted it, and began riding it. I was enchanted by that and determined to use it.

In an early version of the *Roar* script, there was a scene on the African house veranda in which the big cats demolish the newly arrived family's luggage, ripping the bags to pieces and scattering clothing everywhere. Needless to say, that was an easy one. All we had to do was turn them loose with that luggage and let them be themselves, and sure enough, they destroyed it perfectly and had a great time doing it.

There was a skateboard among the family's possessions. I excitedly suggested that we simply place it among the luggage and let one of the cats discover it.

Noel said no. Skateboards, he said, were "out of style," and it would make the scene look dated.

I know, right?

So just before we shut down production for the winter, I privately asked Jan and the crew to come in for a few hours while Noel was occupied elsewhere. Cameras were set up, decimated luggage and clothing were scattered around on the veranda, and the cats were let in. They milled around, they sniffed everything, they batted the debris around, while we waited, and waited . . . and finally, it was our lion cub Lena to the rescue. She closely examined the skateboard, put her paw on it, and felt it move, and off she went for a few minutes of skateboard play that was as much fun for us as it was for her. Even Noel "Skateboards Are Out of Style" Marshall had to admit it was irresistible, and that scene ended up in the final cut of *Roar.*

A scene that was supposed to be funny that still makes me cringe was the result of Noel's bright idea to get inspiration from some of the old silent-movie Mack Sennett comedies while he was writing the script. A sequence he enthusiastically borrowed involved an actor falling down, a shelf above him collapsing, and everything on the shelf raining down on him and knocking him out. Ha-ha.

In Noel's interpretation, I'd be the hapless victim of the collapsing kitchen shelf in the African house, with a jar of honey being one of the items crashing down on my head. But according to Noel, the jar of honey would tip over and pour honey on my head instead, and one of the big cats would stroll over and lick it off as it dripped down my face.

The day came to shoot the scene. I got into position beneath a shelf filled with lightweight prop bottles and jars and the glass honey jar. The direction was given to "Roll film," several big cats were let loose around me like a gang of goofballs, and the shelf collapsed on cue. The props bounced harmlessly off my head, and then here came the honey jar, which, instead of tipping over on the rigged shelf and pouring honey all over me as it was supposed to do, stayed upright and came plummeting down and bonked me on the top of my head, raising a bump that lasted for days.

I was livid at Noel and at the inexperienced propman, who admitted that they "hadn't had a chance" ahead of time to make sure the shelf and the honey jar were rigged properly. In other words, I thought, they forgot, which, as far as I was concerned, was as lame an excuse as the scene itself.

The bump on my head went away, I reunited with my sense of humor and my determination, and a few days later we tried it again. This time everything worked perfectly—the shelf collapsed, props bounced off of me, the honey jar tipped over on the shelf, and honey began dripping down my head and face while five or six leopards and cougars leaped around the room, bouncing off the walls.

As luck would have it, the first one to notice me was Pepper, a stocky black lightning-fast leopard with what I'll politely call an edgy personality. I sat on the floor with my eyes tightly closed and held perfectly still while I felt his claws on my right thigh, followed by his sandpaper tongue licking honey off my cheek. I couldn't let myself breathe, nor could I let myself think, even for a moment, "What the hell am I doing?!" The handlers were about eight feet away, but what possible good could they have done if Pepper had suddenly decided to simply open his jaws and clamp his teeth around my face?

I remember how deathly quiet the set was that morning.

I remember the smell of Pepper's breath and the feel of his rough tongue.

I remember wanting desperately to jump up and escape but knowing my life depended on my not moving a muscle.

I remember Noel quietly saying, "Cut," opening my eyes, and finding the huge, cold hazel eyes of that black leopard staring back at me, less than four inches away.

And I remember being helped to my feet once the cats had been removed and realizing, whether anyone else did or not, that we'd just shot one of the most dangerous scenes in the movie, and for the rest of the day I silently seethed at Noel for asking it of me.

In the end, though, there was no way around it—I was the one who said yes.

Finally it was Timbo's scripted turn in front of the camera, time for his first written scene.

He'd already improvised a scene that we'd managed to capture on film. Jan had long since become accustomed to photographing anything the animals did, which was often more inventive than anything Noel had planned for them. So Timbo had actually made his film debut when he came across a metal camper shell a workman had temporarily removed and placed on the ground near the elephant barn. Something about that camper shell either attracted Timbo or enraged him, and he promptly ripped it to pieces, folded it, and flattened the remains. It made for some dramatic footage and a very chagrined workman, who couldn't imagine how he was going to believably describe this to his insurance company.

We'd already had to warn everyone never to park near Timbo's territory. He seemed to resent vehicles of any size, and he'd already sat on two hoods, totaling them and the cars they belonged to. If he could get to the smaller cars, he would overturn and demolish them. If he couldn't, he also happened to have some expertise at rock throwing, so not even distant windshields were completely safe.

Timbo's major scripted scene was a big one. Once the family had escaped from the cats in their rowboat (despite Tongaru's improvised best efforts to keep us on dry land), they would paddle their way into a cove, only to find themselves confronted by an elephant. To their horror, the elephant would overturn the boat, dumping all of us into the lake, pick me out of the water and drop me back in again, and then destroy the boat. Very dramatic, and even though Timbo was a novice, we were sure we had exactly the right elephant for the job. He'd been with us for five years, and he and I had become great pals by then.

Unfortunately, as we discovered during what we loosely called rehearsals, Timbo didn't have the slightest interest in destroying the rowboat. It took us a while to figure out that, based on his unfortunate encounter with the camper shell, he might be more inclined to destroy a metal boat than a wooden one. Off went the propman to buy several metal boats, which we aged a little for authenticity, and we were ready to roll film.

With a whole lot of practice, I'd finally learned how to be properly picked up by a trained elephant, thanks to Tim Cooney.

"All you do when he comes toward you," he said while coaching Timbo and me, making it sound so simple, "is quickly cross your right leg over your left one. Otherwise, his trunk will go between your legs and you'll end up hanging in midair in a very, uh, awkward position."

I knew my right leg from my left one, so how hard could this be? "Okay, let's try it," I announced, full of false bravado.

Timbo came toward me. I "quickly" crossed my right leg over my left one, but apparently not quickly enough, because I ended up in that exact, uh, awkward position.

I started yelling at Timbo to let me down, prompting a half-dozen crew members to come running. Their reward was the sight of me hanging desperately on to an elephant with his trunk between my legs.

It took a whole lot of rehearsing, but Timbo and I finally mastered "the lift" enough times in a row that I assured Noel we were ready for our close-up. So, with the film rolling, here came the family into the cove in our metal rowboat. Timbo overturned the rowboat and dumped us into the water, then picked me up as I screamed and flailed . . . and refused to drop me back into the water. Instead, take after take, he lifted me up, ran onshore, and dropped me into the sand.

We couldn't figure out what the problem was. It didn't occur to any of us until later that my sweet elephant pal had no way of knowing that my screaming and flailing were *just acting*. How was he supposed to figure out that I wasn't really frightened and in danger? Having to do take after take was only making him more confused and more upset, and frankly, I felt exactly the same way.

On *take number thirteen*, when Timbo lifted me, I didn't quite manage to get myself pulled up onto his head. I tried to adjust by holding on to his ears, arms outstretched, while my right leg ended up under his trunk on top of his right tusk. He then brought his trunk down and, in the process, pinned my leg between his trunk and his tusk.

The pain was instantaneous and excruciating. John and Noel raced over to try to help, which only confused and upset Timbo even more than he already was and caused him to freeze in position so that my leg continued to be crushed.

Mercifully, I blacked out.

I was told later that I continued to hang upside down in midair, unconscious, swinging back and forth, until Tim Cooney finally yelled, "Trunk up! Trunk up!" Timbo obeyed his trainer, lifted his trunk, and let me go. I have no memory of hitting the sand.

I was rushed to Palmdale Hospital in the back of a van, in terrible pain. At first all they observed was a pink area between my ankle and my knee, where it had been pinned against the tusk, but an X-ray showed a hairline fracture of my fibula.

It was late afternoon by the time I got home, limping badly and still in severe pain. I was just settling in when Alex Newman, our vet tech, reluctantly broke the news to me that Cookie, one of the Knobhill lion cubs, had finally lost her long, brave battle with cancer. I was devastated, but relieved for Cookie.

Noel, trying to be helpful, asked if he should cancel the crew party we'd scheduled for that night, a party we held twice a month in the crew dining room to keep up morale.

The combination of my pain and sadness felt like anger. "Don't you dare," I snapped at him. I needed the distraction, maybe even some laughter, to take my mind off Cookie and my throbbing leg. It worked, a little, temporarily.

The next day we filmed another sequence, disguising the fact that I could barely walk. My leg had turned black and blue and was horribly swollen.

Two days later I tried to do a kitchen scene on crutches with Boomer, our inherited lion, but the pain became too much to handle.

The day after that we announced that we were shutting down production again, blaming it entirely on my ghastly purple leg.

But the truth was, we were out of money.

Thirteen

It was late May. Noel was in Japan, virtually going door to door trying to raise money for us to continue production on *Roar.* I was sitting quietly with my leg propped up when Jerry arrived with a pretty new blond girlfriend named Mona Emigh. The ostensible reason was to introduce her to me. The real reason was to show off with the big cats, to let Mona see him walk into a compound and roll around in the sand with a few lions and tigers. What could be more macho than that? It had worked effectively on previous girlfriends, so why not with Mona now that she'd entered the picture?

Sadly, Jerry forgot two very important things. He was wearing tennis shoes, and he happened to stroll into a compound in which

Mike was living—former Knobhill lion cub Mike, tennis shoe freak, who had to possess every tennis shoe he came across, whether it was under a bed or on someone's foot.

The instant Jerry stepped into the compound and closed the gate, Mike was on him, determined to separate Jerry from "his" tennis shoes with his teeth. In the process, he bit Jerry in the thigh, close to the groin, inflicting deep, serious wounds.

I heard yelling and hobbled out on my crutches to see what had happened; I arrived just in time to see John helping his brother into a car to rush him off to Palmdale Hospital. Mona hurried up to me and said, "Mrs. Marshall, would you like me to drive you to the hospital?" She was sweet and thoughtful and refreshingly calm under the circumstances, and as we climbed into Jerry's car to follow him and John to Palmdale, I wondered what on earth she must be thinking. Her new boyfriend had just been pounced on by a lion with a sneaker fetish, and now she was taking care of his badly limping stepmother, who'd been disabled in an elephant mishap. If she'd run screaming for the exit, I wouldn't have blamed her a bit.

The doctor on duty in Palmdale happened to be the same doctor who'd sewn up both Noel and Jan de Bont, and while I waited for word about Jerry, I decided it might be a good idea to have him check on my leg, which was still extremely painful and looked like it had been made up for a horror movie.

He examined it, with that facial expression doctors get when they're about to give you bad news.

"Tippi," he said, "I'm afraid I can't let you go home. Not even for a toothbrush."

"What are you talking about?" I asked. "I just came here to be with my stepson."

"You have gangrene."

Oh, for God's sake. Gangrene? Was he kidding? *Gangrene?* To be fair, I guess gangrene was the one thing that hadn't happened to us yet, but what was next, Noel getting amnesia while he was in Tokyo and wandering off to Tibet to become a monk?

Jerry and I were both sent to Antelope Valley Hospital in Lancaster. He needed more medical care than emergency services could provide, and I needed to be treated for gangrene. (*What?*) We were checked into rooms across the hall from each other so we could visit back and forth. I'm sure Dr. Esfandiar Kadivar, a plastic surgeon who'd be tending to both of us, appreciated the convenience, and we certainly came to appreciate him. A lot of people have GPs as their family doctors. We ended up having plastic surgeon Dr. Kadivar as ours.

Here's a bit of information I never wanted to know: There are apparently two types of gangrene, black and green. If you get to choose which type you'd prefer to come down with, black is better. I had black. Yippee. I was hospitalized for two weeks to receive and recover from the skin graft Dr. Kadivar performed on my leg, while Jerry was released after just a few days. We both had to steer clear of the compounds until we were healthy enough to keep the big cats from perceiving us as infirm, aka potential prey.

Independent films are often shot intermittently due to lack of money, and that's exactly how we proceeded with *Roar* when Noel returned from Japan with no success to report. We managed to accomplish five days of filming in two months, Jerry and I gamely limping our way along, and with about 70 percent of the movie completed, I insisted on believing that somehow, sooner or later, our luck would turn and all this hard work would pay off.

Apparently it would have to be later. Word arrived that EMI, after carefully screening the footage we'd sent them, didn't just disagree with our pride in what we'd accomplished so far, they actually wanted their half-million-dollar investment back. It was a devastating, sickening gut punch. We didn't have half a million pennies to send them, let alone half a million dollars.

I can't explain it, I just know it happened—instead of discouraging us, that latest setback made us more defiant and determined than ever.

Noel, resourceful as ever, started a new TV commercial production company called the Film Consortium, spurred on by the fact that the commercial business was booming at the time. Chuck Sloan, head of production on *Roar*, was put in charge, and we finally had some steady income to feed the animals and keep up with the canyon payroll.

Our cast, film crew, and animal handlers caught the same defiant determination fever, and morale was at an all-time high that summer. They all knew about the EMI rejection, and that their paychecks might be more sporadic than they would have liked, but with few exceptions, they made it clear that they were in it for the long haul, and in it to win it. Some combination of the big cats and the challenge of finishing the film kept them driving down that rutted dirt road off of Soledad Canyon every day, and I grew to love them like family. Several of them even moved onto our property, creating a little village of small trailers we named Gumpsterville, in honor of the portable toilets set up nearby.

But then came August 19, one of those days full of images that woke me up at night for years.

It was about five p.m. Jerry, John, Melanie, and I had just finished a scene with twenty-five or so young cats.

Melanie casually knelt down to play with and scratch one of the cubs.

In a heartbeat, a three-year-old lioness named Sheila, apparently wanting some attention of her own, rose up and jumped Melanie from behind, essentially hugging her head with both paws on her face and holding on while the two of them went down.

We rushed Melanie to Antelope Valley. Dr. Kadivar, whom we should have just put on retainer, started carefully repairing the claw damage while I kept having to remind myself to breathe, especially when I saw how close one claw had come to my daughter's right eye.

I wished a thousand times that it had happened to me instead of her.

I wished a thousand times that I had never mentioned the word *Roar* to her. Yes, she'd known the risks involved, and yes, she'd come back on her own with absolutely no pressure from me. But there was no way around the fact that she wouldn't have been there at all if it hadn't been for me, and the guilt was crushing.

Several hours later, back home again, Melanie looked at me and said, "Mom, I'm not quitting."

"You should," I told her, choking back tears. "You've been through more than enough, and I can't ask you to."

She put her hands on my shoulders. "You're not asking me. I'm telling you. This is my movie, too, you know, and we're going to finish it no matter what."

I felt such a surge of pride, love, and gratitude. Here stood my girl, pale, blood still on her shirt, her face full of stitches, reassuring *me*. Here stood my girl, who'd been a target of countless often malicious gossip columnists and tabloids. Here stood my girl, whom I'd often found so stubborn and strong-willed and impossible to understand, and now here stood my girl, brave, responsible, selfless, and grown up. Just when I thought I couldn't possibly love her more.

So much for soaring morale—another crew member quit that day. As always, I hated to see him go, and as always, I couldn't blame him a bit.

Besides, I was too preoccupied with Melanie's injuries, and with shooting an upcoming scene I'd been dreading for months, to worry about much else.

Yes, it was time to reshoot the scene in which I was sprawled on a log across the river while a single-file parade of lions and tigers jumped over my back. I made sure the handlers had Cherries securely locked up, but I couldn't shake my memory of the sound of her canines scraping against my skull. I was more afraid that morning than I'd ever been in the compounds. With or without Cherries, I'd still be below the big cats' eye level, their cue that they had total control, and who was I to argue with them?

Jan de Bont sensed it and put his arm around me. "It'll go well this time," he promised, and I managed a smile at this amazing man. He'd never lost hope, not once. He'd never said a word about quitting, although he'd had offers for other films that paid a whole lot more, and a whole lot more reliably, than we could.

I did pause, though, before I took my place on the log, to yell to the handlers and crew, "Watch these cats! If one of them decides to do something, don't just stand there!"

Then, after a long, deep breath, I laid down, Noel announced, "Roll film," and Jan kept his promise—it went beautifully. Twenty-six lions and tigers, one after another, filed along the log, leaped gracefully over me, and moved right on along.

When Noel yelled, "Cut!" I felt months' worth of anxiety lift off me as we moved on to the next sequence. Lynn, a lioness, was to come back and lie down on top of me, for no other reason than that she felt like it. Then Noel/Hank would heroically rescue me by pulling her off me, and, because I was so angry with him, in the script, for allowing the whole family to be scared senseless, I would knock him into the water.

As scripted, Lynn flopped down on top of me. A fiberglass shell had been built to protect me, but it was visible on camera and I had to abandon it. So there we were, 100 pounds of me beneath 450 pounds of lion, for what must have been ten minutes, waiting for Noel to get the shot he wanted. (By the time he came to "rescue" me, being angry with him required no acting at all.) All I remember of it was straining to breathe under all that weight and the putrid smell of Lynn's mouth from her diet of raw meat. Other than that, my mind shut down, presumably to prevent me from panicking. Not once did Lynn make an aggressive move toward me, which made me think Cherries's attack on me had a lot more to do with her difficult personality than it did with my being lower than she was when it happened.

Finally Noel/Hank raced onto the log to pull Lynn off me, and as the script dictated, I knocked him into the lake.

Lynn, scene-stealer that she was, then made a spontaneous, unscripted decision and pushed *me* into the lake. It was a much better ending to the sequence than Noel had written, and God bless Jan de Bont yet again for capturing every second of it on film.

It had been a relatively easy, fun day of filming, and we'd desperately needed one of those.

We wouldn't have another one for a very long time.

It was January 29, our first day of filming in the new year. The scene involved Noel and Kyalo sitting on the front steps of the African house, a few cats sprawled around them, talking about the impending arrival of Noel/Hank's family.

For the first time since we'd started shooting, Noel had decided to wear shorts instead of his usual jeans. His stark white legs required body makeup to prevent camera glare. He was a little concerned about the cats' reaction to the smell of the makeup but not concerned enough to refuse to wear it. That was a very, very bad decision.

When I screened the footage later, I could clearly see that the cats in that scene were in a bad mood that day. They looked annoyed, possibly just tired of this whole tedious moviemaking thing we humans had inflicted on them.

Cameras were running and dialogue was being recorded as Togar's son, a young, rough, tough lion named George, approached Noel, who was now standing. Noel tried to ignore him and press on with his dialogue while George started sniffing the makeup on Noel's leg, with an expression that said, "Okay, buddy, what's the story with this smelly brown stuff on your skin?"

Then in an instant, he clamped his jaw around Noel's knee and dragged him off the steps and into a corner, where the handlers raced to pull George away and return him to his compound while everyone else rushed to help Noel.

Despite the eight puncture wounds in his leg, Noel wanted to keep working, driven to compensate for the previous two months when no film had been shot. But wiser heads prevailed, and he was treated by Dr. Kadivar in Palmdale, refused hospitalization, and was home again within a couple of hours.

A few years earlier, my mom and dad had moved to a perfect, comfortable house in Palm Desert. I was visiting them and didn't know a thing about Noel's latest crisis until I got home to the canyon later that day. Even with puncture wounds as severe as his, the pain doesn't set in for about ten or fifteen hours. Then it's excruciating. So the next day, when we entertained Banjiro Uemura and the other Japanese investors he brought to meet us, Noel greeted them on pain pills, in a wheelchair, and chatted away with them thanks to the adrenaline of desperately needing money, only occasionally speaking through tightly gritted teeth.

I checked him back into the Palmdale Hospital the next day, where the doctors managed to keep him for a day or two. He came home from there worse than before and utterly miserable to live with. The puncture wounds weren't healing, his knee looked like an eggplant, and finally I insisted on taking him to Cedars-Sinai Medical Center, where he was diagnosed with severe blood poisoning.

The doctor wanted to immediately hook him up to an antibiotic IV drip and hospitalize him.

Noel said no.

The doctor warned him that he had two choices—cooperate or lose his leg.

Noel was immediately hooked up to an antibiotic IV drip and hospitalized.

I didn't think a thing about the rain that was falling when I drove back to the canyon from Cedars-Sinai that day. The hills around the canyon were dry and could absorb a lot of water.

But five days later, when the steady downpour hadn't stopped, the ground was saturated, and the modest little Santa Clara River that wound through the canyon was looking almost threatening.

There was a twelve-foot wooden bulkhead on the far north side of our property, with a visible high-water mark from the Soledad Canyon flood in 1969. Since then, houses, buildings, and trailers had been built, for the most part, three or four feet above that high-water mark, but some of the animal compounds were below it.

And there were a couple of things we didn't know.

One was that over the past eight years the Southern Pacific Railroad had built berms to direct water away from the tracks and roadbed in case of floods—and straight toward our property. We'd seen some flooding from those berms over the years, but it never did anything more than scare us for a few hours and then recede, and there was no reason to believe that this storm would treat us to anything more than that.

Another was that eight miles upstream at Aliso Canyon, where an unpaved road crossed the river, the county had built up the road with large pipes underneath it to divert heavy rains and keep the road from becoming impassable, as it often did. Apparently no one at those planning meetings ever thought to ask the question "What happens if those pipes get clogged with debris?"

The rain was still falling hard, without a single break, on the morning of February 9. According to the weather bureau, the forecast was for the eye of the storm to pass over us at around midnight, with clearing expected the next day.

I put on my waders and took a long walk to check on the animals. Most of the cats were in their houses. The tigers were out and about, dripping wet and enjoying every minute of the rain. Timbo was contentedly tucked away in his heated barn. I allowed myself a long exhale as I stood for several minutes beside the gray, swelling river.

Back in the house again, I freshened up, changed clothes, and headed off to see Noel in the hospital. I'd driven only a mile when I stopped to look at the river again and saw water flooding over some of the roadways in the trailer park. My heart sank, and I turned around, went home, and called Noel.

"I'm not coming," I told him. "It's not good out here."

A couple of hours later, Jan's wife Monique and I drove out to check on the river again. It was getting uglier by the minute. There was no way around it—it was time to mobilize, just in case.

John began calling in cattle cars and horse vans while I started calling our "regulars"—Gardner McKay, Chuck Sloan, Leo Lobsenz, and a dozen others—to say that we might be in trouble and hoped they'd be available to help move the cats. Not one of them turned me down.

Weeks earlier a tall, tough, ponytailed biker dude named Chris Gallucci had come roaring onto the property on his Harley-Davidson, looking for work. He was an ex-drifter and intensely private, with no apparent purpose or direction in his life, and he offered us his welding and general manual labor skills. We could use all the help we could get, so we hired him, while I privately doubted he'd stick around too long—which goes to show how gifted I am at predictions. He became invaluable, and he's still with me almost forty years later.

So when cattle cars and horse trailers began arriving midafternoon, Chris got to work with his welding torch, closing the gaps along the sides of the cattle cars with chain-link fencing to keep the cats from wriggling through and escaping while they were being transported to safer ground. A chain-link chute was made from portable fence panels to funnel cats from the compounds to the vehicles, and a few cats were safely moved to higher ground in emergency cages and den boxes.

Filming had been suspended indefinitely, so very few members of the film crew were on hand. Jan de Bont, Jerry, and three members of the sound crew, residents of Gumpsterville, had been busy editing, but by midafternoon Jan took every inch of sound tape to higher ground in John's house. Bill Dow, in the meantime, emerged from his darkroom at about five-thirty, stepping out into heavy, wind-blown rain and numbing cold, and immediately began helping handlers and the fence crew. In no time at all the water was above his ankles.

Alexandra Newman had parked her camper-top truck up on the

paved road, which safely housed two of the leopards. Then she went right back to work with the rest of the crew, moving cats and wiring protective plywood against the compound fences.

I put in a call to the 49er Bar and Grill in Acton, ten miles away, and asked if we could use their parking lot for our cat transport vehicles if it turned out to be necessary. God bless them, they said yes. Never underestimate high desert people when it comes to being rugged and sticking together in a crisis.

Darkness was falling, and we were racing against it. Except for the area around the commissary, kitchen, and animal support buildings we called Up-Front, there were no outside lights on the property, since big cats couldn't care less about lighting. Volunteers were scrambling to gather flashlights. About forty of our biggest feline troublemakers were still down in the compounds needing to be moved, so tranquilizer guns were being loaded just in case. People ventured down to the river throughout the evening to check it out with their flashlights and report back to Up-Front, where we kept hot food and coffee available, and the dryers in my house and Monique's were constantly running to keep up with the steady influx of water-soaked clothing.

Moving the troublemaker cats in the darkness was made even more difficult by the fact that it was sometimes difficult to tell them apart in the beams of our flashlights—they were soaked and matted, and very nervous. We'd learned the hard way over all these years that it was dangerous to put random cats together, so we were having to temporarily secure some of them along the upper perimeter fence, about ten feet apart, to keep them safe from each other until we could identify them and take them to safe cover. The only good animal news was that the water was staying away from the elephant barn, so Timbo could remain in his house.

There were gaps in the chain-link corridor that led from the compounds to where the trucks were parked two hundred feet uphill, and humans began filling those gaps. Bill Dow, Chuck Sloan, Gardner McKay, Liberato Torres, and a half-dozen volunteers, some with no experience with big cats, stood guard as the soaked troublemakers made their way through the darkness to the trucks.

The night was surreal. Pounding, wind-driven rain. Blue-red sparks from the welding torch. Random beams from scattered flashlights. Long stretches of fencing, part chain link, part human. Grumbling, upset cats moving tentatively, single file, through the corridor, while the experienced humans yelled to the novices, "Stay steady. If a cat comes up to you, don't move!"

And all the while, without knowing it, we were fighting a battle we couldn't win. A few miles upstream at Aliso Canyon, more and more water was collecting behind the clogged, debris-filled pipes beneath the county roadbed.

Just as the rain stopped, all that water let loose.

I'll spare you, and myself, all the details of that horrible, horrible night. But by the time it was over, a ten-foot-tall wall of water roared into the canyon. I had time to grab only a few clothes and belongings before it crashed into the house. The commissary building, crew kitchen, editing building, and sound building and all their contents were swept away. Fences, cages, and animal compounds collapsed, along with the chain-link chute from the compounds to the rescue vehicles. The teardrop trailers of Gumpsterville were overturned and thrown around.

Thanks to the depth of its foundation of telephone poles, the African house survived, but it was tilted at one end. A huge tree and a dressing-room building rammed into it, and a car and a tree were embedded in what used to be the dining room.

More than 100,000 feet of film were scattered as far as five miles away. Thank God the negative was safely stored in a lab in Hollywood. Tranquilizer guns were used to stop numerous fights among terrified cats waiting to be driven to safety. Four members of the sound crew had to be rescued from the raging waters by firemen with a grapple rope.

Noel, alerted by Bill Dow, got dressed and literally bullied his way out of the hospital, hours before his scheduled knee surgery, and summoned a friend to drive him home. The road was washed out for the last quarter-mile, so he hobbled the rest of the way and immediately went to work moving animals. The second cat he freed from the perimeter fence where she'd been restrained managed to wrap her five-foot-long lead chain around his injured leg, squeezing and forcing pus out of his swollen, infected knee. He no longer needed surgery. A frightened lioness took care of it for him.

Twenty-eight panicky, disoriented cats escaped. Twenty-five of them were finally rounded up. The other three—Mary, Melanie, and Robbie—were shot to death by sheriff's deputies, who, I had to admit despite my grief, had no choice.

And I finally found myself standing in the middle of the road, screaming hysterically, until someone—I don't know who—took me to John's house, above the flooded area. The next thing I remember was Monique, pounding me on the back, yelling, "Breathe! You have to breathe! You have to breathe!"

The sun came up, the waters finally receded, and Noel and I started walking around our decimated property. Neither of us said, "We're wiped out." Neither of us needed to.

He looked terrible. His eyes were sunken, with circles around them so dark it looked as if he'd been beaten. His face was ashen behind his damp, stringy beard, and the severe pain he was in furrowed his face.

I was a zombie. I vaguely remember driving to Acton to call my parents, my sister Patty, and Melanie to fill them in, and their shocked, helpless silence on the other end of the line. I vaguely remember stumbling through debris and stepping over fallen cottonwoods to uselessly pick up a frying pan, a crew member's T-shirt from Hussong's Cantina in Ensenada, and some wet, torn lion and tiger posters that had hung on the now-exposed interior walls of the editing building.

But there's one thing I remember with crystal clarity.

I remember that not one member of the maintenance crews or the animal crews or the film crew, not one volunteer, not Marty Dinnes or Steve Martin or Martin Downey, not a single one of them had left. Beyond exhaustion, sleep-deprived, scratched and damp and hungry, they were all still there, and I marveled at their courage and loyalty.

Jan and Monique found a place to stay in town so that Noel and I could sleep in their still-intact house on high ground that night. We were too bone-tired and in shock to talk, except for one brief, quiet exchange.

"We don't have any choice but to finish it, do we?" he said.

"No, we don't," I replied.

Sunday morning's *Los Angeles Times* reported the Soledad Canyon devastation and the plight of our homeless lions and tigers. Friends and literally dozens of complete strangers responded. Truckers offered vans and trailers. Ranchers and hardware stores showed up with portable fencing. The Southern Pacific Railroad office in Omaha called, ready to send railway cars to house the cats. Friends came to begin shoveling sand out of our house, and one of them even found our supposedly waterproof seven-hundred-pound safe five miles downstream. Herb Dorfman, one of the most important men in our lives at the time, owned a place called Mission Meat in the San Fernando Valley, and he agreed to carry us so that we could keep the animals fed. Handlers and maintenance men started hauling food to the cats in the 49er Bar and Grill parking lot every afternoon and worked in shifts so that one of them was always there twenty-four hours a day. We were overwhelmed with gratitude.

A day or two later, to no one's surprise, a man from the insurance company declared our house a total loss. By week's end, President Jimmy Carter declared parts of Los Angeles County, including Soledad Canyon, a total loss, which could potentially make us eligible for a low-interest loan.

Even with all the amazing help, we knew it would take months to restore the compounds and weeks before our house would be livable again, so Jan and Monique rented an apartment in Los Angeles and Noel and I moved into their mobile home.

Every day I'd think of another piece of my life that had been lost in that river. When it was all said and done, the only one I really mourned was a reel of black-and-white film that had been housed in the demolished editing room—commercials I'd done in the 1950s, including the Sego commercial that had attracted the attention of Alfred Hitchcock.

Did that really happen in the same lifetime I was living now?

The stress, anxiety, and grief were widening the chasm between Noel and me. We seemed to have very little to say to each other, and what we did have to say was invariably sharp-edged.

"I don't know why I'm so angry with you," he said one night. "You didn't cause the flood."

"No, damn it, I didn't." I simmered over that for hours. I didn't like him anymore, but this was hardly the time to deal with it.

The crisis at home was only one piece of the crises that were building up around us. Crises attract the press. And our crisis was no exception.

On March 5 the *Los Angeles Times*'s Wayne Warga wrote:

> Noel Marshall, with his ferocious intensity, his thick wavy hair, his long unkempt beard, and his watchful eyes, actually looks something like a lion. It is as if he is some rogue human being who has come to try to dominate the animals that surround him, and instead they have metamorphosed him.
>
> He is a man passionately obsessed to complete the film called "Roar," one of the most improbable productions in an industry long ago given to the unlikely.

A few weeks later William Arnold's story appeared in the *Seattle Post-Intelligencer*:

> With a kind of Ahab-like single-mindedness, a Hollywood producer named Noel Marshall has been sinking millions of dollars and herculean effort into making a unique and deeply personal kind of wild animal picture . . . Many Hollywood insiders are betting it will be the grandest unfinished movie since "I, Claudius."

A *Daily Variety* editor was quoted as saying:

> People in this industry simply do not understand a man who'll gamble everything on a personal vision. They don't know if he's a gutsy genius or a colossal madman. He's already broken every rule of big-budget moviemaking, and in a town that always plays it safe, that alone is enough to be considered a lunatic.

We literally couldn't afford that kind of publicity. We screened what we had so far of *Roar* for Wayne Warga, and to his credit, he did admit, in print, "What has been completed contains some of the most remarkable—and frightening—photography of animals and people that has ever been produced."

Thank you!

But of course we hadn't completed the film yet, and, with the exception of Jack Rattner and Banjiro Uemura, our few remaining money people dropped us as fast as they could dial their phones. "You're in too much trouble" was the consensus, and how could we disagree with that?

Then, to our complete surprise, two longtime friends, a married couple, gave us a check for $50,000. Gifts like that lifted our spirits and, for better or worse, kept us going.

Noel threw his "ferocious intensity" into raising money, which we needed more desperately than ever, while the rest of us threw our shoulders into rebuilding. I learned to operate a backhoe and fill a dump truck and work shoulder to shoulder, shovel to shovel, with our loyal, underpaid crew. I fell into bed every night with blistered hands and aching muscles and the satisfaction that comes from knowing you've put in a good, hard, honest day's work.

Not once did any of us think of giving up. Our animals needed us to keep going. *We* needed us to keep going. And with *Roar* 80 percent complete, there was no way around it, we had to finish that movie.

Fourteen

Eight months later we were finished rebuilding. Our house was livable again, the African house was intact, our homegrown African location was a perfect match to what we'd already shot, our animals were relieved beyond belief to be back in their compounds again, and we were relieved beyond belief to have them there.

We even had a new addition to the family. Her name was Kura, and she was a notoriously uncooperative elephant who'd worn out her welcome at Circus Vargas. We had a crowd of vets and handlers here to greet her, all of us praying as she emerged from the back of the huge transport truck that Timbo wouldn't resent her usurping his status as the only elephant in the canyon.

It was instantly apparent that status meant nothing to Timbo. If he'd been capable of doing backflips, he would have done them all the way to Hollywood and back the moment he laid eyes on her, and thank God the feeling was mutual. He trumpeted to her as she strolled down the ramp, and she called back. They walked to each other, and he touched her all over with his trunk as if he were making sure she was real. Then they intertwined trunks in the sweetest elephant hug and began making happy rumbling noises in their bellies. It was joyful to watch.

It's a popular East Indian belief that elephants bring good luck. Now we had two of them. There were days when we started sharing that belief, and days when we wondered if maybe having two of them meant they canceled each other out.

Now that President Carter had declared us part of a disaster area, we could at least apply for a Small Business Administration loan and hope for the best. We needed it, and we certainly felt we were qualified for it. But when the SBA appraisers came to visit the compounds, appraisers who were accustomed to assessing damages at shoe stores and pizza parlors, they had no idea what to make of us, or of this "moviemaking is a business" nonsense Noel kept blathering about.

The only way we could legitimize ourselves with the Washington bureaucrats was to appeal to an actual human being, one to one, so we made an appointment to screen what we had of *Roar* for California representative William Ketchum. He watched it, fascinated. He studied the still photographs of the flood damage. He listened sympathetically to our tale of woe, and he promised he would do absolutely everything he could to help us.

Two days later he dropped dead of a heart attack.

Eventually our case found its way to Senator S. I. Hayakawa, who persuaded the SBA that yes, we really did warrant a disaster loan.

We spent the summer of 1978 getting ready to start filming again in the fall. We needed only ten more minutes of footage and *Roar* would be completed. We were almost afraid to say it out loud, but it was possible that we were headed for the finish line.

On Friday, October 13, 1978—the seventeenth anniversary of that phone call asking if I was the girl in the Sego commercial—cameras in the canyon started rolling again. And for the first time I was beginning to wonder why we even bothered.

In October and November we trotted around town with the 80 percent of *Roar* that was ready to show and screened it for every studio in town, as well as independents like Francis Ford Coppola. The response was unanimous—"No, thanks."

Studio heads wanted sex and violence, not furry family entertainment. They all admitted that *Roar* contained the best animal footage they'd ever seen, but "even Disney has given up on animal flicks—they never make back negative costs." Of course, only one out of ten Hollywood movies ever turns a profit, and studio heads have been proven wrong more often than right when it comes to what audiences want to see, but why get in a debate we didn't have any hope of winning?

And then, as a reminder of what *Roar* was *really* costing, there was another near-death attack in the compounds, and our last, thank God.

Our handsome twenty-seven-year-old assistant director Doron Kauper had been raising cubs for us, and he'd made friends with several of our four-legged cast members. So he was respectful but confident when he stepped into a compound where Steve Miller and Darryl Sides were preparing two of the lions—Zuru and the notorious Tongaru—for a mock fight scene. All Doron wanted to do was talk to Steve about something. He almost paid for it with his life.

When Doron swung the compound gate open, Tongaru was stretched out on his stomach, relaxing in the sand. Doron said hello to him and bent down to scratch him under the chin as a passing friendly gesture. But when he stood again to talk to Steve, still bent at the waist, Tongaru leapt at him and rammed the left side of his head, breaking three teeth. Doron went down, with a 475-pound lion on top of him, and Tongaru plunged his canines into Doron's throat a few millimeters away from his jugular vein, almost severing his left ear in the process.

Steve and Darryl jumped onto Tongaru and pulled him away while Doron started crawling toward the gate. He'd just reached it when Tongaru broke loose and sank his teeth into Doron's butt, until Steve and Darryl managed to restrain Tongaru again and a maintenance man dragged Doron out of the compound.

After a five-hour surgery by Dr. Kadivar and three weeks in Palmdale Hospital, that brave, resilient man didn't just survive, he was back at work eight weeks after the attack, back in close, happy proximity to the big cats. He even wanted to see if he and Tongaru could make friends, but I ordered him to never go anywhere near that lion again.

Being broke is one thing. Coming within a few millimeters of a good man losing his life for the sake of a movie nobody even seemed to want was quite another. There was no way around it—the future of our blockbuster looked very, very bleak.

Christmas of 1978 looked bleak, too—rainy, with a cold wind. Noel and I didn't even go through the motions of exchanging gifts, neither of us in a mood that was on the same planet as "festive."

Then, at about eight a.m., Brad Darrington, one of our handlers, knocked on the door, holding a gift that instantly raised my spirits.

It was tiny. It had stripes. It weighed one pound, ten ounces, and it looked like a thoroughbred tiger.

"I found her hidden behind the den in Nikki's compound," Brad said. "She was screaming."

I couldn't have been more surprised—as far as any of us knew, none of the cats was pregnant. "Who's the mother?"

"Debbie, I think." Debbie was an orphan lioness we'd had for four years. I hadn't noticed any difference in Debbie's appearance lately, but she wouldn't be the first cat to surreptitiously give birth.

If Debbie was the mother, there was no doubt that 600-pound tiger Nikita was the father, which meant that the cub Brad was holding was a rare tigon, the offspring of a tiger and a lioness. So far as I knew, there were only three other tigons in the United States.

"I don't think Debbie wants this one," Brad added. "She didn't even look at me when I picked it up and carried it away."

The orphan tigon, a clearly premature female, was wet, cold, and shivering. I wrapped her in a thick towel, rubbing her vigorously to speed up her circulation. Then I pulled a heating pad around her and held her in my arms for three or four hours.

In honor of both the holiday and Noel, we named her Noelle. It was a safe assumption that since Debbie had obviously rejected her, she'd also refused to feed her. I was an old hand at that by now, and within a couple of hours the tiny warm, dry cub was contentedly nursing from a bottle.

Noelle was unique from the beginning, unlike any other cub I'd known. She spoke both the lion and the tiger languages. When she was five days old she began making those delightful nasal puffing "ff-fuff" tiger sounds, but she also started making the happy little lion "aa-oow" sounds. While tiger cubs don't like to be held under any circumstances, Noelle loved to be cuddled. She definitely had a tiger's nose, though, not as blunt as a lion's.

She was magic from the first moment I saw her—without even trying she turned a gray, gloomy Christmas into one I'll never forget.

In early January, Noel and Jan de Bont and I flew to Kenya for some location shots that could never be captured anywhere but in Africa. There's something indescribably sacred about seeing wild animals en masse in their natural domains, especially during the annual migration at Masai Mara. As many as 100,000 zebras, gazelles, antelopes, rhinos, giraffes, hippos, jackals, lions, and other wild creatures can be seen traveling in slow congregations, and while we didn't get to witness the full migration, what we did see and film held me spellbound.

For the briefest moment, I wished that somehow I could release all our animals from their steel-wire compounds, jet them to Africa in some kind of state-of-the-art Noah's Ark, say my tearful good-byes to them, and set them free where they belonged. But after being in captivity, they would never survive in the wild. It was just a futile fantasy, inspired by watching those great herds move across the plains, and if nothing else, it was a good reminder of why we were making our film.

Jan got a spectacular array of footage for the "establishing shots" of *Roar*, and on the first day of photography he also got a wonderful "gift shot," one of those little additions to the film created and performed by the animals that we could never have dreamed up ourselves.

Noel was on a motorcycle, going right to left across the screen, with some of the migration as part of the backdrop. Suddenly a huge bull giraffe split off from its herd and decided to race him. He joyfully galloped at thirty-five miles an hour and kept up with the bike for almost a quarter of a mile, his head about eighteen feet in the air, having the time of his life, providing us with an opening sequence it would have been impossible to stage.

I was abruptly yanked away from the obsessive, addictive drama of *Roar* when, on April 1, 1979, Daddy passed away at the age of eighty-six. Even though he'd struggled with his health for much of his life, he'd been doing better, we thought, so his death seemed sudden and shocking. Mom and Patty and I, the three women he loved, who loved him right back, were with him when he peacefully left this earth. It didn't feel real that he was gone, and for weeks if not months afterward I just went through the motions of being alive, hoping it wouldn't show too much how numb I was inside. The grief of losing him was as deep as my gratitude that I'd had the privilege of being his daughter. I've never known a finer, gentler man. I have framed photographs of him in my bedroom, and I smile at him every day.

In late June I joined Food for the Hungry again, this time in Singapore, to board the SS *Akuna* and search the South China Sea for more refugees from the Communist regime in Vietnam.

Those poor, brave people, packed into those overcrowded boats with very little food and even less hope, were being beaten, raped, and robbed by a network of Thai fishermen, as if they hadn't already been through more than enough. Holding a starving, badly sunburned baby or a raped pregnant woman is an instant cure for self-pity, believe me. And coming upon the wreckage of a makeshift wooden boat and finding a tiny sandal floating nearby makes struggling to finish a movie in Hollywood seem embarrassingly trivial.

Those two weeks on the *Akuna* were humbling and inspiring, exhausting and energizing. Once again, I flew home from a Food for the Hungry trip hoping I was able to give as much to the refugees as they gave me.

Call it karma, call it justice, call it sheer stubbornness, but while I was gone, the lawsuit Noel had filed years earlier for his fair share of *Exorcist* profits was finally settled out of court. As soon as all the legal paperwork was properly signed, sealed, and delivered, Warner Brothers would start making direct payments.

It was almost impossible to believe, but we were about to have enough money to finish *Roar* in this lifetime.

September in Southern California typically brings the hot, dry Santa Ana winds that make fires a constant danger. The floods had taught us a lot about being prepared for natural disasters, so by the time September rolled around, we were as ready, just in case, as we knew how to be. We had forty horse trailers and cattle cars lined up to evacuate the animals. We'd gathered firefighting tools and pumps and high-pressure hoses, and we had a long list of volunteers who promised to be on call. We kept the property well watered and irrigated and the low brush cut back to a safe perimeter.

On the morning of Thursday, September 13, as Noel was getting ready to shoot the final sequence of *Roar*, two fires broke out, one named Sage and one named Monte by the Forest Service, both of them on the Angeles Crest Highway—some distance away, but too close for comfort. We were awake throughout the night, watching the ominous glows west of us and listening to radio reports on the progress of more than a thousand firefighters as they battled the flames on the ground and from the air.

On Friday morning I was scheduled to leave for a weekend Food for the Hungry board meeting in Dana Point, south of Los Angeles. Anti-famine representatives from all over the world would be there, along with Dr. Larry Ward, and I didn't want to miss it. But when I looked out at the column of smoke about five miles wide and thousands of feet high spreading across the sky, I told Noel I was thinking I should stay home where I might be needed.

"Go to the conference," he assured me. "We'll be fine." Between the film crew, the handlers, and the maintenance crew, and John, Jerry, and Joel, he reminded me, there would be more than sixty people on hand for the next two days to move the animals if it came to that. He repeated, "We'll be fine," and with some reluctance I left. Gray ash was floating onto my windshield, and I could smell burned brush until I'd driven about half an hour of the 130-mile trip. According to the radio, the two fires had become nine, and the Sage Fire alone had already consumed twelve thousand acres.

I was tuned in to the news again the next morning while I dressed for a breakfast meeting and heard a Forest Service official say, "This is a perfect day for a fire." My heart sank. Oh, Lord, not again.

I immediately called the canyon office and asked our bookkeeper Nancy Landry, "How close are the fires?"

"Nothing to worry about," she told me. "There's a breeze, but no heavy wind, and everything's fine. In fact, Noel's filming."

I was so relieved. I went on with my day feeling much better and enjoying every minute of the valuable time I was spending with this extraordinary group of people.

But then at two p.m. I was summoned out of a board meeting for an emergency call from Nancy Landry.

Out of breath, voice trembling a little, she managed to get out the words, "Tippi, we're completely surrounded by fire. Noel's evacuating the cats."

"I'm on my way," I said with a lump in my throat.

Two of the board members, Don and Fritzi Simonson, had flown down from Santa Barbara in their twin-engine Cessna, and they immediately volunteered to fly me to a small airfield less than ten miles from Soledad Canyon.

As I left the conference room my good FH friend Larry Ward put a reassuring hand on my shoulder and promised, "We'll have a prayer session for you."

"Thank you," I said from the bottom of my heart.

I believe in the power of prayer.

By midafternoon, twelve fires were burning over an area the newscasters reported to be 250 miles long. As we approached the airstrip near Acton through columns of roiling black smoke I could see our preserve far below in the canyon, and I prayed, pleaded for the safety of our animals.

Nancy met me at the airport. She'd clearly been crying, and we gave each other a long hug before we got in the car and headed home. We'd been driving for only about five minutes when we found ourselves stopped at a roadblock. One of the deputies on duty stepped up to the car.

"Sorry, lady, you can't go up there."

"Yes, I can, Officer. I have to. My animals are there. My husband is there." I explained, talking a mile a minute, and they let me through.

When we pulled onto our property we could see fire in the canyon on both sides of us, but it was being knocked down by aerial tankers and county fire crews.

Nancy looked around, gaping. "I don't believe this. When I left here, we were surrounded by flames, and the smoke was so thick I could barely see well enough to drive."

Burning ash was still falling here and there, and the air was yellow-gray with smoke near the compounds. I ran up to Noel, who was directing traffic for the evacuation vehicles. About half the animals had already been moved, he said, and Tim Cooney had led Timbo and Kura westward, with a police escort, to one of the trailer camps upriver where the cats were being housed until the danger passed.

A half hour later we were all busy loading and trying to calm the rest of the cats, calling out to each other over the whir of the overhead choppers and coughing our way through the acrid smoke, when someone yelled, "Oh, my God, everybody, look!"

We shifted our attention from the animals and to the hills around us. The flames that had been bearing down on us were miraculously flickering and dying, almost literally at the perimeters of our property line. The smoke was starting to recede. We couldn't believe it, but the danger was over.

I heard one of the volunteers say to Noel, "You finally got lucky."

I don't think luck had anything to do with it.

Thank you, Dr. Larry Ward, for the prayer session. I may not have been a practicing Lutheran since I was in my teens, but I believe to the core of my soul in God and the power of prayer.

It worked.

Profits from *The Exorcist* allowed us to start shooting again and to pay back some loans.

On Tuesday, October 16, 1979, one month after the fire, I wrote in my datebook, "Finished filming 'Roar.'"

That same day one of Noel's brothers was killed in a car accident. Somehow, through all those years of filming, it seemed as if every win was followed by a loss. Noel and some of the crew started calling it "the *Exorcist* curse." I don't believe in curses. I don't really believe in luck, either, good or bad. I believe life happens, and you shoulder through the worst of it with your head held high and give thanks to God for the rest of it. I learned part of that lesson in Soledad Canyon and the rest in the South China Sea.

I celebrated the completion of *Roar* with a walk through the compounds, congratulating the most important members of our cast and doing a nose count: seventy-one lions, twenty-six tigers, ten cougars, nine black panthers, four leopards, two jaguars, one tigon, two elephants, six black swans, four Canadian geese, seven flamingos, four cranes, two peacocks, and a marabou stork.

Thank you, God.

Now that filming was completed, a relative quiet settled in over the property on Soledad Canyon. It deserved a name of its own, and my friend Elaine Newman suggested a Sanskrit word that means a meeting place of peace and harmony for all beings, animal and human.

The word was Shambala. Shambala it became in 1980, and Shambala it remains today.

In the meantime, Roar still needed editing, a sound effects track, and a musical score. Jan and our editors were hard at work on cutting the film and attaching the sound effects. We hired a young composer named Terrence Minogue to write the score and another young talent, Robert Hawk, to write lyrics for some of Terry's music. They both moved to Shambala for a while to get added inspiration from the movement and sounds and magic of the cats. The National Philharmonic in London beautifully recorded the perfect score Terry and Robert created for us.

Now all we needed was a distributor.

The search began in September of 1980, when we finally had a fully completed movie.

My datebook for September 20, 1980, reads, "Screening 'Roar' everywhere. Charlie Bluhdorn (Paramount/Gulf & Western) saw it last night."

A month later I wrote, "Paramount wants 'Roar.' ABC wants 'Roar.'"

Two months later, a slightly less optimistic datebook entry: "Screened 'Roar' for Warners."

The reaction was favorable across the board, despite the fact that instead of the sex-and-violence movies they were looking for, we just had a family film, "an animal show," as one of the executives described it.

It was great news that some networks and studios wanted *Roar*, but as usual, there was a catch. According to the deals they offered, they would keep the lion's share (pardon the pun) of the profits, even though they hadn't spent a dime making the movie. That made absolutely no sense to us, so it was back to the drawing board.

On February 22, 1981, Noel and John started screening *Roar* all over the world, and it worked. We made deals in England, Japan, Germany, Italy, Australia, and a handful of other countries, but not a single deal in the United States.

The slowly dawning reality was devastating: We hadn't made an international blockbuster after all. We'd captured wild animals on film in an awesome, unprecedented way. But the human story, the story line about the people that would drive the film forward from beginning to end, wasn't there. We two-legged characters seemed like nothing more than an excuse to show off, react to, and interact with our four-legged cast, and it just plain wasn't enough.

We'd gambled everything. We'd risked our lives, the lives of our children, and the lives of our crews for eleven long, painful, joyful, incomprehensible years. Our personal financial stake was staggering, and we were deeply in debt to several investors. We'd defied the odds and countless warnings from people who knew infinitely more about what we were getting into than we did, and we'd lost. The damage to our pride was crushing.

I spent that summer with the animals, knowing I could count on them to help me heal. I walked around the compounds for hours every day, and swam in the lake with Timbo and Kura, talking to all of them, sitting with and touching the cats who could safely be sat with and touched. I needed them every bit as much as they needed me.

I've heard it said that the loneliest place in the world is on the inside of a bad marriage, and I believe that. Even now I can honestly say that I've never experienced loneliness when I've been alone. But my marriage to Noel had collapsed, and for the first and only time in my life, I was lonely, and I ached from it. The goal of seeing *Roar* through to completion had kept us together. Now that the goal had been accomplished, there was nothing between us but bitter arguments, recriminations, and tense, hollow silence.

Somehow, in late October, we managed to put on a good front for the world premiere of *Roar* in Sydney, Australia. Melanie, John, Kyalo, and Robert Hawk joined us for the traditional press parties and interviews. We were welcomed with such enthusiasm that I almost convinced myself that maybe, just maybe, the future of *Roar* might not be as dismal as we thought, that it might come charging out of Australia with a life of its own and become an international blockbuster after all.

The day after the premiere, *Daily Variety*'s representative critic telegraphed his review for publication in the Hollywood trade paper:

> The noble intentions of director-writer-producer Noel Marshall and his actress-wife Tippi Hedren shine through the faults and

shortcomings of "Roar"—touted as the most disaster-plagued pic in Hollywood history.

Given the enormous difficulties during production—devastating flood, several fires, an epidemic that decimated the feline cast and numerous injuries to actors and crew, it is a miracle that the pic was ever completed.

Here is a passionate plea for the preservation of African wildlife, meshed with an adventure-horror tale which aims to be a kind of "Jaws" of the jungle. If it seems at times like a "Born Free" gone berserk, such are the risks of planting the cast in the bush surrounded by 150 untrained lions, leopards, tigers, cheetah and other big cats, not to mention several large, ill-tempered elephants.

Pic is flawed by lapses in continuity and silly dialogue.

Hedren and her daughter, Melanie Griffith, have proved their dramatic ability elsewhere; here they and their costars are required to do little more than look petrified.

The film's strongest selling points are the spectacles of wild animals and humans filmed at such close quarters, something akin to the perverse fascination of going to the circus and watching agog as the lion tamer puts his head into the beast's mouth. That, plus the Marshall family's laudable desire to focus attention on the slaughter of many animal species.

When *Roar* opened in England, David Robinson of the *London Times* wrote:

It is better to forget and forgive the story. The animals, though, are superb, and shamelessly skillful in all techniques of upstaging; and there is an irresistible thrill in seeing an understanding between humans and animals that overturns centuries of preconceptions about relationships in nature.

When all was said and done, *Roar* cost seventeen million dollars and grossed two million dollars worldwide.

It would take a very long time to recover, financially and emotionally. But as long as the animals at Shambala were safe, content, and well-fed, I could handle it.

As for Noel and me, it turned out we had one more drama to deal with before we both moved on.

Fifteen

I promise that there's a reason I'm telling this story.

I had a very, very handsome older cousin named Jimmy Hedren. He was a pilot in World War II, and his plane crashed when they were flying over Germany. He survived, but half of his face was burned and he was terribly disfigured for the rest of his life.

I was in my teens when he came home from the war. I hadn't seen him until he and his wife came to visit us. I was really looking forward to giving him the warm, loving welcome he deserved. But the instant he stepped in the door, I saw his face and fainted. I was so ashamed and so embarrassed, and I apologized over and over again. He was very understanding about it, but I never quite forgave myself. I kept reminding myself that it wasn't as if I chose to faint, it was completely involuntary. It didn't help. I wouldn't have hurt his feelings for anything in the world, and I was sure I had.

I remember asking his wife, who'd married an incredibly handsome man before he left for the war, how she handled his awful disfigurement. Her amazing answer was "I never saw it."

Since then, of course, between the animals and the injuries they'd inflicted and the Food for the Hungry victims around the world and the many veterans hospitals I visited, I'd seen a lot, and as hard as it always was to witness, I'd never fainted again, not until one day early in 1982, and I paid a stiff price for it.

Noel was in the hospital. It wasn't the big cats' fault this time. He was there for serious kidney surgery. I was waiting in his room for him to come out of recovery. Finally they wheeled him in, and he must have still been under the effects of anesthesia, because, very uncharacteristically, he was screaming at the top of his lungs in what sounded like mortal pain.

And I fainted. I went down like a bucket of rocks and, on my way to the floor, hit my left temple on the metal guardrail at the foot of his hospital bed.

I was in a coma for three and a half days and woke up in the room across the hall from Noel's. He was recovering well and was standing beside my bed when I opened my eyes. I was stunned when he told me what had happened and how long I'd been unconscious.

A nurse brought me a tray of food. IVs had been keeping me fed and hydrated while I was out cold, but I was hungry and eagerly dived in. After a few bites, though, I pushed the tray away and said to the nurse, "I'm sorry, I know I'm not in a five-star restaurant here, but this is the blandest food I've ever eaten. There's no taste to it at all!"

I expected her to shrug and leave with the tray—I could only imagine how many complaints about the food nurses have to put up with in a hospital full of patients. Instead, she looked a little concerned, briefly left the room, and returned a few minutes later with a doctor and a collection of small vials of liquid.

One by one the vials were put under my nose and I was told to sniff each of them and, if I could, identify the smell. I did, and as far as I could tell, every vial was filled with nothing but water. They had no odor at all . . . not even the one the doctor showed me that, according to the label, was filled with formaldehyde.

The way the doctor put it was "You're in serious trouble with your olfactory senses."

The way I put it was, and is, that since that day I fainted and hit my left temple in early 1982, I've had absolutely no sense of taste or smell.

I know there are far, far worse things that can and do happen to people, but from the very beginning I can honestly say that the psychological effects are even worse than the physical ones.

I put up a constant fight against anorexia. I make sure to put a certain amount of healthy food on my plate, just to keep up my weight and my stamina. Otherwise, believe me, food is of no interest when you can neither taste it nor smell it, which makes Thanksgiving dinners and meals in gourmet bistros no fun at all. In fact, when I eat in restaurants I have to be sure to order what someone else orders, so that on those very rare occasions when the food tastes or smells a little off, they'll notice and alert me not to eat it. It's boring, and it's painful knowing that I'll never be able to look forward to another meal or some special treat I used to love.

One day, trying to be a good sport and cook a nice healthy lunch for myself, I fixed myself a casserole, slid it in the oven, and *kaboom!*

The stove exploded, burning off my left eyelashes, my left eyebrow, and the left side of my hair because I couldn't smell the gas leak. I had to have all the gas appliances in the house switched to electric.

Rain, flowers, freshly mown grass, fresh-baked cookies, perfume—all those smells I used to love are just memories now. It took me years to stop walking over to a vase of roses to take a nice long whiff. I still enjoy having them around to look at and appreciate how beautiful they are. I'm sure they fill the house with that wonderful aroma. I wouldn't know. I love Joy perfume. I've worn it every day since I was in my teens, and I still do—just because I can't smell it doesn't mean other people shouldn't enjoy it.

It's amazing how much of life is based on taste and smell, and I miss those senses terribly. I'm resigned to the fact that they're irreversibly, irretrievably gone. I resent it when I let myself think about it, which is why I refuse to let myself think about it very often. What earthly good does it do?

Noel and I were divorced on January 19, 1982. Happy birthday, Tippi.

I'd filed months earlier, when it had become impossible to ignore the fact that there was nothing between us anymore to support and sustain a healthy marriage. The divorce's being finalized on my birthday was a sad gift of relief to both of us.

There was never a question of which of us would be leaving. Noel moved to a cottage in Beverly Hills and continued with his TV commercial business, the Film Consortium.

I stayed right here in Shambala with the animals, more beautiful than Beverly Hills any day as far as I'm concerned.

Once the marriage was over, once the anger and the hurt and the turbulence were over, I felt the most peaceful relief, a deep inner sense of freedom. I believed in myself again. I was in charge of my own life again, after seventeen years of nonstop impulsive chaos at a dead run. There had been enough excitement, enough surprises and challenges, to fill several lifetimes, so I didn't regret those seventeen years. I'd just reached the same moment that still resonated in me from a hill in Minnesota when I was ten years old: "I'm not going to do that anymore."

And how could I ever regret my years with Noel, when if it weren't for him, there would be no Shambala?

In 1982 I had the joy of giving Melanie and her fiancé Steven Bauer a small, wonderful wedding in New York. I'd missed her first wedding, and I didn't just want to attend this one, I wanted to make it as special as possible. Melanie was a breathtaking bride, she and Steven were glowing, and I was the proudest mother of the bride in the history of weddings. I remember waving good-bye to the newlyweds as they left the church in a horse-drawn carriage and sending off a silent prayer for their happiness, and for Melanie and me to always stay as close as we were that day.

Three years later I had the awesome thrill of being in the hospital room when Melanie gave birth to my first grandchild, Alexander Bauer. Maybe it's because I saw him take his first breath, maybe it's because he's been so uniquely *him* from the day he was born, but Alexander and I have always had a special connection that I treasure.

I've never been a woman of leisure, or even aspired to be one. Part of reclaiming control of my life after Noel and I divorced was getting back to work and starting down the long road toward financial recovery.

At the top of the priority list was making sure the wild animals were taken care of—not just our animals at what was now the Shambala Preserve but wild animals everywhere. I did a lot of research and a lot of footwork, and in 1983 the Roar Foundation, a 501(c)(3) nonprofit organization, officially came into being, with a mission statement that reads, "The Roar Foundation supports The Shambala Preserve and shares its mission: to provide sanctuary to exotic felines who have suffered from gross mistreatment and neglect so they can regain their physical and mental health and live out their lives in dignity; to advocate no buying, selling, breeding or trading of exotic felines; to educate the public about exotic felines; and to advocate for legislation to protect them. P.S. And elephants too!"

Noelle, our tigon, had already become one of the Roar Foundation's greatest goodwill ambassadors, a celebrity in the cat world. Photos of her were being published all over the world, from Moscow to Bombay to Manila, and with good reason—she was exquisite. Full-grown now, she was a little larger than the average tigress, tall and long-legged. Her stripes had softened from coal black to subtle brown. Her base coat was orange, with a pure white belly and some mottled spots on top of her head. I'd never seen a big cat quite like her, and apparently neither had anyone else.

Her personality was as unique as her looks. She spoke fluent "lion" and "tiger," both with an almost feminine shyness. She loved to swim, and she was the best jumper at Shambala—she startled me awake more than once by leaping up on the roof of my house at dawn, seemingly just for the fun of watching me and Liberato or Penny or Jesus try to entice her back down to the ground again. She was affectionate and playful with humans, especially skilled at the lions' art of tripping innocent passersby with her paw.

I was in Orange County at a breakfast meeting one day when I got a call from Penny, who responded to my hello with an urgent, "Are you sitting down?"

Oh, God, I thought, what now? Cats were loose? Another fire in the canyon? Someone was injured? I braced myself and asked, "What's wrong?"

"Noelle just had a cub."

Within minutes I was on my way home to Shambala.

I'd visited the Royal Melbourne Zoological Gardens while I was in Australia for the opening of *Roar*, and I had a long talk with their head veterinarian, Dr. Ray Butler, about the population problem in the compounds. Thanks to a birth control pill called megestrol acetate, not a single cub had been born in the Melbourne Zoo for more than two years, and there were no potentially harmful side effects. The minute I returned to Shambala, we put every female big cat on the pill . . . except Noelle, who, as a tigon, was supposedly sterile, with an obvious emphasis on the word "supposedly." We knew she'd mated many times with a very handsome tiger-about-town named Anton, but since she "couldn't get pregnant," their sex life was none of our business.

Now, though, I suppose it was. Noelle's cub was a male. I named him Nathaniel, a derivation of my given name Nathalie, and according to the zoologists I contacted he was very possibly the only "ti-tigon" in existence at the time.

I was mesmerized by that cub and by Noelle's approach to parenting. She was understandably possessive about him. He was about ten days old when Noelle saw Penny sitting on the floor beside Nathaniel, leaning toward him, talking to him and petting him. Noelle walked up behind her and took Penny's neck in her mouth, her teeth closed firmly without puncturing the skin. Penny was experienced enough not to move a muscle; she just quietly said, "I understand, Noelle," and Noelle let go of her neck. But Noelle wasn't done yet—she then used her paws to move Penny to the middle of the room and away from her cub.

Noelle was also diligent in teaching Nathaniel about manners and proper behavior around humans. While she loved playing with him, she also didn't hesitate to box his ears and literally sit on him, nonchalantly gazing around and ignoring his screams of protest at being pinned to the ground, when he got too rowdy. A lot of the credit goes to her for the fact that our one-of-a-kind ti-tigon, who had the physique of an NFL linebacker when he reached adulthood, was transformed from a wildly rambunctious cub into an absolutely angelic grown-up.

Another transformation at Shambala I had the privilege of witnessing had its roots in the elephant barn, of all places.

Chris Gallucci, our welder/handler/maintenance worker, had proved his dedication over and over again, especially on that horrible night of the flood, when he worked nonstop in a blinding rainstorm for what must have been fifteen hours straight. He still seemed to be looking for some kind of real purpose, but there was something special about him that I hoped we could find a way to harness; we didn't want to lose him, and he was too good a man to live a disconnected drifter's life.

Suddenly one day our elephant handler was gone, and to my complete surprise Chris spoke up and said he'd like to give it a try. I thought of it as a huge help, nothing more, until we could find someone experienced and permanent.

Not long after Chris became Timbo and Kura's fill-in handler, I stopped by the elephant barn one evening at feeding time. There was Chris, just finishing preparing their dinner. He'd arranged a giant semicircle of oat hay for each of them. On top of the hay were separate mounds of a grain and molasses mixture, and inside all that, he'd hidden four apples, three oranges, six bananas, and a half-dozen carrots. Dessert—four fresh coconuts—was waiting near Chris's feet to be served when the elephants had finished their meal. The only things missing were candles and monogrammed linen napkins.

He'd gone to so much trouble, and it was so sweet and unexpected. I asked if he did this every night.

He grinned, a little sheepish. "Not *every* night," he said, and I walked away not sure which of them I was happier for—Timbo and Kura, or Chris.

A few months later I came home around one a.m. and noticed a distant light that wasn't usually visible. I investigated and quickly picked up the phone to call Chris.

"I'm sorry to bother you at this ungodly hour," I told him, "but Timbo's smashed the barn door to pieces. Kura's fine."

I waited with the elephants for Chris to arrive, explaining to Timbo that this behavior was unacceptable, not to mention expensive, as if he cared, and reassuring Kura that I knew she hadn't participated in this act of vandalism.

Timbo was obviously feeling guilty, because he started making low rumbling noises when he heard Chris's car pull up. Chris marched toward us, and the minute he was close enough, Timbo gently wrapped his trunk around Chris's head, then placed the top of his trunk on Chris's head, then rubbed his cheek, then pulled Chris's head toward his mouth, almost engulfing it. Finally he lifted one of his giant feet and held it above the ground, almost begging Chris, who had yet to say a word, to please forgive him and tell him they were still friends. There was clearly a connection between Chris and those elephants, and a lot of love and trust and affection. The only remaining question was who had conquered whom.

Former loner/drifter/biker dude Chris Gallucci, the man I thought would move on a few short weeks after he roared up to our door on his Harley, is still here forty years later, director of Shambala, vice president of operations, and one of my closest, most trusted, most valued friends.

In the meantime, after a few months of regrouping, I wanted to work beyond my work at Shambala—something that would actually bring home some money. I needed to work, and I still didn't know how to type.

It was time to do what I'd learned how to do and see if Hollywood still remembered me.

They did, and within a happily short time I was cast in a movie called *Foxfire Light* with a wonderful group of actors who included Leslie Nielsen, Faye Grant, and Lara Parker. After all those years of insanity making *Roar*, with coproducer responsibilities on top of performing, I was overjoyed to just act and leave the rest of the work to the crew.

We shot *Foxfire Light* in Branson, Missouri, and as often happens when you least expect it, fate stepped in and changed my life again.

I'd made some lovely new friends in Branson, and one of them lost a close family member just as we finished shooting the movie. I stayed for the funeral and the wake, which was actually a series of amazing parties celebrating the family member's life.

Picture this scene accompanied by Rossano Brazzi singing "Some Enchanted Evening": On the third day of these celebrations I walked into a room full of people in cocktail wear, and there stood a tall, impossibly handsome man in his early fifties. Our eyes met, and he immediately approached me and introduced himself.

His name was Luis Barrenechea. The gorgeous offspring of a Basque father and a French mother. Seventeen days older than I was. Divorced. Smart. Wonderful sense of humor. Charming. Romantic. Attentive. A Korean War veteran. Wealthy and successful from decades in the steel fabrication industry. I mentioned "gorgeous," right? Used to be a drinker. "Used to be" worked for me. Or, to put it another way, if I'd made a list of everything I was looking for in a man, even though I wasn't looking for one at all, Luis Barrenechea had every single quality on the list.

We never left each other's side at that party.

After several spellbinding hours, he glanced at his watch and said, "I'm going back to Los Angeles," then turned to me and asked, "Are you coming with me?"

"Yes," I answered without a second thought.

We were in love and inseparable from that moment on.

It was thrilling.

His daughter and I were alone in the car one day, on our way to do some shopping several months into Luis's and my relationship, when out of nowhere she said, "Don't marry my dad."

I didn't ask her why. I didn't ask her what she meant. I just chose to pretend she hadn't said a thing and quickly changed the subject. I guess we don't hear what we don't want to hear.

Luis and I were married on February 15, 1985. It was a small, lovely wedding. Melanie was my matron of honor.

We had a beautiful house in Arcadia, a few miles northeast of Los Angeles, and a fantastic party house built around a pool, formerly owned by William Holden, in Palm Springs. I loved both those houses, but Shambala was still my home, and we spent three or four nights a week there, without a single complaint from Luis. He quickly fell under the spell of the animals and couldn't have been more supportive of my passionate dedication to them.

He was just as supportive of my desire to work, and I had the best time doing guest-starring roles in TV movies and series and a few feature films. I did one episode of *The Bold and the Beautiful* and have been addicted to it ever since. Melanie and I even got to work together a couple of times, once on a movie called *Pacific Heights* with Michael Keaton and once on, of all things, an episode of *Alfred Hitchcock Presents*, a reprise of Hitchcock's hit series in the 1950s and early 1960s. Hitchcock had passed away by then, and I wondered if he was spinning in his grave knowing I was working again, especially on something that bore his name.

Luis was every bit as supportive of my deep love for my family. He couldn't have been more gracious when my mom came to stay with us for a while, and he cheered me on when I insisted on taking a trip to Texas for one of the most important events of my life.

Melanie and Steven Bauer had divorced in 1987, and thirteen years after their brief first marriage, she and Don Johnson reconciled. On October 4, 1989, in Austin, Texas, Melanie gave birth to their exquisite daughter, Dakota. She asked me if I could come, as if there's a force on this earth that could have stopped me. It meant the world to me to be there, and it speaks volumes about the inclusiveness Melanie inspires that both Melanie and Steven's four-year-old son Alexander and Don and Patti D'Arbanville's seven-year-old son Jesse were in Austin as well to meet their new baby sister.

For several years I woke up every morning so peacefully, ecstatically content. I was happily married to a man who was everything I'd ever wanted in a husband and partner. We had a large group of fun, stimulating, lovely friends and a busy social life. My awesome daughter had given me two precious grandchildren. My mom, at her own insistence, had moved to a nursing home, where she was happy and fairly healthy and even had a boyfriend. I had my beloved animals and staff at Shambala, and the Roar Foundation was off and running. My acting career was picking up steam again. I almost had more blessings than I could count.

But sometimes I can't even believe how naive I can be. I thought I was marrying a sober man. It honestly never occurred to me that "used to be a drinker" meant "might be a drinker again someday if I feel like it."

I didn't even ask, "Why?" when Luis's daughter said, "Please don't marry my dad."

Luis and I had been married for eight years when he started drinking again. There was nothing subtle about it. I've never seen a human being change so quickly and so dramatically. When he was sober, he was the most wonderful man I'd ever met. When he was drunk, he was a cruel, vicious monster. He never raised a hand to me in anger, it was all verbal, but that doesn't make it hurt any less.

I walked out on him several times.

I didn't just send him to rehab three times, I went with him to rehab three times to be supportive, because I really, *really* wanted him to beat that demon in him so I could go on living with the man I married and loved so much.

The demon won.

Luis and I had a terrible fight one night in our house in Arcadia. It ended when he passed out drunk on the floor.

I stepped over him, went home to Shambala, and after nine years of marriage, filed for divorce.

"I'm not going to do that anymore."

Sixteen

I took a lot of long walks through the compounds when I left Luis and settled back in to Shambala full-time. The animals always helped me reset my compass to true north. They still do.

Maybe, I decided, I'm not good at marriage.

Or maybe I'm just not good at picking the right man to marry.

I certainly didn't get married three times because I felt less than whole without a man in my life. I'm already whole, all by myself. I'm enough. It's no one's job but mine to fulfill me. I'm content being alone. I always have been, and I always will be. So enough marriages for me. I was done. Luis made his choice to start drinking again and let alcohol turn him into someone I couldn't and wouldn't live with.

I made my choice to help as best I could and, in the end, refuse to live with an abuser. We were both entitled to make our choices, move on and let it go.

I'm not one to harbor old hurts and resentments. If nothing else, as a friend of mine once said, it's *terrible* for the complexion. Clinging to anger, being rigid and vengeful and unforgiving, shows up on the face, and it's not a good look. Aging takes enough of a toll without piling on sags and wrinkles because of past wrongs I can't go back and change. I've had some tightening done around my neck and jawline, with a little scar behind each ear, but I'm not about to subject myself to a facelift at the age of eighty-six, especially when we've all seen how badly those can turn out. So, if for no other reason than sheer vanity . . .

Thank you again, Peter, for Melanie.

Thank you again, Noel, for Shambala.

Thank you again, Luis, for eight of the best years of my life. Eight out of nine is better than none.

Besides, I was too busy and had too many blessings to sit around feeling sorry for myself.

The acting jobs kept right on coming, with appearances in a lot more TV series episodes, TV movies, and feature films.

Mom passed away on October 31, 1994, at the age of ninety-five—devastating for Patty and me, of course, but we were so happy for her. She died with the greatest peace, and she lived every moment of her life until the very end. She played the piano every single day at her nursing home in Las Vegas to keep her fingers limber, refusing to let her arthritis limit her, and she'd taken up oil painting in her seventies. (Daddy good-naturedly took up complaining about the price of frames when she first started.) She loved painting landscapes and castles, and she won a few blue ribbons at art shows. I have several of her paintings, and pictures everywhere of that infectious smile of hers. She's with me every day.

Melanie and her new husband Antonio Banderas presented me with my third grandchild, my darling Stella.

And, in the meantime, the population of Shambala continued to grow.

We gladly took in two of Michael Jackson's tigers from Neverland Ranch—Thriller and Sabu. I was really disappointed that he didn't call, not once, to check on them, nor did he ever send a dime for their food and upkeep.

We acquired a very special liger (lion father, tiger mother) named Patrick. He came from a horrible roadside zoo in Illinois, where he'd been badly abused, and we moved him into the compound right next to my house. I'll never forget the day he arrived. I opened the gate to his new home, and he stared in at it for a long time as if he couldn't quite believe his eyes. Then he jumped up in the air and joyfully ran the full length of it, just because he could. It became our daily tradition that I would go out and sit beside him, with the fence between us, and just talk to him, about life and love and my promise to make up for every bad day he ever had. At some point he would look at me with his big, beautiful, playful eyes as if he were saying, "Let's run!" and he'd run the length of his large compound with me running right alongside him, chain link between us. Within a few weeks he learned the sound of my car, and I'd arrive home to find him eagerly waiting for me at the corner of the fencing. There was a very special connection between Patrick and me, that's one thing I knew beyond the shadow of a doubt.

Then one late afternoon Patrick was being given his medication, with his huge roast beef dinner waiting for him nearby. I happened to glance over to see that his roast was being swarmed by what looked like dozens of yellow jackets, so thick that I couldn't even see the meat beneath them. "Oh, no you don't," I thought, "that's my Paddy's dinner, not yours," and I marched over to reach through the chain link and brush them away.

Patrick, in the meantime, was watching me with his usual adoration . . . until I apparently got too close to his food. Suddenly his expression changed from adoration to rage. The most bloodcurdling sounds came out of him as he charged at me like a locomotive and leaped up on the fence. He was fully prepared to rip me to shreds, and I jumped back in the nick of time.

What absolutely amazed me was that even after the decades I had spent working and living with wild animals, even after Ozzie Bristow's comment about Dandylion all those years ago, "He loves me, but he could also kill me," *my feelings were hurt*. My Paddy, my close, dear friend, my great pal, my buddy—how *could* he?

After about five minutes I slapped myself and came to my senses. What was I thinking? It wasn't personal! I should have known that as well as anyone! It's not that wild animals in captivity can't be trusted. They *can* be trusted—to be wild animals, to have countless centuries of genetic instincts in their DNA. We humans who expect anything more of them—or more accurately, anything *less*—are arrogant, naive, and downright stupid . . . all of which I'd been, all the way back to letting a full-grown lion named Neil have free rein of my Knobhill house and close proximity to my daughter, trainer or no trainer just a few short feet away.

I started thinking a lot about the fact that our government was allowing apex predators at the top of the food chain, some of the most dangerous animals in the world, to be bred and sold as pets and/or as an offbeat way to make money. I knew it was wrong, I knew it was obscene, and I knew I couldn't live with myself if I didn't take action and try my damnedest to do something about it.

I coauthored a bill with one of our zoological veterinarians, and we made a four-minute video—four minutes, we were told, was as long as we could expect any politician to give us their undivided attention. I took the bill to my congressman, Buck McKeon, in Washington and gave him a quick synopsis of our concerns. He didn't seem too enthusiastic until he watched the video. Then he turned to me, looked me in the eye, and said, "I'll do it."

The Captive Wildlife Safety Act became a law in 2003. Of course, laws are only as effective as the people who enforce them, but it's made a difference, and I'm proud of that.

The more I researched, though, the more I realized that while the Captive Wildlife Safety Act was a valuable law, it didn't go far enough.

There was a horrifying, highly publicized tragedy in Ohio in which a man with seventy-some wild animals threw open the gates to their cages one day, let them out, and then committed suicide. In the terrible resulting chaos, the police came in and killed all the animals.

A four-year-old boy in Texas lost his arm to his uncle's "pet" tiger.

A ten-year-old boy went with his father to visit a friend who had a collection of lions and tigers. The friend enjoyed bringing out a lion or tiger to be photographed with visitors. Tigers happen to be very interested in children, so the instant the friend opened the gate, the tiger blasted out of its cage and headed straight for the little boy. The friend raced to help the child and, in the process, left the gate open. The lion came charging through the gate as well, and both the lion and the tiger attacked the ten-year-old. The boy survived, but he'll spend the rest of his life as a quadriplegic.

An eleven-year-old girl went into a tiger's cage, under her stepfather's supervision, to groom the tiger. The instant the stepfather closed the cage gate behind her, the tiger jumped on her, sank its teeth into her neck, and killed her. Her heartbroken biological father was on the news, sobbing, "Why aren't there laws against this?!"

Why indeed?

Not one of those horror stories should have happened, and not one of them is the animals' fault.

And yes, obviously, there but for the grace of God go I.

So, armed with all these facts and more, I coauthored another bill, the Big Cat Public Safety Protection Act, the original intention of which was to stop the private possession and breeding of big cats.

As I write this, in 2016, the bill is still languishing in Congress, years after I took it to Congressman Buck McKeon.

They haven't heard the last of me yet.

We don't discriminate at Shambala. You don't have to be a big cat or an elephant to melt our hearts and find a home here.

A man from nearby Acton called one day to ask for help. A feral cat had given birth to a litter of six kittens in his garage. He'd caught the cat and had her spayed, but he couldn't begin to care for all those kittens.

"They're about eight weeks old," he told me. "I was wondering if you could help me find homes for them."

"Absolutely. Bring them over," I assured him. Between the staff and our visitors, there's no shortage of animal lovers at Shambala.

Wouldn't you think I'd know myself better than that by now? I took one look at those six incredible little kitten faces meowing up at me saying, "Hi, Mom!" and thought, "God help anyone who tries to take these babies away from me."

There were five males and one female, and I decided this was a perfect opportunity to pay homage to various costars and loved ones. In no time at all I was sharing my home and my bed with Rod Taylor, Sean Connery, Marlon Brando, John Saxon, Antonio Banderas, and Melanie Griffith. As soon as they were old enough, I had them spayed and neutered, and I have to say, it felt like a luxury to watch six kittens play without doing the thousands of dollars worth of damage, as even one lion or tiger cub is capable of. Their favorite things to do were wrestle, pounce on each other and my head, cuddle, and last but certainly not least, sit in the windowsills and tease the big cats living closest to the house, which I had to teach them very early on was *not* a good idea.

A few years later a very handsome adult male cat came strolling into the house, looking around as if he were trying to decide whether or not to buy the place. To this day I have no idea where he came from, but he's been in charge here ever since. I deviated from the tradition of naming him after costars and loved ones and named him Johnny Depp. Antonio and Dakota have worked with him. I haven't, nor have I ever even met him. I'm just a fan. He and I were both at an event recently, but somehow I couldn't quite work up the nerve to walk over, introduce myself, and say, "I named my cat after you." On one hand, he might have taken it as the compliment I intended. On the other more likely hand, he might have thought "Yikes!" and suddenly remembered that he was late for an appointment as far away from me as possible.

And then there was my smart, funny, adorable potbellied pig Winston Churchill, in honor of Churchill's quote, "I am fond of pigs. Dogs look up to us. Cats look down on us. Pigs treat us as equals." Winston shared a little house adjacent to mine with my beautiful serval Ariel, and they were great friends.

This should go without saying, but in case it doesn't—none of the adopted domestic animals are ever, *ever* allowed to wander freely around Shambala. No good could possibly come from that.

It's a source of some fascination to visitors here that the property is also home to a large number of very loud, very entitled ravens. They're not at Shambala because they happened to see *The Birds* and thought it would be funny to gather at my house. They're at Shambala because we serve meat to the big cats, and ravens happen to love meat. In fact, they're very aggressive about dive-bombing the meat in the big cats' compounds at mealtime, and yes, an occasional raven has lost its life to a huge swatting paw in the process. I hate to see it, but I have to admit, some part of me always wishes I could ask them, "What did you *think* was going to happen?"

I apparently needed a good lesson in "Never say never," because, believe it or not, I got engaged again.

In my defense, this time it really did seem like a great idea.

We'd known each other very well and admired each other for many years.

It's an understatement to say that we had a lot in common.

We lived less than a mile from each other, just close enough, just far enough away, which suited us both.

We had one of those rare relationships that evolved slowly and reciprocally from friends to lovers.

You've read his name several times in the last many chapters.

I got engaged to Dr. Marty Dinnes, Shambala's first official veterinarian, brilliant and internationally renowned for a practice dedicated to the care of nondomesticated animals.

I'm not sure which of us was more surprised when we realized we'd fallen in love, but everything felt so right about it.

We'd been romantically involved for about a year and a half, and we were celebrating New Year's Eve together, ready to ring in the year 2000. I was on the phone with my sister Patty when, in the middle of the conversation, Marty said, "Here," handed me a little black velvet box and I opened it to find the most gorgeous engagement ring I've ever seen. It literally took my breath away, and caught me completely off guard. We'd talked about getting married, but we'd never made any decisions or plans.

I quickly wished Patty a happy New Year, hung up the phone and said yes.

Neither of us was in any hurry to get married. In fact, Marty had known me through two different husbands, both Noel and Luis, so he understood why I wasn't leaping up and down to set a date and start picking out china patterns.

It was a busy, stimulating, interesting engagement. I was a working actress and, at the same time, committed heart and soul to Shambala, the Roar Foundation, and wild animal protection legislation. Marty was keeping up with his local practice while being flown all over the world to care for the widest possible variety of nondomesticated animals at preserves, zoos, and marine parks. We were two independent, strong-willed people, both of whom enjoyed our privacy, so there was no clinging, no neediness, no arguments if one or the other of us wasn't available. Most of all, we respected each other, and we were unflinchingly honest with each other . . . I thought.

It was eight years into our engagement.

I was very hard at work on legislation that would make it illegal to declaw wild cats, which, to oversimplify my opinion on this, is like sending soldiers into battle but not allowing them to take their weapons with them. How dare we humans disable wild cats to make them easier and safer for us to deal with, when the truth is, thanks in part to big-game hunters and poachers, they're in a lot more danger from us than we'll ever be from them.

I wrote an impassioned letter to the lawmakers in Sacramento outlining the bill I was proposing and the reasons behind it.

Marty and I had many long conversations about the declawing of wild cats. He was as strongly in favor of it as I was opposed to it. He'd even declawed countless wild cats himself. It was one of those issues between us in which the only compromise we ever reached was agreeing to disagree.

I was entitled to my opinion.

Marty was entitled to his.

What he wasn't entitled to do was write an eleven-page letter to Sacramento, as impassioned as mine, defending his advocacy of declawing nondomestic big cats and essentially encouraging lawmakers to dismiss my letter—*and sending that letter behind my back, without mentioning a word about it to me.*

I don't think I've ever been so angry or felt more betrayed in my life. If he felt morally compelled to write the letter, fine. I wouldn't have liked it and would have tried to talk him out of it, but in the end, I would have understood that we all do what we have to do when issues come up that really, really matter.

But behind my back? Really? It was sneaky, it was premeditated, it was a huge lie by omission, it was something I would never have tolerated from someone who called himself my friend, let alone someone who claimed to love me enough to want to marry me.

I wasn't about to commit the rest of my life to a man I clearly couldn't trust.

I broke off the engagement.

He wasn't happy about it. I didn't care. Two nights later I was alone in my office at seven p.m. when he marched in and said, "I want the ring. Now."

It was a gorgeous, gorgeous ring, but he'd taken away the intention and the meaning behind it anyway.

I gave him the ring, and that was the end of that.

We still live less than a mile from each other, and we run into each other at the supermarket from time to time and make polite small talk. He recently told me, for example, that he's currently boarding and treating a kangaroo, which is as far as the conversation went.

I have conflicted feelings about him. I don't miss my fiancé, but I think I'll always feel the loss of a friend and brilliant, dedicated veterinarian who taught me so much and saved animals' lives at Shambala.

Since that engagement ended, I've been the most contented single woman I know, and mark my words, this time I'm staying that way. I've already got all the headaches I can handle, and you have no idea how much I wish I were kidding.

It's hard to pinpoint exactly when I started suffering from chronic debilitating headaches. I'm sure being bitten on the back of the head by a lion contributed to the problem, and the collision between my left temple and the metal rail of Noel's hospital bed that cost me my senses of taste and smell couldn't have helped. But despite the best efforts of a lot of very capable doctors, starting in the early 1990s the severe headaches became my almost daily companions. They weren't migraines. They started at the back of my head and worked their way toward my forehead, and I tried everything to get rid of them—acupuncture, chiropractic, a variety of prescribed medications, Botox shots, you name it. Nothing helped.

In 2005 I had a spinal fusion. For the first time in years I had hope.

It made a huge difference, and I actually started imagining a pain-free life.

Then, on June 22, 2006, I was on a soundstage in San Diego, filming a short-lived TV series called *Fashion House*. I was in a nightgown and slippers and using a walker for the scene, just standing there minding my own business waiting to hear the word "Action!," when suddenly, from somewhere high, high above me, a powerful deluge of water came flooding down directly on my head. If I hadn't been holding on to that walker, it would have knocked me off my feet, and incredibly, it didn't hit anyone but me.

I found out later that it was caused by an accumulation of water from a blocked air-conditioning condensation tube. The press couldn't resist commenting on the irony that the blockage seemed to have been caused by a bird's nest, with a variety of headlines like "Tippi Hedren, Star of 'The Birds,' Injured in Bizarre Stage Accident Caused by Birds." I didn't much care what caused it, I was just devastated that, through no fault of my own, the headaches came roaring back.

I hired a lawyer to file a lawsuit against the obviously negligent studio facility. This was a highly recommended attorney, referred by a close friend, so it was very confusing when I kept hearing nothing from him and kept getting the same response when I'd call to ask what was going on: "It's coming along."

I'll spare you—and myself—the *seven years* of legal wrangling it took to put this nightmare to rest once and for all. The highlights are simply that the studio was let off the hook based on the statute of limitations, and I ended up winning a lawsuit against my attorney for malpractice. The jury awarded me $1,483,708.

The lawsuit and the amount of the award were highly publicized, and almost immediately we saw that donations to the Roar Foundation dropped significantly. It was understandable—how hard up could a foundation possibly be, after a sudden influx of almost a million and a half dollars?

Which might be true if we'd actually *received* a sudden influx of almost a million and a half dollars. The truth is, as happens in so many court settlements, we ended up seeing only a small fraction of that amount over a period of time.

So just to set the record straight, the Roar Foundation is still alive and well and deeply grateful for, and in need of, any and all donations to support our precious animals.

Since the deluge accident, I've had countless tests, X-rays and MRIs. One doctor, after examining the MRI results, asked if I'm left-handed. I explained that I'm actually ambidextrous—I sew and do other crafts with my right hand, but I write with my left.

"You lucked out," he told me. "If you weren't consistently using the left side of your brain, the concussion you suffered from that fall in 1982 would have left you unable to walk or talk."

Suddenly losing my senses of taste and smell didn't seem quite as horrible compared to what might have happened.

In late 2014 another doctor took a look at my X-rays and asked incredulously, "How are you holding your head up?"

He strongly recommended neck surgery, as soon as possible. If he'd strongly recommended I take up nude skydiving, I swear I would have agreed to that if it would make this pain go away.

In February of 2015 I underwent neck surgery. I was too excited to be nervous about it, thinking finally, after two decades of searching, someone had finally found the source of the problem and come up with the solution.

It was a ten-hour surgery, ten nonstop hours of anesthesia essentially polluting my body. I ended up with two steel plates in my neck.

I was in a neck brace twenty-four hours a day for eight months and still wear it when I sleep.

It didn't help. In fact, the aftermath has been headaches that sometimes immobilize me, so that it's hard to commit to invitations, knowing that I might wake up that morning in too much pain to get out of bed. I had to cancel a private Oscar party and a trip to London this year, both of which I was really looking forward to.

I fight my way through perpetual exhaustion and depression. I don't have time for them, and I refuse to live like that. I'll continue to blame all that anesthesia for some of these aftereffects—but I'll be damned if I'm going to let them get in the way of living my life the way I want to live it.

I can't begin to count the number of doctors, orthopedists, neurologists, and headache specialists I've been to. When even Scripps Health can't help you, you start to get discouraged. I did have to laugh at a very recent headache specialist who, after looking at all my medical records, X-rays, and MRIs, handed me a bottle of pills he thought would be helpful and added, "although you might find that they make you forgetful." Sure, I'll start taking those right away, while I'm in the middle of writing my memoir. That would be a big help. I left without the pills, whatever they were.

There are hours now and then when I feel discouraged enough to just resign myself to living like this. Then I get over it. "I'm not going to do that anymore." I cannot and will not believe that no one can help. I know there's someone somewhere who will run exactly the right tests, look at exactly the right results in some new way, and say, "Oh, *here*'s the problem! And here's what we can do about it!" I'll keep looking, and someday I'll find that someone. You're out there, I know you are!

I did get some relief a few days ago from a certified hypnotist named Catherine Hickland. I wouldn't claim, nor would she, that she cured my headaches. What she did do, though, was give me a very welcome respite from the constant stress that comes with chronic pain. I hadn't realized how much tension I was living with until I felt it leave my body, and I'll be diligent about the relaxation techniques she gave me.

None of this is intended to be my way of inviting you to my pity party. Don't bother showing up—I'm not throwing one. I just wanted to share my experience and let you know that if you're one of the countless people who suffer from chronic pain, you're not alone, and I promise not to give up the search for a solution if you don't. The only caveat is, a solution that turns us into zombies is absolutely off-limits. We owe ourselves, and the people and animals who love us and count on us, a whole lot better than that.

Seventeen

All in all, it's been a pretty amazing life for a small-town girl from Minnesota whose only dream was to be a figure skater. And I'm not done yet.

I never set out to be famous, or a model, or an actress, or an animal rights activist, or a humanitarian. I just went where my heart led me, once I decided that being afraid was something I wasn't going to do anymore, and it led me on an extraordinary journey.

When I was preparing to write this book I did some research on myself and made a list of awards I've received for—you guessed it—acting, animal rights activism, and humanitarianism, all of which

I would have missed out on if I'd let fear rule my life. (In case you're interested, you'll find the list in the appendix of this book.)

Every one of those honors is on proud display in my museum at Shambala, including the most recent one that truly left me speechless. In 2016 Melanie invited me to be her date at the Hayari Paris Hollywood Beauty Awards. The Timeless Beauty Award winner: Melanie Griffith. When she went to the podium to accept that lovely trophy, my daughter didn't just dedicate it to me, she *presented* it to me.

As if my daughter of great fortune hasn't already given me enough by being the love of my life and then compounding that love with my three precious grandchildren, Alexander, Dakota, and Stella, who call me Mormor (the Swedish word for grandmother). After all she and I have been through, separately and together, the fact that we're closer today than we've ever been is a daily reminder that mistakes, second-guesses, question marks, and all, I am so blessed.

Melanie gave me the two greatest birthday parties of my life, one for my seventy-fifth and one for my eightieth, both of them in her gorgeous house in Hancock Park. No one throws a party like Melanie. Family and friends flew in from everywhere, including Minnesota, Oregon, and New York. There were magicians and fortune-tellers and palm readers—I've never seen anything like it. Yes, there were seventy-five candles on the first cake and eighty on the second, and yes, Antonio had to help me blow out eighty candles. But how can I possibly mind growing older with my generous, creative daughter on hand to surround me with so much fun and so much love?

I wake up grateful every morning to the sight and sounds of the big cats enjoying their twice-daily playtime, once just after sunrise and the other at twilight—several minutes of silly wrestling, chasing, pouncing, and standing on their hind legs for the big-cat version of patty-cake, accompanied by affectionate moans and growls.

I get out of bed and never, ever miss doing my exercises—a lower-body routine to keep my legs strong, and an upper-body routine with weights to strengthen my arms. (I do think there's a design flaw to us Women of a Certain Age, by the way, when it comes to our upper arms. No exercise in the world seems to get rid of that unsightly, pendulum-like droop, and I miss wearing sleeveless clothes in public.)

Once I'm showered and dressed, I put on mascara, whether I'll be seeing anyone that day or not. I have very long eyelashes. I can't take any credit for them. They were a genetic gift, and I express my appreciation by giving them a little attention every day. And then, of course, there's the fact that without mascara, I have no face at all.

I also put on Joy perfume every day, even though I can't smell it myself. It's a habit since my teens, and I'm not about to give it up now.

Then I dive into a day that's as busy as my headaches allow, with time out for *The Bold and the Beautiful*. I'm sure there are other daytime shows I would enjoy, but a half hour is all I'll allow myself. There are interviews, meetings, and doctors' appointments; there's correspondence to be taken care of; and there are hours in my office administrating a private wildlife preserve—not very glamorous, but never boring, either.

As often as possible there are fundraising activities for the Roar Foundation, including our wonderful monthly Shambala safaris. Come take a safari with us next time you're in Los Angeles. You won't see any "funny" animal tricks or big cats in ridiculous costumes. You'll just see, and probably hear, some of the most exquisite creatures on earth, dignity intact, living out their lives loved and cared for and safe.

And at the end of every day, I set aside time for meditation—my way. I don't sit on a mat with my legs crossed. I've tried that, and all I ended up meditating about was how much I wished I weren't sitting on a mat with my legs crossed.

My daily meditation is a long walk along the paths and footbridges between the spacious compounds of Shambala's forty acres, checking on the big cats, talking to them, and soaking in the privilege of knowing each of them so well. They're each so different, each with their own distinct personalities and sounds, as individual as people. Those who are awake come to the fences, I put the back of my hand against the chain link so they can lick me hello and we walk and talk side by side to the end of their compound. Those who aren't awake are often snoring like buzz saws, which always makes me smile—so much for dignity.

There's life among the compounds, and history and strength and survival. There are graceful creatures all around whose every move and every sound are honest, uncomplicated, unapologetic inspirations of lives lived without pretense. There are beautiful four-legged reminders of where I've been and the seemingly haphazard path I took to get here. But looking back, I can't help but wonder if there was anything haphazard about it. Maybe I planned it ahead of time without realizing it. Maybe I just got lucky. Maybe all that matters is that I'm here.

The only thing I'm sure of is that this is where I belong.

Thank you for taking this walk with me through my last eighty-six years.

I have to admit, when the idea of writing a memoir first came up, I didn't exactly leap at it. I wasn't afraid of it, I just found it daunting. There was so much to tell and so much to say, I couldn't imagine how to sort it all out, let alone make sense of it.

But finally, in the spirit of "Don't think about it, just do it," I decided to just hold my nose and dive in, with one hard-and-fast demand of myself—to tell the truth and let the chips fall where they may.

Now here I am on the last page, and I have to say, I've enjoyed every minute of spending this time and my life with you. I hope you enjoyed it as much as I did.

I want you to know that by buying this book, you've made a difference, too, since the proceeds will be put to great use by the Roar Foundation. Thank you again for that.

I wish you love and health and fearlessness and a kind, forgiving heart and, however it manifests itself, your own Shambala . . .

"a meeting place of peace and harmony
for all beings,
animal and human."
With gratitude and so much love,
Tippi

ACKNOWLEDGMENTS

My eternal love and gratitude to . . .

FAMILY

Carl Eckhardt, M.D., Julia and Charles Eckhardt, Bernard Hedren, Dorothea Hedren, Patty Hedren Davis, Melanie Griffith, Alexander Bauer, Dakota Johnson, Stella Banderas, Heidi Hanzlik, Beni Hanzlik, Tipper Hanzlik, Steve Hanzlik, David Hanzlik

FIRST LOVES

Richard McFarland, Jimmy Lewis

HUSBANDS

Peter Griffith, Noel Marshall, Luis Barrenechea

CELEBRITY FRIENDS

Antonio Banderas, Don Johnson, Steven Bauer, Marlon Brando, Sophia Loren, Rod Taylor, Jessica Tandy, Louise Latham, Betty White, Sean Connery, Suzanne Pleshette, Sigfried & Roy, Joanne Worley, Diane McBain, Kieu Chinh, Lily Tomlin, Sienna Miller, Gardner McKay, Donald Trump, Loni Anderson, Eric Murphy, Barbara Eden, Linda Blair

AGENTS, PRODUCERS, DIRECTORS, AND DESIGNERS

Rita LaRoy, Eileen Ford, Lew Wasserman, Alfred Hitchcock, Alma Hitchcock, Charles Chaplin, Edith Head, Rita Riggs, Bud Moss, Jules Stein, Thierry Mugler, Mary Ellen Marks

BEAUTY MAKERS

Jim Brown, Peggy Robertson, Bob Dawn, Howard Schmidt, Virginia Darcy, Rita Riggs

BUSINESS ASSOCIATES

Jeanette Laslovitch, Terri Camerano, Lindsay Harrison, Fred Hill, Harlan Boll, Jennifer DeChiara, Ben Mankiewicz, Melissa Giordana, Thunn Lee, Robert Klorizak, Kay Zigrang, Karen Cadle, Eileen and Jerry Ford, Lisa Sharkey, Matt Harper

ANGELS AND LIFESAVERS

Lillian and Hubie Boscowitz, Steve and Cathi Shultz, Pastor Anderson, Vietnam veteran Tom O'Keef, Thomas and Toni Polacki, Dusty Butera, Shirley and Pat Kubly, Dr. Larry Ward, Catherine Hickland, Blanca Monge

FELLOW FRIENDS AND ADVOCATES OF ANIMALS

Dr. James Kayvenfar, M.D., Sandy and Kent Madsen, Chris Link, Ella Knot, Paris Sneider, Donald Spoto, Brian Barfoot, Florence Lambert, Chris de Rose, Vernon Weir, Melissa and Steve Whitmire and The Muppets

SHAMBALA PRESERVE STAFF

Preserve Director and Guardian Chris Gallucci, Bill Dow, Trudy Farley, Chui Torres and all our loyal volunteers

SHAMBALA PRESERVE VETERINARIANS ON CALL

Jon J. Bernstein, D.V.M., Gay Naditch, D.V.M., Martin R. Dinnes, D.V.M., Chris Gauble, D.V.M.

ANIMAL CARETAKER FRIENDS

Ray Burwick, Penny Patterson, Birute Galdikas, San Diego Zoo Curator Werner Heuschle (Director of CRES for San Diego Zoo Global), Ron Oxley, Steve Martin, Frank Tom, Sylvie Loboda, Liberato Torres, Ben Sanchez, Claude Roberts, Eve Rattner, Yvonne Garner, Marina Malchin, Betty Rose, Danil Torpe, Merrie Post, Sue Barton

ANIMALS (to name just a few)

Corky (first dog), Partner (dog), Puss (cat), Peter (cat), Forio (horse), Demitasse (toy poodle), Buddy (raven), Neil (first lion), Casey (lion), Needra (lion), Pharaoh (cheetah), Timbo (elephant), Kura (elephant), Billy (lion), Buster (leopard), Noelle (tigon), Patrick (liger),

Boomer (lion), Zeus (lion), Kermit (frog), Natasha (tiger), Winston Churchill (pig), Ariel (serval), Johnny Depp (cat)

THE *ROAR* HEROES

Ozzie Bristow, John Marshall, Joel Marshall, Jerry Marshall, Jeff Haynes, Tim Cooney, Banjiro Uemura, Jan de Bont, Monique Van de Van, Kyalo Mativo, Alexandra Newman, Charles Sloan, Darryl Sides, Rick Glassey, Steve Miller, Mike Vollman, Robert Gottschalk, Patsy Nedd, Pat Breshears, Penny Bishonden, Leo Lobsenz, Dr. Steve Kadiver, Mona Emigh, Martin Downey, Doron Kauper, Brad Darrington, Nancy Landry, Don and Fritzi Simonson, Herb Dorfman, Gary Dartnell, Robbie and Ellen Little, Elaine Newman, Ted Taylor

To anyone I might have forgotten while writing this list,
please know it will haunt me for the rest of my life,
and remember, I'm 86.

Appendix

THE AWARDS

- The *Photoplay* Most Promising Newcomer Award
- The Golden Globe Award for New Star of the Year
- The Life Achievement Award at the Beauvais Film Festival Cinemalia in France
- The Helen Woodward Animal Center's Annual Humane Award
- The Life Achievement Award in Spain's La Fundación Municipal de Cine
- The Founders Award from the ASPCA
- The Woman of Vision Award from Women in Film and Video
- The Presidential Medal from Hofstra University for my work in film
- The Lion and Lamb Award from Wildhaven
- The Humanitarian Award at the Las Vegas International Film Festival

- The Best Actress in a Comedy Short Award at the Method Fest, Independent Film Festival (for *Mulligans!*)
- The Best Actress Award from the New York International Independent Film Festival (for *Tea with Grandma*)
- A star on the Hollywood Walk of Fame
- The "Hope Is a Woman" Honor from the Women of Los Angeles
- The PAWS Companion for Life Award
- The Best Actress Award from the Los Angeles TV Short Film Festival (for *Rose's Garden*)
- The Animal Rights Advocacy Award at the Activist Film Festival
- The Living Legacy Award
- The Conservationist of the Year Dino Award from the Las Vegas Natural History Museum
- The Lifetime Achievement Award from the Riverside Film Festival
- The Jules Verne "Nature" Award from the First Annual Jules Verne Adventure Film Festival of Los Angeles
- The Academy of Art University's Second Academic Film Festival Award
- The Jules Verne Legendaire Award
- The Thespian Award from the La Femme Film Festival
- The "When a Woman Wills She Will!" Award by the Woman's Club of Hollywood
- The Workhouse's first Lifetime Achievement in the Arts Award
- The first star on the Orinda Theatre Walk of Fame
- The Lifetime Achievement Award at the 24th Annual Genesis Awards Show from the Humane Society
- The Brave Heart Award
- The Who-Manitarian Award

- The Lifetime Achievement Award from the Hollywood Chamber of Commerce at its 90th Annual Installation and Awards Luncheon
- The "Women Together" Award from the United Nations
- The Vietnamese-American Matron Saint Award from the Boat People SOS Organization
- The Omni Youth Humanitarian/Career Achievement Award
- An Honorary Master's of Fine Arts Degree from the New York Film Academy
- The Mayor's Career Achievement Award from Starz at the Denver Film Festival
- The Legacy of Style Award
- The "People Helping People" Award from the Touching Lives TV Awards Show
- The Lifetime Achievement Award from the Bel Air Film Festival
- The Special Recognition Award from the Acton Women's Club
- The Women's International Film & Television Showcase Foundation International Visionary Award
- A tribute called "Choreography of Desire" at the Vienna International Film Festival
- The Believe, Achieve, Empower Award